60

Also by Joan Solomon Weiss

Your Second Child

RAISING A SON

The Essential Guide to a Healthy Mother-Son Relationship

JOAN SOLOMON WEISS

SUMMIT BOOKS
New York

Several names and identifying details have been altered to protect the privacy of the children and parents mentioned in this book.

Copyright © 1985 by Joan Solomon Weiss

Published by SUMMIT BOOKS
A Division of Simon & Schuster, Inc.
Simon & Schuster Building
1230 Avenue of the Americas
New York, New York 10020

SUMMIT BOOKS and colophon are trademarks of Simon & Schuster, Inc.

Designed by Jennie Nichols/Levavi & Levavi

Manufactured in the United States of America

10 9 8 7 6 5 4 3 2 1

First Edition
Library of Congress Cataloging in Publication Data

Weiss, Joan Solomon.
    Raising a son.
    Bibliography: p.
    1. Child rearing. 2. Mothers and sons. 3. Oedipus
complex. 4. Interpersonal relations. 5. Family.
I. Title.
HQ769.W434 1985   649'.132   84-24084
ISBN 0-671-45269-X

Acknowledgments

S o many people have helped me in the preparation of this book—from the inspiration that sparked it to the ideas that gave it life to the hard work that gave it shape. My husband, Allan, helped to get me started with his enthusiasm and his encouragement; my children, Michael and Brian, helped to keep me going as they carefully tallied how many pages I had written, hoping they could count as high as I could pile the pages up.

The names of the people who inspired and assisted me would number even higher than that. I would like to thank them all, all who have shared with me their time, their energy, their ideas, although their names would go on too long to list them separately here. But I would like to list and give special thanks to the following relatives, friends, and professionals who went far beyond the call in helping me transform *Raising a Son* from compelling thought to completed book: Leo Solomon, Pauline Solomon, Diane Swatzburg, Emil Weiss, Gerta Weiss, Jules Weiss, Dr. Daniel Araoz, Jane Besher, Dr. Hooshang Bonheur, Diane Carr, Jerie Charnow, Dr. Susan Coates, Shirley Cooper, Dr. Lloyd deMause, Helen Dubinsky, Ted Dubinsky, Susan Frankel, Dr. Roger Gittelson, Dr. Amy Horowitz, Richard Hill, Phyllis Jonas, Dr. Hanna Kapit, Dr. Milton Kapit, Professor Leah Lauter, Sylvia Lehrich, Fran Levinson, Pat Levinson, Madeline Firetag Lizt, Barbara Lowenstein, Dr. Steven Meltzer, Dr. Robert Mendelsohn, Dr. Ildiko Mohacsy, Ruth Mohr, Dr. Ruth Neubauer, Dr. Karl Neumann, Ruth Newman, Wendy Nicholson, Susan Philliber, Anne Rosberger, Dr. Britt Rosenbaum, Dr. Joel Sambursky, Dr. Lorelle Saretsky, Dr. Lydia Seggev, Dr. Gary Seltzer, Miriam Seltzer, Dr. Robert Sherman, Larry Siegal, Dr. Harry Wachen, Janet Wein, Martin Wein, Dr. Reed Welson, Dr. Eleanor Yacchnes, Donald Ziccardi, Sheilah Ziccardi, the Austin Street Senior Center, the Institute for Psychohistory, and Parents of Gays.

Finally, I would like to take this opportunity to welcome the newest son into the family, my nephew Joseph David Weiss.

Joan Solomon Weiss
October 1984

To my newest and oldest friends,
my parents

Contents

Introduction

*W*hen a newborn son is placed in his mother's arms he may seem at first like a stranger to her, as her mind floods with memories of other boys—boys from her past, boys she hardly got to know. Most mothers of today were brought up in an era when the differences between the sexes were emphasized and magnified. We were taught that boys were more important than girls but at the same time not quite as human, nor as loving, nor as understanding. And so they existed on the peripheries of our lives until we became aware of their romantic possibilities. We went ahead to meet them as adult men, never to look back at the boys we left behind.

But those of us who go on to have sons find ourselves, by necessity, looking back. It is not to look back, as the mothers of daughters do, at the children we ourselves were, but at the boys who teased and taunted us and kept us at a distance—boys who may even have included our own brothers. Now that we have our own little boys, how are we to develop this relationship that has previously eluded us? Strange as our sons are to us, how are we to help them negotiate the challenges of growing up from baby to boy, and then from boy to man?

With the birth of a son, the intimacy with the opposite sex that was denied us as girls now comes at us with full force. The bond we have with our male child starts off as the closest between the two sexes, with mother and son literally sharing a single body. And the closeness continues throughout the boy's childhood, embodied most dramatically in the sexuality of his Oedipal years.

But soon, the closeness begins to dissipate. The son takes leave of his mother for another woman, for another home, for a life of his own. Some women fear this separation almost from the time their sons are born. They quote the old adage, "A son is a son till he takes a wife, but a daughter's a daughter all the days of her life." Indeed, one psychologist questioned about the lack of attention given the mother–son relationship told me, "No one wants to touch it because it's simply too painful. The natural instinct of a son is to reject his mother. The natural instinct of a mother is not to want to give him up."

The dual themes of sexuality and separation run through the mother–son relationship from its earliest stages up until its last. To some extent the sexual differences force the separation, as they did the girl–boy split of childhood, but the separation from our sons need not be as complete as we fear it might be. Though the challenge is a formidable one, it is certainly possible to raise a son who will lead a life of his own and still not forget his mother. The challenge begins the minute we are handed our infant sons. First, we must accept the baby's sex, even if we had wanted a girl, even if he seems a stranger. Then we must learn to relate to the child even though we have had no previous experience with a relationship just like it. The mother of a son, unlike the mother of a daughter, starts fresh, with only her experiences with other males—her father, her mate, her brother—to draw on. And though she may be influenced by her mother in raising her male child, it is her image of her father that will guide her in shaping the image of her son.

When her son grows up, the mother who will be remembered with love is the one who nurtures his human qualities, not just his "manly" ones. She is the one who helps him through his stages of close attachment to her and doesn't abandon him at the times he seems to be abandoning her. As he changes from adolescence to manhood, she too is changing, as a woman; she is enlarged by the experience of having a son.

Of course, the challenges do not end when the boy becomes a man. In some ways, the job gets tougher as a woman relinquishes control over the child she has mothered for so long. There is the challenge of establishing an adult relationship with him, and of relating to the important people in his life. Whether a son is married or not, gay or straight, it is possible for a mother to accept his manhood without losing his love.

The relationship between a mother and her son is a unique one which this book will explore in depth as it takes us from before the birth of the son to after the death of the mother. It will show not only what sons gain from their mothers but also what mothers gain from having sons. It will address all of the challenges implicit in the relationship, as well as challenge that old saw about losing a son. The subject of mothers and sons is *not* too painful to touch. So don't be discouraged by all those books you see lining the shelves on the subject of mothers and daughters. If you are a mother of any age of a son of any age, this is a book for you.

1

Preference and Obsession: The Birth of the Mother-Son Bond

*A*s a native New Yorker, I'm used to hearing all sorts of strange unsolicited comments from passersby. I've learned to walk briskly on, keeping my face in a protective mask of nonexpression. But toward the end of my first pregnancy I had a different kind of comment made to me, as sexual innuendo gave way to sexual prediction: "It's going to be a boy!" came at me from every city soul who had nothing to do but to observe and remark on the life passing him or her by. At that time, I didn't even try to suppress my smile. I was happy I was pregnant; I was happy it showed; I was happy that someone out there thought I would have a boy, even though I never acknowledged a preference in myself.

During both of my pregnancies, every stranger or friend who ventured a guess predicted I would have a son. Perhaps that was because all of the telltale signs were there: I carried each baby high and in front; my face remained free from the "distorted" quality attributed to the mothers of daughters, and my babies kicked both frequently and ferociously. So the multitude of sexual seers may have foretold a son because they really thought it would be one—or perhaps because they were telling me what they thought I wanted to hear, believing that deep down every woman wants to have a son.

Although it is not popular to express a sex preference in these supposedly egalitarian eighties, there were no such compunctions throughout most of history. In fact, it was almost always simply taken for granted that it was better to have a male child than a female one, better to be the mother of a son. In most cultures, it was the son who carried on the family name and the family tradition. It was he who hunted for food or grew it; it was he who proved the potency of his father and who assured his mother's place in the family. Had Anne Boleyn succeeded in birthing a boy, she might have had more than a thousand days, and Henry VIII but a pair of wives.

So countless methods were devised to tempt the gods and improve the odds. Women were ordered to drink a concoction of wine and lion's blood and then to copulate under a full moon. They were told to lie on their right side during sex, to copulate before midnight or when the north wind blew. In pre-Christian Sweden, to encourage the birth of males, brides-to-be slept with small boys on the eve of their weddings. Young brides of the Pelew Islands dressed in male garments before intercourse—an act so adorned would, no doubt, bear male fruit.

But nine months seemed a long time to wait to measure success. And so history's mothers-to-be were closely watched for signs of the sex of the child they were carrying. The lucky woman, it was believed, would have a right breast larger than her left, with dark areas around the nipple and early secretion of milk from that breast. Her right eye would be brighter and her right nostril would bleed frequently. According to seventeenth-century English prognosticators, the color of such a woman would be good. Her body temperature would be warm. By contrast, a woman thought to be carrying a girl would be pale and listless, her face spotted with red, her abdomen heavy and drooping. Her body was telling her that she was unworthy, that she had failed in her mission to produce a male, that her husband would be displeased with her.

But while she might pay a price for not producing a son, the daughter she produced might well pay a price dearer. Throughout most of history, female infanticide has been a common practice, horrifying proof of the premium placed on males. Female babies were flung into rivers, plunged into latrines, tossed onto dung heaps, left to die on hills and roadsides. In ancient Greece, a second daughter was rarely allowed to live.

SEX DETECTION, SEX SELECTION

Trying to determine or influence a baby's sex is no longer fashionable. Ask most expectant parents about their preference for a son or a daughter, and they'll look at you accusingly and say, "We don't care about the sex, as long as it's healthy." Yet that reply may cover up strong desires— ones that the parents-to-be are often barely aware of or unwilling to discuss. Whether such desires are met with the child of choice or not, they are certain to influence the relationship of parent and child. In these times of changing sexual mores, it is often the mother who is most in conflict about her role, a conflict that may coalesce around the sex of her unborn children. And it is often the son, whether he is wanted or unwanted, who bears the brunt of her confusion. The mother–son relationship, even before the birth of the child, is born in the mind of the mother.

It is clear that sex preference is still alive. In the privacy of their homes, couples are still trying to figure out the sex of the fetus before the nine months are up. A new array of superstitions has become popular. If a wedding ring suspended over the woman's abdomen swings from side to side, it means a boy; if it goes in circles, it means a girl. A fast heartbeat is thought to be the sign of a boy racing to come out; a slow one, the sign of a girl biding her time.

But science has done what superstition hasn't—it has provided an almost foolproof way of detecting the sex of an unborn child. Through amniocentesis—a medical procedure that involves withdrawing amniotic fluid and examining fetal cells for their chromosomal content—couples can learn with almost complete certainty whether the fetus is male or female. Few women have the procedure done solely for that purpose, but it is an extra piece of information most people seek when the technique is performed for other reasons.

Going beyond sex prediction, there are books available that stress sex selection. They tell couples when to have intercourse, in what position to have it, and what the after-sex douche should consist of in order to improve the odds of conceiving a child of a particular sex. The problem is that the advice given in one book often contradicts that in another. More scientific methods, involving sperm separation and artificial insemination, are being developed and refined, but they are far from foolproof. A few couples are taking a more definitive approach. They are having amniocentesis done to find out the fetus's sex, and then aborting it if it's not the right one. Most physicians will have no part in this, but there are some who are willing to do it, maintaining that they are simply going along with the wishes of their patients. While this practice seems barbaric, some form of scientific sex selection will most likely be a popular trend in the future.

THE POPULARITY OF SONS

Studies conducted over the last half century have shown that the preference for males still exists, though its strength has diminished somewhat. A study from the 1930s showed that if parents were to have children of the sex they wanted, 165 boys would be born for every 100 girls. Recent surveys show a lower preference ratio—ranging from 106 boys for every 100 girls to 138 boys for every 100 girls—but it is still almost always higher than the natural one, approximately 106 boys born to every 100 girls. (Males being more medically vulnerable, that ratio narrows during the first year of life and after, and in older age groups females outnumber males.)

One might assume that a man would want a child born in his own image, someone to carry on both his name and his masculine attributes. But more pertinent to this discussion is what *women* want, and why. Even if they had once wanted boys, wouldn't the women's movement have opened their eyes to the advantages of a daughter? A study conducted in the 1970s—when the feminist movement was perhaps at its height—addressed just that question. The researchers were surprised by what they found. Of those college students questioned who stated a preference, 92 percent of the women wanted their first child to be a boy, even higher than the 90 percent of men who wanted a first-born son, according to a report in the journal *Psychology*. When asked their preference for an only child, 64 percent of the women who had a preference would have liked a son. The only significant difference the researchers noted between their findings and findings from twenty years earlier was a drop in preference by men for a male only child. The women's preferences seemed untouched by a feminist consciousness.

A 1980 study described in the journal *Psychological Reports* confirmed these findings. More than half of the first-time expectant mothers questioned had a definite sex preference for the child they were carrying. Of those, about 60 percent said they wanted a son. Perhaps even more telling, three out of four of the mothers stated that they *believed* they were carrying a boy. Beliefs and fantasies may tell a truer story of our innermost desires than do consciously stated choices.

In a 1981 study described in the book *The First Birth*, sixty-three of the mothers followed gave birth to boys and fifty-seven to girls. Most of the women said they were satisfied with their baby's sex. But where boys were concerned, the satisfaction ran deeper. Three times as many mothers of sons said they were "overjoyed" with the sex of their baby.

Although most women *do* want a daughter at some point, they want a son first, and they want one more. If it's only one child they want, the preference is most often for a boy. Why should this be so, even today, when daughters have virtually the same opportunities as sons? Some of the reasons are not very different from what they were in generations past. A son is viewed as the child who will carry on the family name, bring status and prestige to the family, perhaps take over the family business. He is the one who will help his mother please her husband, since most men want sons. Moreover, a boy is still viewed as easier to bring up than a girl and as having an easier time of it later in life, with more of a chance for success.

Sometimes, the reasons are rooted not in the son's future but in the mother's past. Memories of childhood make some women long for boys—memories of a brother being favored by a doting mother; memories of boys batting and boxing their way to school championships with girls cheering on the sidelines; memories of boys wrestling little girls to the ground, and bigger girls to bed, forever asserting their alleged superiority. By identifying with "the aggressor," mothers of sons sometimes feel more powerful themselves.

Tied to this feeling of power is a feeling of pride that is

hard for many women to admit. As one feminist mother acknowledged, "There's that feeling that a boy is worth more, that you can be prouder of him. It's a vestige of the past, but it's there."

I was glad to hear her admit this, because it made my own admission easier. Though I hadn't even realized it until my first child was born, I too was proud that I had helped create a son. I was proud of all the religious fanfare that attended the birth of a boy, proud that he was long and husky and had the look of a bruised boxer. And I was proud that I had given my father, who had never had a son, a grandson.

The irony of course is that the women's liberation movement has not made a significantly greater proportion of women want daughters. In fact for some women it may have even strengthened the desire for sons. As Claire, the mother of two boys, says, "I simply may not be liberated enough to have a daughter. Whenever my older son, Danny, opens the vitamin bottle, I tell him how big and strong he is. I think it's cute. I have him carry heavy packages and fix things for me. A liberated woman wouldn't do that. So would I be doing a daughter a favor? I don't think I'm 'liberated enough' for a daughter of the future." She says this even though she was feminist enough to become a lawyer, to set up her own practice, and to balance the demands of her profession with the demands of her family.

UNHEALTHY OBSESSIONS

In most cases, preference for one sex or the other is simply that—a preference. As one psychologist put it, "It's like hoping to land a job in Manhattan but finding one in New Jersey instead." Some women would *like* a son, others would *like* a daughter, but they make peace with what they get. They may feel momentary disappointment, but the beauty of the baby and the joy of parenthood soon overcome it.

Nevertheless, some women are obsessed with the sex of their unborn child and fiercely determined to have it turn out the way they want. If it does, there is great exaltation, focused more on the sex of the child than on the child itself. If it doesn't, there is deep disappointment, rage, and even depression. Feelings of sadness and loss may last for months, years, or a lifetime, and they will strongly influence the mother–son relationship.

When a woman's wish for a son reaches the point of obsession, it may be the result of a troubled relationship with her father. According to Dr. Joseph Schonberger, a New York psychiatrist, a woman may want to have a son in a desperate attempt to win her father's love and to rid herself of guilt: "By giving her father a grandson, she is trying to assuage his disappointment in her for being a girl. She is saying, in effect, 'Well, if I couldn't be your son, at least I'm giving you one.' " Or, in the case of a woman whose mother had only daughters, she may believe she has done her mother one better, that she has pleased her father in a way her mother never could. Though she may have lost her childhood battle to wrest her father away from her mother, at least she has won an important skirmish in adulthood.

Early family dynamics played a very important role in the attitude of Carolyn, a thirty-year-old computer programmer who had desperately wanted her firstborn child to be a son. She was disappointed, however: She gave birth twice, both times to girls. Fortunately she is insightful enough to understand some of the origins of her disappointment.

Carolyn was the younger of two children. The firstborn was a boy and, as she remembers it, her brother was very much favored: "He was like my mother's shining knight. He could do no wrong while everything I did was wrong in the eyes of my mother." When Carolyn thought about having a family, she realized the intensity of her wish for a son and traced it to a desire to duplicate her family of origin. "During my pregnancy I had a very clear image of the kind of child I wanted," she says. "He would be a very clever, active little boy. He would love me and amuse me. I'd get a lot of pleasure in watching him become a man. Now I realize that to some extent the son I wanted was my brother. But there was also another aspect to it. I couldn't face having a girl. When I thought of a girl, I thought of all the difficulties my mother and I went through. I just couldn't go through it again. I was afraid that my daughter, like my mother, wouldn't like me, that I would repeat my childhood with my own child."

Upon discovering that her first child was female, Carolyn went into a deep state of depression. When the nurses told her that she could see the baby, she didn't want to. Just as she had predicted, she couldn't face her daughter, at least in the beginning.

What seemed to bother Carolyn the most during the next few years was her daughter's femininity, a characteristic she tried to downplay. She encouraged her child to roam around the house, not to stay in the playpen, to use the slide and jungle gym at the playground, not to sit passively in the sandbox. She remembers one particularly painful incident: "At a birthday party for two-year-olds I was playing ball with the kids. My daughter just sat on a swing watching us. She didn't join in. I couldn't stand it and kept screaming for her to come and play. My friend finally said I should just leave her alone. When I was a child I was also shy. That's what got me so angry. To see that in her reminded me of what I had gone through. I didn't want to see myself as a child. I wanted to see my brother."

Carolyn showed great insight into the origins of her negative feelings toward her daughter. She recognized the competitive relationship between her mother and herself and her dread of living it again. She also recognized the male worship she had grown up with. Carolyn was raised to believe that her brother was better than she was. If only she could produce someone as good, a powerful firstborn son, the glory would rub off on her. She was also aware of her reluctance to see herself again as a child in her own child, to reexperience her early feelings of inferiority and inadequacy.

Psychologists saw still other things when they heard her story. Carolyn *said* she wanted things to be different—but perhaps she really wanted them to be the same. According to Dr. Lydia Seggev, a New York psychologist, "She seemed to want to recreate the situation of her youth, recreate it and redo it. By having a first son, a son like her brother, she could identify with his power. It's a case of repetition compulsion—the need to repeat what has happened to us."

Carolyn's insight did, ultimately, work to both her and her daughter's benefit. She came to see her child as more than a repository of feminine traits. "Gradually I came to realize what I was doing," she says. "I was identifying certain characteristics as masculine, and assuming that they couldn't be found in a girl. But they can appear in a boy or a girl. I've come to understand my daughter and to accept her for the child she is. I've separated the reality from my expectations. Now I'm concentrating on bringing out the best in her."

The strong desire to have a son sometimes relates to a more current situation—a woman's relationship with her husband. If that relationship is troubled, a woman may want a son to replace the partner who has failed her. She imagines that her son's love will compensate her for what she isn't getting from her mate. In some cases, the son comes to represent the extramarital lover his mother dare not take on. She cannot be considered "unfaithful" to her husband by loving her son too much. But while this may serve the mother's purposes, it is fraught with peril for the son. "The boy who becomes the love object of his mother becomes confused," says Dr. Schonberger. "Constantly being hugged, kissed, petted and held close to her bosom produces a lot of anxiety and guilt in a youngster."

A woman who is determined to have a son may come to use the child as an extension of herself. She cannot afford to let him go or she will lose part of her own identity. "The child may develop serious problems, sleep problems, school-reluctance problems," says Dr. Stuart Asch, professor of psychiatry at the Paine Whitney Clinic in New York City. "He may have a hard time going away to camp or to college. Because he is held so tightly, he'll have a difficult time breaking away and becoming an independent human being."

There may also be problems with sex-role development if a son is wanted chiefly because of his sex. He may be forced into a sex role that is too rigid, one that is too much a function of his mother's vision of what a boy must be. He *must* play sports, he cannot ever cry or reveal his feelings. As a result, an important part of his inner self is stifled before it has a chance to develop.

MOTHERS WHO WANT DAUGHTERS

Of course, not every mother wants a son. Some mothers believe that boys will be more likely to abandon them. To these mothers boys signify separation and girls connection. With daughters there may be a feeling of physical as well as emotional attachment. As one pregnant mother of a three-year-old girl wrote, when asked about her preference for the sex of the new baby, "I have always felt that a son would be a bit of a stranger to me simply by virtue of his being male. The greatest thing about having a daughter is feeling physically close to her. In some ways I still feel part of one body with her. I don't think there is any other person in the world other than my husband—and sometimes

not even him—that I feel as comfortable with physically. I
don't see that changing as she gets older the way I fear it
would with a son." This woman may have gone further
than most in her expression of it, but the feeling of one-
ness between mother and daughter that she describes is
quite common.

Most women do find satisfying ways to relate to their
sons, but some women don't even try. Those are the
women whose desire to have a daughter instead of a son
has reached pathological proportions. They can't get over
their disappointment, and their sons will suffer. According
to Dr. Seggev, such feelings are often rooted in a problem
of identity. "Women have both feminine and masculine
traits within them," she says. "But some women have a
hard time with this. Those who have difficulty with the
masculine part are generally not very aggressive or assertive. They suppress or deny their masculinity, fearing that
if they express it they will lose their femininity. Those are
often the women who do not want sons. On the surface,
they feel they would have nothing in common with a boy.
But on a deeper level, they are afraid that a son would
somehow unmask their own hidden masculinity."

One of Dr. Seggev's former patients was a perfect example. Although she was bright, beautiful, and wealthy, and
the mother of four lovely boys, she was utterly miserable.
"The root of her problem was the inability to separate
from her mother," says the psychologist. "Her mother had
held on to her for dear life. This woman, her daughter, was
her pride and joy. The mother never praised her for her
intellectual accomplishments, only for her beauty. She
wanted her daughter to fill her life, to take up the empti-
ness inside. The daughter, in turn, wanted a daughter of
her own for the very same purpose." A daughter would be
a monument to her femininity and would complete her
unfinished identity.

The birth of each son was a blow to her womanhood.
She felt she had nothing in common with them. She hated

them for not being girls. She didn't want to join in their talk about baseball and batting averages. When she saw toy trucks in the house, she got so uptight she would start to cry.

The unhappiness of this woman was not lost on her sons. She tried to compensate for her feelings by spending a lot of time with them and by satisfying all their demands. But her disappointment showed through. "You hate me," her second child would shout, sensing the feelings she could not entirely mask. Through therapy, this disappointed woman has begun to understand the source of her emotions and to deal with her children better. She has assured her sons that her problems are hers and have nothing to do with them. In taking responsibility for the problem, she is releasing her sons from the guilt of being boys.

We saw earlier how an unhappy marriage can make a woman want a son. Ironically, a similar situation can lead to the exact opposite desire. Some women, feeling alienated from their husbands, want a daughter for companionship. "It'll be us girls against the man," is the rationale. Any boy she has is born into a booby trap. Whatever he does—cry loudly, smile crookedly, run quickly—may serve as an unpleasant reminder of her husband. Says Dr. Seggev, "Because such a woman doesn't like her husband, she can't have a 'good' son. In her mind, all men are bad. Her father treated her badly, her husband treats her badly, her son will treat her badly."

FROM OBSESSION TO ABUSE

A son born to a woman who most definitely does not want one is inevitably in for a difficult time. He may be emotionally rejected, physically abused, or even abandoned. And even if the mother tries to overcome her negative feelings, her depression may prevent her from doing so. The result may be a feeling of inferiority, of unworthiness, of low self-esteem in the boy. "I'm not good enough. Something is wrong with me because I can't make Mother happy," he will be forced to conclude.

The subsequent birth of a sibling of the preferred sex may make matters worse. It's hard enough for any child to adjust to a new baby, but if the new baby is mother's "hope and redeemer," big brother or sister may justifiably feel left out in the cold. One four-year-old boy could not seem to adjust to the arrival of his baby sister, the daughter for whom his mother had prayed desperately. Jeremy had seemed a happy enough child before the new birth, active and bright and even-tempered. But after his sister came on the scene, his jealousy went well beyond the bounds of normal sibling rivalry. "You don't love me anymore," he would tell his parents, over and over again. "Ever since Nicole was born, you give all the attention to her. There's just nothing left for me. I know you hate me." He took out his feelings on his sister as well, hugging her with a vengeance, kissing her more with his teeth than his lips, "accidentally" knocking her down one time too many. Did the son see what the parents didn't, or wouldn't? Was the answer to a mother's dreams the beginning of a child's nightmare?

Dr. Martin Fisher, a psychologist at Adelphi University's Institute of Advanced Psychological Studies, was one of those sons who "should" have been a daughter. When a daughter was born seven years after his birth, it took some of the pressure off him, but in some respects it made matters worse. As Dr. Fisher recalls, "I remember my mother telling me that she had cried when the doctor said I was a boy, but that that was now gone. I've come to realize that it was *never* gone, though she seemed on the surface to get over it when she had another child who was a girl. Her daughter was her little doll to play with as she grew up. I had a lot of ambivalent feelings toward my sister because it was inferred that I would somehow have been more lovable if I had been a girl. No matter what I did, if I was cute, if I was bright, if I stood upside down, I still couldn't be a girl."

Sometimes a mother's rejection of her unwanted son is expressed in an unexpected way. She may try to hide the hurt and angry feelings she has toward the boy for being male, as Dr. Seggev's patient did, thereby developing what is known as a "reaction formation." Dr. Fisher explains, "Since it's considered such a terrible thing for mothers to hate their own children, they may become extra good, extra kind, and extra loving toward them. Years later these mothers may say, 'I did everything for him. Why doesn't he feel as if I loved him as much as I loved his brother or sister?' But the message was communicated in a whole variety of other ways, unspoken and otherwise, which the child was picking up. He develops a sense that he wasn't good enough, or didn't feel special enough. She's rejected him on some level, and then later in life he rejects her."

Some women just won't accept a boy for what he is. If they can't give birth to a girl, they will mold their son into a daughter. They will dress him and treat him as they would a girl, a situation that contributes to gender confusion. In extreme cases, the unwanted boy may grow up to be a transvestite or transsexual. Research conducted by two Welsh psychiatrists has shown that the mothers of transvestites and transsexuals were more likely than the mothers of normal heterosexual men to have wanted a daughter instead. (The fathers' preferences did not have the same impact on the sons' development.)

Acting out a desire for a girl can have serious consequences. But denying such a desire doesn't seem to help the situation very much. What helps is for a woman to try to understand, before the birth of her child, why its sex is so important to her. Would she see a son as the rivalrous brother of her youth? Would she see him as the masculine part of her own personality? Would she see him as a substitute for a disappointing mate, or as her husband's ally? It is not until she sees him neither as sinner nor savior but as a child that she is ready to begin an honest and loving relationship with him.

2

Our Fathers, Our Brothers, Our Sons

*H*e may look like just another newborn to the casual observer—a bit punch-drunk from his recent fight to get from womb to world, stubby-nosed and puffy-eyed and pigeon-toed. One adorably squashed baby face looks very much like another. But to a mother such confusion is impossible. She may look at her son and see her father in the curve of his cheek or the blue of his eyes. Or she may listen to him cry and hear an envied brother's squawks from the nursery that was once hers. Or she may nurse him at her breast and feel the pleasure of her husband's embraces. This baby boy arouses the male imagery that has accumulated, layer by layer, since her own earliest years. He is born not only into her genetic heritage but also into the legacy of the men who have peopled her life.

How a mother reacts to this latest male in her life will be powerfully influenced by the way she was treated by the first male in her life, her father. Whether he loved her too much or too little, and whether or not he is alive to celebrate the birth of his grandson, his hand is on the cradle. The kind of man he was sets up his daughter's expectations of what men in general are like and what this baby boy will be like. The way her father treated her, the way he treated her mother, will all have bearing on the way she treats her son. His denigration of her femininity, or his appreciation of it, will help to determine whether she fears or fosters her son's masculinity. According to psychoanalytic theory, a girl develops her style of relating to males at a very young age, during the first three to five years of life. And while this style can be modified by later experience, her basic feelings about men come from this early period.

A study recently conducted at the University of Lund in Sweden examined the relationships between sixty-nine women and their fathers, husbands, and sons. How does a woman's relationship with one affect her relationship with the others? First, it was discovered that women who were dissatisfied with their marriages often reported poor early emotional relations to their fathers. (Their early relations with their mothers were not as potent in predicting future happiness with a mate.) Second, a mother's attitude toward her son was strongly bound up with her early experience of her father. She was more likely to see her son in a positive light if her relationship with her father had been good, more likely to be rejecting of her son if her relationship with her father had been poor. Such feelings were not lost on the son. At the tender age of four, he was more likely to describe his mother negatively if her relationship with her own father had been negative.

Interestingly, the study found that a woman's relationship with her father was not a good predictor of her relationship with a daughter. The researchers stressed the very specific impact of a woman's image of her father on her way of relating to other important males in her life. They

pointed out that a girl's image of herself as a woman is de-
rived in large part from her interaction with members of
the opposite sex, primarily her father. "This implies that
the father will be considered the prototype of men in general and that the relationship to him will be considered as
'typical' for relationships to men," the researchers determined. Barely out of the womb, the newborn baby boy
may be seen in terms of the loving father, the playful
father, the rejecting father, the punishing father, or the
father who was never there.

If the boy is lucky, things were going fairly well for his
mother twenty or thirty years back. She was not a disappointment to her father, not a girl who should have been
a boy. She was loved for herself and for the woman she
would become. "If she felt valued and accepted, she's more
likely to accept her child," says Dr. Lorelle Saretsky, a psychoanalyst on the faculty of Adelphi University's Institute
of Advanced Psychological Studies. "If she feels that men
are warm and soft and giving and kind, she'll expect her
son to be that way, too. Her perception of what maleness
is about comes mostly from her father, from the traits she
sees in him and from how he treated her. As a mother to
a son, she draws on that experience."

Justin is one of the lucky ones. He's the three-year-old
son of a woman whose father loved her and showed it. The
woman is in her midthirties now, but she has not forgotten
her father's nurturance and praise. "I always had the feeling that my father approved of me," recalls Anne. "When
I got dressed for a date, he always told me how pretty I
looked. If I told him something that was on my mind, he
would let me know that he valued what I said and respected me." Despite her positive experiences with that
first male in her life, her father, she was not so sure what
it would be like to have a male creature for a child. She
wondered how a son would compare with the daughter she
already had. "I loved my daughter so, I couldn't imagine
what it would be like to take care of a son. How would

I raise him? How could I avoid being sexist? How would I react to buying boring boys' clothes? How would I react to taking care of a penis?" But one look at her baby boy and her anxieties disappeared. "I adore him. I find myself giving him lots of hugs. I just think he's precious. His physique is so cute, his personality is all his own. And there are scenes right out of my past. If I'm getting dressed to go out he says, 'Mommy, you're beautiful.' I just love that. I could hear it every day." Justin is certainly getting his fair share of mother love. One reason for his good fortune is that his mother was loved as a daughter.

But there can be too much of a good thing. If a girl is loved too intensely by an adoring, overpowering father, she may set impossible standards for the other males in her life. With such a beginning, what man could measure up to Daddy? Who could accomplish as much and love her as well? Women who have examined their pasts may go on to have healthy relationships with husbands and sons alike. They may realize that what they had with their fathers was unique to that relationship, that the other men in their lives will offer them something different, their own special kind of love. But women unwilling to explore their pasts may spend their lives looking for someone like Dear Old Dad. Most likely, such a woman will decide that her husband does not fill the bill, and she will make his shortcomings obvious to her growing son. Perhaps it is in that *son* that she will find what she's been looking for. Perhaps *he* will meet the standard of her father—that is, if he's willing to protect her and adore her and grow up in the image of his grandfather. His task is set for him, even before he arrives.

Ironically, when things sound too good between father and daughter, often they weren't very good at all. There may well be an unconscious cover-up of those *other* times, the times he humiliated her with a look or a word, or made her feel unworthy because she was a girl. By idealizing him she is canceling out those painful past experiences, but she is also setting a trap for the men of her future. Her son may be expected to live up to totally unrealistic expectations. Either she may blind herself to her son's faults, as she did to her father's: He's male, and he can do no wrong. Or she may react in the opposite way, becoming unreasonably critical. If she takes the latter path, then nothing he does would be good enough for her because "Dad would do it better."

Sometimes a woman's feelings of rage toward her father have not been repressed. She remembers all too well the feeling of being unloved, rejected, or even abused by him. It may be her little boy who will bear the brunt of her rage. She may try to take charge of him and make him into the "right" kind of person, someone very different from her father, even if it means making him miserable in the process. But not all women react to an unhappy relationship with their father in the same way, points out Dr. Lyle Greenman, a New York psychoanalyst. An alternative reaction is for the woman to fantasize that her son will be the good father she never had; she may expect things from him that a child cannot and should not provide a parent. Both of these reactions are unconsciously motivated, says Dr. Greenman. The woman does not understand why she's acting the way she is. But in both instances the boy serves to satisfy his mother's unconscious emotional needs, not to develop into his own person. Only if his mother begins to understand and modify her behavior will he be free to live his own life. A woman who can see, really see, what has happened to her, can do her best to see that it does not happen to her son.

LIKE BROTHER, LIKE SON?

Although a girl's father is usually the primary male figure in her life, there is sometimes another important masculine influence to be reckoned with. Need your bed short-sheeted? Need a good dose of unmerciful teasing? A brother would doubtless be happy to oblige. Need an ally against an unreasonable parent or a protector from a bully at school? Again, it's brother who will most likely volunteer, even if it means risking a sore fist and a black eye. The impact of siblings cannot be underestimated, though it has been in the past by psychologists and other researchers. But now siblings are getting recognition for their important role in shaping each other's personalities, abilities, and ambitions. And siblings who are of the opposite sex inevitably help shape each other's concepts of masculinity and femininity.

If a girl's relationship with her brother is a "normal" one—that is, horrible but not so bad—then it will help give her a positive image of what maleness is about. One woman I spoke to recalls with fondness the days she helped take care of her baby brother. He was a "good child" she says, and she remembers the fun they had together. "I have sweet memories of that period," she told me. "So I like when people compare my son Joshua to my brother. Joshua reminds me of my brother, and that has a good connotation for me." In the family she grew up in, the children were treated in an evenhanded fashion. She was not favored over her brother nor vice versa. But parents can undermine the healthy relationship between brother and sister if they put too much of a premium on one sex or the other; and in the past, more often than not, the premium had been placed on the son. You can be sure that a girl is not going to like her brother much if he always gets the car seat by the window and first crack at the television dial. What's so good about boys anyway, the sister may wonder? Not much, she may decide. Her son may end up the ultimate victim of her parents' sexual favoritism.

A story related to me by a psychoanalyst was a perfect illustration of the link between brother and son. The woman she told me about grew up in a situation of intense sibling rivalry with her brother, who seemed a difficult person to match. "She felt the struggle all through adult-hood," her analyst told me. "When she had her own children she was grossly inequitable, clearly favoring her daughter in the sibling rivalry between her daughter and son. She encouraged the girl to act out flagrant hostility toward her younger brother. Her attitude was not helpful to the daughter or to the son." Sometimes if a competitive sibling situation can be worked out in adulthood, either through family therapy or through a recognition of how the parents set up the rivalry, it can make life more harmonious for the next generation of siblings.

FROM SAVIOR TO SCAPEGOAT

Though the males from a woman's childhood strongly influence the way she feels toward her son, it is the current relationship between a woman and her partner that has the most powerful impact on the mother–son relationship. If a woman's emotional needs are fulfilled through her relationship with her mate, she will not require that those needs be met by a son. She will be free to love him in a healthy maternal way without making unreasonable emotional demands on him. But if she is disappointed with her husband, she may try to make up for it with her son. As we saw in the last chapter, she may turn to him for the affection she craves.

According to Dr. Joel Sambursky, a clinical psychologist at Brooklyn Jewish Hospital's Developmental Clinic, "She tries to get from the child the love she doesn't get from her husband. She tries even harder as the son gets older and more manly. She expects to be nurtured in return for her nurturance. But a child does not give love back in this way. It won't happen, and if she expects it, she'll be disappointed."

Some women in unhappy marriages will move in the

opposite direction. They will become so depressed over the situation that they remove themselves emotionally from their sons and daughters, leaving them with a withdrawn or sad or angry mother. Instead of being mothered too much, the children will be mothered too little.

If the marriage actually dissolves, the son may face a different kind of problem. Sean is only nine months old but not too young to be the scapegoat of his parents' separation. He has three older sisters whom his mother perceives as wonderful children. But Sean, she told me, was trouble from the start. "Every other week there was something else wrong, a cold, a cough, an infection," she related. "He was so fussy. And he wasn't growing properly. The baby put a terrible strain on the family. The whole house was topsy-turvy. The baby was always crying. It was a very tense place.

"My husband is a very demanding person. He always wants things his way. He needs someone to get for him and do for him. I had filled the bill up till then. But after Sean was born, I had nothing left. That's when the breakdown in our marriage occurred. It was because the baby was so hard and my husband was the way he was. We separated when Sean was seven months old."

Was Sean really such a hard baby—or does it just seem that way from the perspective of a wrecked marriage? Is it that his mother is angry at him for the spot she thinks he put her in? Or has he become difficult because she has been difficult with him? In her mind it seems she has merely swapped a husband for a son, one demanding male for another.

When marriages break up, a son is often seen as the "bad" husband. Much of what a woman didn't like about her husband will be projected onto the boy, especially if father and son look or act alike. Some sons who start life with this disadvantage manage to overcome it. But the chances for a son's emotional well-being are best if the mother can come to terms with the truth of who he really is, irrespective of any problems she may have had with his father, or her father or brother for that matter.

THE FACTS AND THE FICTIONS

A woman's relationship with her son is determined not only by her past and present experiences with men but by the kind of infant he is. Is he active or passive? Contented or cranky? Healthy or sickly? The specific temperament of the baby will certainly affect his relationship with his mother. But something else will play an even more signifi-cant role, and that is the prevailing cultural attitudes toward the sexes. Though the gap has narrowed consider-ably, in this culture boys are still thought to be very dif-ferent from girls. They are expected to cry differently, to crawl differently, to throw differently, and even to think differently. And yet scientists have found more similarities than differences between the sexes. In general, baby boys are no more active, competitive, or dominant than their fe-male counterparts, and baby girls are no more anxious, timid, or nurturant than boys, according to numerous studies.

There are some obvious physical differences between male and female babies, however, beyond the ones that make a boy a boy and a girl a girl. Male babies tend to be larger than female babies. They also seem better able to lift their heads early on. But larger and stronger does not mean sturdier or healthier. Males are more likely to suc-cumb to illness or even death during the first year of life. By any nonmuscular measure, males are the frailer sex, and in many areas they seem less developed than their female counterparts. For example, there is some evidence that baby boys are less responsive to auditory stimuli than are baby girls. Also, right from the start, male babies tend to carry on and cry more than female ones. And if their crying seems only infrequently punctuated by the silence of slumber, it's probably not just the imagination of a mother bordering on maternal burnout. Boy babies do tend to sleep less than girl babies.

If you consider these early sex differences less than astonishing, you'll be interested to know that scientists are equally unimpressed. Dr. Michael Lewis, a Rutgers Medical School professor and prominent researcher in infant development, says, "There is just one thing unique to the mother of a male newborn. That is her confrontation with male genitals. That difference is clear-cut. Other than that, there's no way to predict how a woman's daughter and son will be different. That's totally up for grabs. A mother will face more individual differences than differences based on sex."

But more clear-cut differences do begin to emerge in the second and third years of life, differences in activity level, aggression, and play behavior. Could any of these differences be traced back to the mother, to a disparity between the way she handles her son and daughter? Most mothers would deny any responsibility for this, insisting that their babies get identical treatment regardless of their sex. But according to Dr. Rose Caron, the director of the Infant Research Laboratory in Silver Spring, Maryland, mothers of infant sons do focus on their sons' masculine attributes. "Women who come here with their babies show tremendous pride in their children, regardless of the sex," relates Dr. Caron, who is also professor of psychology at George Washington University. "But mothers of sons are more likely to be particularly proud of their son's physical prowess, saying things like, 'He's going to be a football player someday.' They say this especially if the infant is large and well developed."

Studies that have shown mothers sex-stereotyping their children—playing with them differently, giving them "sex-appropriate" toys—typically show that they are not aware they are doing it. But even if they are aware of what they are doing, very few will admit it. As Dr. Lewis puts it, "In this day and age you're not likely to hear anyone say, 'I treat my children differently, as a rule, based on the old wretched stereotypes, and I'm disgusted with myself for doing it.' " But those stereotypes are potent, he adds. "Biology works in a funny sort of way. It informs us and creates a stereotype. Our behavior to the child is then in keeping with the biological stereotype. But the stereotype provides relatively no information that is relevant to the individual child."

PRODUCING A PENIS

One reason that mothers act differently with boys is that they often feel differently about them from the start. From the moment of birth, to mother a son is a different experience from mothering a daughter. It is to know that out of your female body you have produced a male body, which can be a startling discovery. As one psychiatric social worker, who had her two sons almost twenty years ago, recalls, "The production of a penis out of a female body is a shocking experience, a shock that's probably universal. When I had my first son I thought, 'This is not right. How did this happen? What would I do with a boy?' It made more alien the sensation of having a baby. Having a boy added a piece of shock to the whole event."

And yet after the shock of the birth is over, after the feeling of awkwardness in holding and tending the male baby has subsided, many women begin to feel less pressure with a son; they are not as likely to feel that they must be perfect mothers. After all, as a female, isn't there a limit to what she can know about the wants and needs of a male child? Any mistakes she makes can be attributed to the differences between the sexes rather than to any incompetence on her part. One mother of a young son explained it like this: "I was glad I had a son because I had a built-in excuse for not knowing what I was doing. If anyone complained, I would tell them to talk to my husband, that he's the one who should know how to handle the baby. I just didn't feel the pressure to perform that I would have if I'd had a daughter."

A son is easier for a mother on a psychological level, too. As Dr. Joy Osofsky, research and staff psychologist at the Menninger Foundation in Topeka, Kansas, says, "Even though a son is unfamiliar because of his sex, the mother–son relationship generally has less conflict all the way along than a mother–daughter one. For a mother, a daughter is like a re-creation of herself. There's anxiety that the baby will become like her. Through each stage of the girl's development, the mother reexamines herself and reexperiences what she's been through. That leads to conflict. But a boy is different. The mother can relax more. Her thought is, 'I don't know just what it is he's experiencing, but I'll hang in there and support him.'" Having a son means that a mother does not have to look so closely at herself, nor relive a past that she would rather leave behind.

In general, there tends to be more affection shown between mother and son than between mother and daughter, particularly in the first few months of the baby's life. Various studies have found that mothers spend more time feeding, holding, looking at, and exercising baby boys than they do girls. In mothers who are excited about having a baby, the differences are most dramatic. In one study, mothers were first interviewed while pregnant and rated for the degree of excitement and enthusiasm detectable in their speech. Those same mothers were then observed with their new babies three times during the first three months after the birth. The enthusiastic mothers-to-be who went on to have sons were physically affectionate with their baby boys, kissing and holding them frequently. But those who had girls seemed more interested in teaching them than in touching them. They tried to stimulate them with sounds and sights, concentrating more on their intellect than on their emotions.

But before a year is up, something comes between mother and son, breaking into the intimacy, forcing them apart. That something is the cultural message that mothers and sons shouldn't be *too* close, a message delivered with force by neighbor and relative alike. "Don't make a mama's boy out of him," they say. "Don't always be holding him. It's just not natural." And so by six months or so the breakup begins, a breakup that's as hard on the mother as it is on the son. From that time, until at least two years of age, daughters get more from mothers than sons do. They are touched more, rocked more, looked at more, talked to more. Jonathan Segal of the Catholic University of America, writing in a 1981 issue of *The Journal of Psychology,* attributes this "abandonment" of boys to a sudden concern for their masculinization. Based on his research with the parents of infants, he found that "parents placed significantly more emphasis on the importance of their sons' masculinity, and less emphasis on their daughters' femininity, as their children matured through the first year of life. Apparently six months of age is a pivotal period in parental sex-role perceptions of their children." It is when parents no longer see their sons as sexless babies; it is when they begin socializing their sons for manhood.

Dr. Michael Lewis believes the pivotal moment comes when the baby begins to move around and becomes interested in the objects around him. The male child is encouraged by his parents in this orientation toward objects and away from his mother. "You don't want your son hanging around you," says Lewis. "You're uncomfortable with him touching you and you touching him. You want him to move away, to go play with his building blocks. That is the beginning of the push away." A girl is pushed away too but not so forcefully, nor so precipitously.

An Educational Testing Service study conducted by Dr. Lewis and Jeanne Brooks looked at the behavior of opposite-sex twins in a playroom situation with their mothers. The little girls, aged thirteen to fourteen months, looked at their mothers, moved close to them, and touched them more often than their brothers did. But according to the researchers, such sex-related differences in behavior are not innately programmed. Instead, they are based on the teachings of the mothers who allow their daughters to come close and keep their sons away.

As Dr. Joy Osofsky of the Menninger Foundation says, "Women are afraid of holding onto a male child too long or of being overly nurturant. They think it will make the boy too feminine, so they tend to push him away too early and too hard. They encourage him to be a 'big boy' when he's still a little boy and needs mothering. Nurturing and loving are very important parts of the early mother–child relationship, as important for a son as for a daughter." It's not overprotection that Dr. Osofsky recommends but a balance between the security of closeness and the encouragement of independence. "A mother should be aware of the normal developmental times when a child moves away, as well as be alert to her child's own style. She should encourage her son as he explores and moves away, and be supportive when he comes back to her as a secure base. This movement should be neither discouraged by the mother nor forced. A son does not have to fulfill his mother's standards of what a male should be." As an interesting sidelight to Dr. Osofsky's comments, research has shown that a mother's warmth neither increases nor decreases her son's masculinity. Instead, it is a mother's restrictive and punitive behavior that feminizes her son. In other words, to allow a boy maternal warmth is not to undermine his masculinity. Harsh punishing behavior is the threat.

INFANT EROTICISM

At the heart of the relationship between mothers and sons is an erotic force that binds them together early on, relaxes its grip during the "terrible twos," and then binds them more tightly than ever during the years of Oedipal upheaval. Some women are aware of their feelings and delight in them from the first: "What a sexy little baby!" they say of their newborn sons. And as they gaze at the baby's body, they fall hopelessly in love with an image of the man he will become. Other women are horrified at the very idea of an erotic attraction to an infant. Indeed, they may be even more horrified at the notion expressed by Dr. Eleanor Galenson, a clinical professor of psychiatry at the Mount Sinai School of Medicine in New York—that a daughter too may arouse such frightening and forbidden feelings.

"A mother will react erotically to both sexes," asserts this pioneer researcher in infant sexuality. "It's an early and protean eroticism between mother and baby, boy or girl. Every woman who feeds and fondles and bathes a child experiences it. It allows her to do all this caretaking willingly because of the pleasure she gets. We're afraid to call it erotic, but that's what it is. It's absolutely normal. You can see it in any mother on any day of the week as she kisses and fondles and rubs her infant with intense pleasure on both sides." Dr. Galenson is careful to distinguish this normal eroticism from pathological sexual desire for the child, desire based on the belief that the child could actually be a sexual partner.

Other psychologists point to a unique type of eroticism between a mother and her son, an eroticism flavored by their sexual differences, by the sense of "otherness" each feels about the other. The fact that he came from her body is exciting; the fact that his body is the antithesis of her own heightens the excitement. "An eroticized relationship between a mother and a son is very normal," stresses Dr. Osofsky. "If the mother is stable and can be loving to her son without becoming too invested or symbiotic with him, that eroticism promotes normal healthy closeness."

Those sentiments are echoed by Dr. Ildiko Mohacsy, an assistant professor of psychiatry at the Mount Sinai School of Medicine. "Every normal woman has sexual feelings for her son. He's a little man who needs her. It's different from a grownup relationship, where two people have to come together in mood and in emotion. A baby is always available, always needy, always grateful for whatever you do to his little body. The mother has the pleasure of busying herself with his body, or kissing him from head to toe. In our culture, we avoid that somewhat. We're worried about Oedipus, and so we inhibit ourselves. But in primitive societies, they kissed their infant from top to bottom."

In some cultures, male babies have been the focus of a great deal of sexual activity. In medieval society, for example, grandmothers were expected to masturbate their grandchildren. At the turn of the sixteenth century, parents were counseled by Gabriel Fallopius, the anatomist who first described the fallopian tubes, to "be zealous in infancy to enlarge the penis of the boy." Even more recently, in the early twentieth century, some nurses in the United States were known to stimulate babies at the breast to keep them quiet. And to this day, some Navajo mothers masturbate their male babies and kiss them passionately on the mouth while feeding them.

Though this behavior might seem extreme to most Americans today, even in our culture a boy's genitals are more open for discussion and more likely to be touched than are a girl's. "Boys are supposed to have a large penis. Boys are supposed to be sexual," points out Dr. Lorelle Saretsky. "There's a lot of concern about his sexual organ. There's a looking ahead to his sexual appearance. With little girls, we don't think of how big their breasts are going to be. Girls are supposed to be pretty and clean, with nothing showing. Their sexuality is underplayed. With boys, the importance of sexuality is exaggerated."

Even in the hospital, the size of a boy's penis can be a focus of attention. One mother told me of her pride when the nurses pointed out her son's "overendowment." Another mother was concerned that her second son didn't "measure up" to her first. "I'm afraid he's always going to feel inferior because of it," she worried. Still another mother of two sons explained to me, in minute detail, how her sons' genitalia differed not only in size but also in shape.

In everyday routines of washing, diapering, and powdering their sons, some mothers worry about making too much contact. "Will I stimulate him too much?" they may ask aloud, but the real message is "Will I stimulate *myself* too much?"

Dr. Galenson refers to "unconscious fantasies" provoked in both parents, but especially in the mother, in the course of handling the infant's genitals during caretaking activities. Some mothers will respond to their fantasies by cleaning the genitals until they are red; others will avoid the area completely—even if it means a rash for the baby.

For women uncomfortable with their son's sexuality, the feeling tends to start early on, which is not surprising since boys are capable of having erections from the first day of life. (In fact, there is evidence from sonograms—pictures made inside a pregnant woman's body by high-frequency sound waves—that erections occur in utero.) And most boys discover their genitals before their first birthday, an average of one to three months earlier than girls do. During the next year, both male and female babies engage in masturbation, frequently and persistently manipulating their genitals. Sometimes they involve their mothers in their activities, touching her body during or after masturbation. Drs. Galenson and Herman Roiphe, associate professor of psychiatry at the Mount Sinai School of Medicine, have noted sex differences in this early genital play.

A boy's play tends to be more persistent, more focused, and more frequent (probably because of the greater exposure of his genitals, the presence of erections from birth onward, and the difference in parental handling). So if a mother notices that Johnny is "doing it" more than Joanie ever did, it should not be surprising.

Though infant sexuality is hardly a subject that comforts the average parent, it does have an important role in a child's development. According to Drs. Galenson and Roiphe, a child's "pleasure in masturbation seems to expand and fortify the sense of self and sexual identity." Whether a child's sexuality develops as it should depends largely on the attitude of the mother. Several studies have shown that where mothering is inadequate, children do not develop normal autoerotic behavior. Apparently a mother's tender and loving caresses stimulate pleasurable feelings in her infant, which he then tries to recreate through his own erotic stimulation. By allowing herself pleasure in her son's body, a mother makes it possible for her son to experience the pleasures of sensuality from the beginning of his life.

But many mothers are too panicked by the whole subject of their son's sexuality to enjoy it in any way. As Dr. Galenson explains, she saw this clearly in the course of her study: "The striking thing is that a parent and I would together witness a child masturbating and several weeks later the parent would deny she ever saw it. Parents push the memory of that underground. Infant sexuality is a hot potato. It arouses a lot of uncomfortable feelings in adults. For one, it brings to mind the sexual feelings they have toward their children. For another, it's a reminder of their own early sexual feelings which they've spent years getting hold of and regulating. Seeing their infant's sexual activities puts their own control in jeopardy."

Whether the mother of sons experiences discomfort in this regard often depends on the relationship she had with her father. As Dr. Galenson points out, some women have never taken the crucial step in their development from attachment to mother, to a loving, comfortable, and sexual (though not incestuous) relationship with father. She can be Daddy's *little* girl, but she never develops into Daddy's *sexual* girl. "That step has to be made before women can be comfortable with male sexuality. It has to be made for her to allow her son to become a sexual being."

Infancy seems like an innocent period, a period when boys and girls are very much alike, when calmness reigns before the storm of Oedipus. But the challenges of this period are tremendous. It is a time when parents must hold their children close and yet encourage them to begin to separate. For the mother of a son, the challenge is to begin to let go very gently so that the baby never feels abandoned. It is also to let his sexuality develop naturally as he learns to delight in the pleasures of his body. And it is to see him neither as a perfect father, nor an imperfect husband or lover, but as an infant who needs the emotional steadiness and the nurturance of a mother who sees him for who he is.

3

The Oedipal Age

*J*ust as a mother has gotten used to her young son's moves toward independence and a world larger than home after his first three or four years, she may find that he is headed right back toward her and with something other than the intimacy of infancy on his mind. Before Sigmund Freud's illumination of the sexual side of childhood, and his formulation of the Oedipal complex theory, the boy's manner of approach might have caused a great deal of consternation. A mother might have wondered just what kind of little sex fiend she was bringing up: "Want to marry me, do you? Why don't you go propose to someone your own size!"

But today, if a boy doesn't become glassy-eyed at a glimpse of his mother's body, if he doesn't try to persuade her to give up "big bad Dad" for "lovable little me," she may worry that he is not developing as a little boy should. After all, doesn't every normal boy want to sleep with his mother, and get rid of his father in the bargain?

As one of these little boys, now grown up, said for himself: "I loved my mother. I think there would have been nothing better than to have had an affair with her. I think everyone ought to have an affair with his mother." That is not the mythical Oedipus Rex speaking. That is real-life Bob Fosse of Broadway fame, as quoted in a recent book of celebrity interviews entitled *Public Spectacles*.

Some mothers eagerly look ahead to the erotic attentions of their sons. It is certainly flattering to have such an ardent admirer. But other women don't want to believe that their innocent little boy could harbor such unthinkable thoughts about them, that the look in his childish eyes is lust, that his hands are groping for more than maternal softness and warmth. It just can't be true that a young boy sees his mother in a sexual way. Or can it?

THE ORIGINS OF OEDIPUS

In the Sophoclean tragedy of *Oedipus Rex,* an oracle prophesizes that a son born to Laius, King of Thebes, and his wife, Jocasta, will one day kill his father and marry his mother. Although Laius abandons young Oedipus and leaves him to die, the prophesized events come to pass. Oedipus does grow up to unwittingly slay his father and to wed his mother, and then to tear out his own eyes when he learns the ghastly truth. According to Freud, what Oedipus does in this legend is what *all* boys wish to do (but without the punishment of blindness). In the son's desire to possess his mother, the father becomes his rival. But father is big and strong, and can retaliate with the threat of castration. So in order to protect himself from his father's vengeance, the son begins to identify with him, to become like him, which allows his masculinity to flourish. In addition to enabling boys to become men, the Oedipal stage is purported to enable men to become lovers. As written many years ago in a book entitled *Fathers Are Parents, Too* by O. Spurgeon English and Constance J. Foster, "no man has ever yet been able to love another woman unless he has first loved his own mother and wished, in his own childish way, that she were his own." So a child's brush against a breast may prefigure a man's ardent embrace of his lover, and a sleepy good-night kiss may provide the promise of a sexual future with a woman other than Mother.

For some time, Freud's formulation was treated as gospel. His translation of *Oedipus Rex* from Greek tragedy to universal complex was hailed as genius, and anyone who took issue with it was branded a heretic. "For many years, the Oedipus complex was swallowed hook, line and sinker by psychoanalysts," says Ted Dubinsky, a New York psychotherapist. "They really believed it. It became the basis of the whole psychoanalytic theory." As one aspect of this theory, it was thought that an unresolved Oedipus complex was at the root of most adult mental disorders: If a boy didn't come to realize that he could not have his mother, if he didn't come to realize that there is nothing left for him but to be like his father, he was destined for a life of anguish or analysis.

POWER OR PATHOLOGY?

There are still many staunch believers in the Oedipal concept among psychoanalytic purists. "The Oedipal phase is crucial," maintains one analyst. "It is the greatest love affair of a man's whole life. Some people have put it down because of the intensity of the feelings. There is no situation in life as powerful as the Oedipal conflict and the taboo. The little boy does want to marry his mother and give her a baby. Of course, his image of sex is different from the adult one, but he does want to take his father's place."

However, some therapists take issue with the universality, the inevitability, and the significance of the Oedipus complex. It *can* occur, they say, but only as a symptom of an unhealthy family situation. "The Oedipus complex is an extension of competition between the parents," contends Dr. Eleanor Yachnes, an analyst on the faculty of the American Institute of Psychoanalysis, and associated with the Karen Horney Clinic in New York. "It happens when each parent wants more of the child's admiration than the other. It's like when grandparents want to know whether the child likes grandma A or grandma B better. It's a struggle for stardom, and the child is the guinea pig. Oedipal rivalry does not occur when parents are respectful of each other and of the child. It is neither a psychological nor a biological must."

What, then, is the truth about Oedipus? One of the criticisms of Freud's formulation has been that he did not himself work with children who were presumably experiencing the complex; instead, he pieced together the theory out of the memories of his adult patients. But today's child therapists are hearing it directly out of the mouths of babes. "There are those who minimize it, but those who listen to children find continuous evidence of it," says Dr. Peter Neubauer, director of the Child Development Center in New York. "The son recognizes himself not just as a child but as a boy. He looks at his mother not just as a mother but as a woman, and at his father as a male. All those relationships are tested during this period. The boy communicates to the mother, 'I want to be close to you. I want to replace Father. I want to sleep on your side of the bed.' Children are freer in expressing these kinds of thoughts these days. What it means, sexually, depends on a child's developmental state. A five-year-old is not like a fifteen-year-old. But the Oedipal stage is a period of possessiveness, of exclusivity, of jealousy."

Dr. Reed Welson of the Queens Children's Psychiatric Center is another child therapist who says that Oedipal issues come up frequently with the children he works with. In play therapy, for example, young boys often move the father doll out of the scene, leaving the boy doll and the mother doll alone together in the playhouse.

Some boys find it too scary to go after their mothers, so they hide their feelings or express them in subtle ways. Others simply choose a safe substitute. One six-year-old selected Olivia Newton-John as his model Oedipal object. He urged his mother to wear her hair like Olivia, to slim down like Olivia, to look and act like Olivia. Not all boys have such specific Oedipal substitutes in mind. In many cases any female will do, sometimes even an inanimate one. For instance, Jayne, a suburban mother and lawyer, discovered that her sons, aged seven and four, took inordinate pleasure in examining whatever it is that mannequins have under their skirts.

It's not hard to see why a little boy would want his mother all to himself. Dr. Robert Mendelsohn of Adelphi University's Institute of Advanced Psychological Studies explains it from the point of view of the child: "The boy's mother holds him and powders him and feeds him. But then some man comes in at night, spends a few minutes with him, and then distracts Mommy. He takes the attention away. Does the boy want to kill his father? He certainly wants the competition to go bye-bye."

But just because the boy wants the relationship with his mother to be exclusive, does that necessarily mean he wants it to be sexual? We know that genital sensations do occur in little boys, and that they can be very excitable in response to their mothers. They can have erections and even experience orgasms. But these feelings are limited to the genitals. Eroticism is not experienced at a higher level because children do not have the romantic imagination of the mature adult. Our experience of sex is very different from that of our children. What they experience, their feelings for their mother, are perfectly appropriate for their stage of development. Such feelings are not unhealthy or anything to get alarmed about. Says Dr. Henry Paul, a New York City psychiatrist, "There is nothing sick or ill about it. The real illness is if parents get excited about it."

When most people think of the Oedipal period they are referring to the years from three to five, when the boy is too old for diapers but too young for school, just the right age to be Mother's little love. But some boys don't wait until their diapers are off to be turned on by mother. One boy, William, was just nineteen months old when he insisted that his place was next to his mother in his parents' double bed. Every night he would want to climb into bed with her, kissing her, running his hands over her nightgown.

But even more difficult than detecting the exact beginning of this period is pinpointing its end. Is it at five, or six, or seven? The more researchers look at the mother–son relationship, the more it seems that the Oedipal conflict never ends, though it certainly varies in intensity. In this respect it has been compared in the *Bulletin of the Menninger Clinic* to a character in a play: "By no means is it an event which plays a tumultuous but short-lived role limited to the phallic scene of the play of life, but it is rather a constantly reappearing character which comes across the stage in new and changing roles progressing with the ages of man."

FROM SEXUALITY TO SEX ROLES

Just as a boy is dealing with his feelings toward his mother, he is also coping with another important aspect of this developmental stage, that is, the establishment of his sex–role identification. According to Freud, the appropriate sex identification will occur as the boy begins to resolve the Oedipal crisis and model himself after his father in order to ward off his wrath. But what role does the mother play in all this, other than to be the object of both of their affections? What can she do to influence the future of her son's masculinity? The concern of mothers used to be solely that their sons be masculine enough, that they be assertive, independent, and completely unfeminine. But some mothers are now rejecting this macho model in favor of a softened version of masculinity, one that combines the best of both male and female qualities. Interestingly, a number of studies have shown that androgynous males—those who embrace the positive traits of both sexes—have higher self-esteem, more positive attitudes toward sexuality, and are better adjusted than highly masculine or feminine men.

But if a woman thinks she can leave the whole matter of her son's sexual identification to her husband, believing he will be the boy's sole role model, she is underrating her own importance and influence in her son's life. According to the Yale psychologists Dorothy Singer and Jerome Singer, both the persistent aggressiveness of boys and their sense of male superiority are actually fostered by their mothers. Women are often more subservient to their sons than to their daughters, intentionally losing to them at games, comparing their own "weaknesses" as women to their sons' masculine strength. They may also play the traditionally helpless female by being unable to make the simplest repairs around the house or refusing to take the wheel of the car if their husbands are available to drive. As a result of this kind of behavior, sons will begin to see males as the stronger sex and females as second-class citizens. Wanting to be strong themselves, they will take on only clearly masculine attributes.

A woman who has herself embraced the androgynous ideal—allowing both her own masculine and feminine qualities to emerge—will help her son move in that direction. He will see that a woman does not have to be trapped by her gender and neither does a man. He will come to understand that every person is free to explore and develop to his or her fullest human potential.

Another important influence on a boy's sex-role identification is the nature of his parents' relationship. If he sees his parents in an equal relationship, one in which the work is shared, including the work of child rearing, he will probably use that example in his own life and his own relationships, expanding them beyond the limits traditionally set by rigid sex roles. The mother's challenge is thus not only to stretch her own sex role boundaries, but also to allow her mate to explore and exhibit both his feminine and masculine attributes, showing their son all the things a man can be.

This is not to say that a boy shouldn't be encouraged to delight in his burgeoning masculinity. But it is not necessary for a mother to put herself down or limit the range of his play activities or his emotional expression in order to promote this. Trucks, guns, and bravado are not all there is to being a boy. What a mother can do is to express admiration of her son's masculinity and, just as important, admiration of his father. If she defines her mate, as well as other important men in their lives, as worthy people, the boy is likely to develop a positive image of what maleness is all about and what his own maleness means.

As the years pass and the boy becomes more and more independent, the mother is presented with frequent opportunities to reinforce her son's pride in himself as a male. It is her task to accept his moves away from her, to acknowledge him as an autonomous, separate individual. Her confidence in him will make him more confident in himself and in his maleness, confident enough not to have to act all man.

THE OTHER SIDE OF OEDIPUS

Thus far we have focused primarily on the experience of the son during the Oedipal period, on his desire for masculinity and his desire for his mother. But what about the mother's desires for her son? Though she is not likely, on a conscious level, to want to have sex with him, oftentimes she does find him to be very desirable, an attraction that increases as he develops from infancy to manhood. "It's totally normal to feel attracted to a son," asserts Dr. Jerome Kagan, a prominent authority in child development. "He's cuddly. He smells good. There's nothing wrong with feeling that way about a son, as long as the mother doesn't make him feel like a sexual target."

Not surprisingly, the average woman will not admit to her sexual feelings about her son, according to Dr. Robert Dickes, a psychiatrist associated with the Center for Human Sexuality at Downstate Medical Center in Brooklyn. But the attraction between mother and growing son should be nurtured rather than denied. It can help the boy feel good about himself as a male, help foster his developing sexuality, and bring out feelings of warmth, tenderness, and affection in him. Some women, especially ones who are healthy and liberated, will acknowledge that they feel an attraction for their son. But other mothers bend over backward not to acknowledge it or express it, and their fight against their natural feelings can be damaging to their sons. As Dr. Robert Mendelsohn says, "Some women repress their feelings and are cold to their sons. They think of their boys as X-rated movies, and they are filled with revulsion. But they still have to deal with their sons on a day-to-day basis. What will the self-image of these boys be? If they are kept at arm's distance because of their mother's mixed feelings, that spells disaster for the boy." Ironically, it is not unusual for a mother's denial of sexuality to result in an exaggeration of its importance in her son's mind. His sexuality will become the standard by which he judges himself. He will have to perform, he will have to be macho, he will have to be sexy, even though this is what his mother had hoped to avoid at all costs.

Other sons will respond by adopting their mother's anti-sexual stance. The message such sons have heard and learned well is that it is wrong to feel an attraction for someone of the opposite sex. Even if as an adult the son wants to be sexual, he may be afraid to express his sexuality for fear of failure. He hasn't learned the lesson from his mother of how to behave with a woman. So when he grows up he doesn't know how to please women: He just doesn't know what to do. Whatever he finally *does* do doesn't seem right because the message has always been to do nothing at all.

Some mothers cope very well with their infant sons. Unaware of their feelings of attraction toward such a tiny creature, they are not afraid to show their love. But they begin to have trouble as the boy grows up, as he becomes more adept with his body, more social, more verbal, more flirtatious: "Will you marry me, Mommy?"

A mother who acknowledges her feelings can acknowledge such invitations without actually accepting them. She can say, "No, Johnny, I can't marry you because I'm already married to Daddy. But when you grow up you'll find someone you'll love as much as me, and you'll marry her." As well as acknowledging his proposal she will acknowledge his sexuality, letting him know that it's a wonderful part of him. She'll give him the message that he's an attractive male, and that she loves him and adores him for it, as she does everything else about him, from his school achievements to his athletic abilities to his generosity. She'll give him the message that it's all right to be sexual. And she will enhance his sense of self by doing so.

But just as being too cool can interfere with a boy's development, so can being too warm. Affectionate warmth, of course, is wonderful. A mother's hugs and kisses are as nourishing to a boy's soul as food is to his body, and just as necessary. But too much food or affection can create problems, especially when used in an effort to control. Physical demonstrations that play into a boy's Oedipal fantasies will be at once arousing and frustrating to him and ultimately destructive.

Barbara, mother of three-year-old Ted, is someone who

cannot see the problem she is creating through her over-whelming affection for her son. "Everything is great now. Ted loves me so. He kisses me all the time, and I never stop kissing him. But I'm afraid my kisses won't be enough. Someday he will choose another woman."

Another mother, who has a six-year-old son, has already experienced the pain of jealousy. "I went along with Brian's class on a trip to an amusement park and I saw Brian walking along with a classmate, holding her hand. For a second, just a second, I felt terribly jealous. I thought to myself, 'He's still mine, you know.' " Another mother was horrified to hear her son cry out in the middle of a nightmare for a little girl from his kindergarten class. For the first five years of his life it was always *she* he wanted, always "Mommy" he called for when he needed comforting. "It came as a jolt for me," she admitted. "He's only five, but already he's out of the house and he's got his girls."

Of course, a certain amount of maternal jealousy is to be expected, particularly as a boy begins to emerge from the Oedipal period and notices that girls his own size can be even more fun than Mother. But such jealousy can be harmful if used to keep a son too closely bound to home. One woman told her son, as he began to look elsewhere, "You're always going to live here with me. If I don't like your girlfriends, you'll have to stay with me the rest of your life." She claims that she was kidding when she said it, but the message she transmitted to her son was clear: No matter how hard he looks, he'll find no match for Mother.

Other mothers show off their adult bodies to their sons in the hopes that this will persuade them that they need not look elsewhere. But just how will this affect young boys? "The effect of the mother's nudity depends on the context, on how it's done, on her attitude," says Dr. Jerome Kagan of Harvard University's Department of Psychology. "You can't say 'This will happen if you walk around without clothes.' Some children are influenced negatively and some aren't. The principle is that one particular practice, in and of itself, has no effect. It depends on how it's embedded in the culture and in the family's beliefs."

But some parents may be mistaken about their motives for undressing in front of their children. They may think that they are doing it out of a desire to be natural. In reality, they may be doing it out of a very different desire. According to Dr. Susan Coates, director of the Gender Identity Project at New York's Roosevelt Hospital, "Some parents who believe that their nudity is a natural expression are unconsciously using it to seduce and have power over their children. Some children who have been repeatedly exposed to parental nudity feel sexually excited, controlled, and intruded upon."

Other experts maintain that parental nudity will be detrimental to the child, whatever the motivation for it. Whether the mother thinks she is being natural or knows she is being seductive, it is an assault on her child. And even a very young child can be adversely affected, according to this view. One psychologist was surprised by the reaction her own eighteen-month-old nephew had to a single instance of nudity. "He was intensely fascinated when I undressed in front of him," she related. "It seemed too much of a reaction. He seemed to be erotically stimulated. You don't want to repress a child's sexuality, but you don't want all that libido on the surface." What's a child to do with all that libido, anyway? From the perspective of this psychologist, a child who is exposed to adult nudity is being stimulated without being given the channels to express his sexuality.

Dr. Robert Dickes considers frequent parental nudity a form of exhibitionism. "If on occasion a boy walks in while his mother is putting on a robe, that's okay. If the rest of his environment is normal, nothing will come of it. But often there are a number of stimulating things happening at once. A mother will be naked, and kiss and hug her child, and say 'Oh, how gorgeous you are.' Or she'll be naked and have him in bed with her. Children are usually tough enough to handle one thing that's inappropriate, but if there are many, they may be harmed."

THE SEDUCTIVE MOTHER

When a mother does behave seductively toward her son, it usually says more about the woman than about her child, more about her past relationships than about her present one. In all likelihood she herself was seduced as a child by a father who was eager to display to her his body but not his love. And she repeats the pattern with her son—stimulating him inappropriately, loving him inadequately. It may seem strange that sexuality should exist without affection, but that is the hallmark of the seductive family. There is a confusion between warmth and sexuality, and intimacy is possible only in a sexual context. Because of the confusion, the child may be sexually seduced and yet repressed at the same time. Dr. Henry Paul explains how those two apparent opposites can coexist: "A mother will walk naked in front of her son. He gets excited and masturbates. Then she admonishes him for playing with himself. Or she exposes her breast to the boy. If he tries to touch it, she tells him to stop. Why does she do that? It's because of her own upbringing. She is the victim of victims, her neurotic parents. Unresolved conflicts in the parents lead to double and triple messages given to the children."

Dale is both one of those parents and one of those children. The thirty-five-year-old woman seems, on the surface, like the Mom next door. A commercial artist for a West Coast firm, she is articulate, friendly, and caring of her two children, four-year-old Travis and five-month-old Justin. But her talk of her past and her present belies at least part of that image. As she relates it, her father was a classic example of the seductive parent, while paradoxically rejecting Dale for being a girl. "He was so disappointed in not having a son, he'd make jokes like 'You only have a crack, send it back,' or he'd say that he could only make buttonholes, never buttons. He made it clear in many ways that I was not what he had in mind for a child. I used to envy the little 'princess' on 'Father Knows Best.' I was most definitely not my father's little princess. And yet he was always appearing in front of me unclothed."

When Dale fantasized about children of her own, she imagined daughters. So when her sons were born, she was disappointed in their sex, as her father had been in hers. She had particular trouble in accepting her first son. "I wasn't so excited when he was born. I would have been more excited with a daughter. He was such a difficult baby, it made matters worse. He was so fussy. He cried all the time. I was very tense until I went back to work. I felt less stressed when I wasn't with him so much."

And just as she repeated her father's rejecting attitude, she repeated his seductiveness. She walks around naked in front of Travis, she still takes baths with him, she often brings him into her bed to sleep. When she was pregnant with her second son, she would take Travis along to the doctor with her. "He would come with me to my gynecologist, even at the very end of my pregnancy. He stayed in the room with me. He was very interested and watched everything the doctor was doing very intently." Her husband seems to be an accomplice in the seductive behavior; he often walks around unclothed, and takes nude pictures of the son who's no longer a baby.

Dale's story vividly illustrates the continuum described in the last chapter—from father to daughter, then from mother to son, with the mother choosing a compliant husband. Many psychologists believe that a seductive childhood is a necessary ingredient to seductive parenting. "Some-

thing has to have happened in the past to cause seductiveness," maintains Dr. Robert Mendelsohn. "If a woman's
father was seductive with her, would she repeat that with
her own son? If she doesn't work overtime to avoid it, she
might act it out just the same way. But some patients throw
me a curveball. One woman had a distant, cold relationship with her father, without sexual elements. But she
smothers her son. It turns out that her uncle was like an
auxiliary father to her, and tremendously seductive. That
was the key."

But why would women go on to repeat this behavior
that caused them distress whether they managed to repress
it or not? Psychologists believe it may be a way for them
to psychologically undo what happened to them. They are
no longer passive but active, no longer vulnerable but all-
powerful. By turning the situation around, by seducing
their own children, they are trying to reverse the helplessness of their own pasts. To break the chain of events it is
necessary for a woman to look back into that past, to
understand what her father or an amorous uncle did to
her, so she won't do it to her son.

THE SIX-MINUTE SEDUCTION

In a recent study conducted at the University of Minnesota, 173 mothers and their toddler children were observed
in a toy cleanup situation. The researchers found that sixteen of those mothers exhibited some kind of seductive
behavior during the six-minute cleanup period. For example, one mother asked her child for a kiss, grabbed his buttock after he said no, and finally called him to her and
kissed him on the lips. Another mother, whose child
wasn't cooperative in the cleanup, whispered sensually,
"What did you do?" and rubbed his buttock. Yet another
of the mothers put her hand on her child's genital area.

The psychologists, Drs. Alan Sroufe and Mary Ward, had little trouble differentiating seductiveness from affection. The seductiveness was directed, in fifteen of the sixteen instances, toward boys. And it often went along with physical punishment and threats of punishment. The same mothers who were inappropriately sensuous were most likely to strike their children or shake them, and yet this behavior did not help them achieve any special results. In fact, they were generally less able than other mothers to set and maintain limits in the cleanup situation.

Of the sixteen mothers who exhibited "seductive" behavior, eight were interviewed in depth about their family background. Of those, seven provided some evidence of "seductive" parenting in their own pasts. For example, two of the women, as children, had been victims of actual incest. One had been sexually abused over a long period of time by someone outside the family. One had incestuous siblings. The other three had been "parentified"; that is, as little girls they had been put in the role of their father's wife and used to meet his emotional needs, his sexual needs, or both.

"These mothers learned two things from their pasts— that their own emotional needs were not met, and that it's all right for parents to meet their emotional needs through their children," explains Dr. Sroufe, a professor of child psychology at the University of Minnesota. "These women are needy women, but they don't know how to get their needs met appropriately. As they were exploited as children, they've learned how to exploit. That's all they know. They don't know about mutual relationships. So the mother is vulnerable and the son is vulnerable. He is the substitute for what she really wants."

Dr. Sroufe and his colleagues will be looking at these children, who are now of school age, through their adolescence to gauge the effects of the seductive behavior. The investigators expect to see significant effects. What they already see is the power of the seduction. "These children are really hooked. Their relationship with their mother is very interwoven, very intense. Neither of them can let go. In some ways, seductiveness is more powerful than physical abuse. These kids are definitely not indifferent to Mommy."

To seduce a son, either verbally or physically, is to give him neither love nor sexual satisfaction. It is not to have respect for his independence. It is not to support him and nurture him and help him grow. On the contrary, it is to infantilize him. It is to lock him in a power struggle that he is destined to lose. It is a trap a mother sets, unconsciously, which pulls her son into a neurotic relationship with her and undermines his natural development.

Seduced sons have shown various symptoms: anxiety, aggression, rage. In some cases seduced sons have become incestuous fathers. In others they become men who don't like women. According to Dr. Lorelle Saretsky, "They may wind up backing away from women because they feel threatened. Despite Oedipus, no boy wants to end up with his mother. It's called the Oedipal triumph, but it's not triumphant at all. It's a turnoff. And he turns off to women."

Dr. Britt Rosenbaum, director of the Human Sexuality Center at the Long Island Jewish/Hillside Medical Center, has worked with many of these men, and she confirms this interpretation. A turned-on boy can, indeed, become a turned-off man. "These men may have their sexual desire turned very low. They're frightened of women because their mothers were so overpowering to them. The mothers become larger than life, and women seem like frightening, powerful figures to them. They're overwhelmed by these powerful creatures. So these men hold back and become very passive."

Some men show variations of this pattern. Instead of being frightened by women they're angry at them, angry because of the way they were teased. Instead of avoiding sex altogether they may develop a sex problem, such as premature ejaculation. The point is that they don't really *want* to gratify women. They *want* to tease them, to frustrate them, as they were teased and frustrated as boys. It's a way of identifying with the aggressor, of doing as their mothers did.

Seduction is generally destructive of more than a man's sex life. It can also play havoc with his sense of self and his view of what his mother—and by extension, the world—is all about. It can lead to pathological behavior and even to criminal behavior, including sex crimes. "Many sex offenders, especially those who beat or maim or kill their victims, act in response to their mother's seductiveness," says Dr. Hooshang Bonheur, senior psychologist at the Forensic Psychiatry Clinic of the New York State Supreme Court. "Seduction involves a power struggle in which the sons are the losers. But now, as grown men, *they* have the power. 'Enough is enough' these sons are telling their mothers through their acts against women. Now I'm going to *take*. They take because they want to humiliate their mothers. They are venting their rage and anger against them." And yet sexual messages from father to daughter are taken more seriously and considered far more dangerous than similar messages from mother to son.

THE INCEST TABOO

When seductiveness goes one step further, to actual incest, the situation is reversed. Although there are strong cultural taboos against all forms of incest, the most strictly censored activity in civilized society is incest between mother and son. Only in certain primitive societies are such relations tolerated. For example, the Northeast Bantus of East Africa may marry their mothers, the Kalangs in Java encourage mother–son marriages, and the Gaboon queens marry their sons. But these are the rare exceptions.

The reason for the pervasiveness of this stricter taboo

can be found in the nature of the mother–child relationship. The child must separate from the mother in order to form an individual identity. The father, by contrast, is viewed as one of the agents of that separation. So a sexual relationship with the father is not regarded as inimical to a girl's identity and sex-role development. She can be his sexual partner and still be her own person. While a taboo against father–daughter incest certainly exists, it is not quite as absolute as that for mothers and sons. But for a boy to be sexually involved with a mother is to be bound to her, unable to resist the symbiotic pull, unable to develop his own identity. It is for him to remain, psychologically, an infant.

There is yet another way in which mother–son incest is particularly ominous. It is to the mother that most children turn for comfort and for nurturance, for rescue out of bad situations. But it is the mother whom the seduced son needs rescue from. Just when he most desperately craves a loving mother as savior, her love has turned into something else, and he has nowhere to turn.

To safeguard the sons, as well as to preserve the sanctity of the family, society has decreed mother–son incest forbidden, punishable by legal sanctions, by social ostracism, by extreme levels of guilt. But there is another taboo against it, an internal one, which is even stronger than the cultural barrier. According to Dr. Rosenbaum, there is something deep inside most mothers that makes incest unthinkable. "Such a strong aspect of mothering is nurturance, of taking care of the needy child," says the sexuality expert. "The caretaking overpowers the erotic. For fathers, the sexual aspect can be stronger. Also, women tend to be more in control of their sexual impulses. In relation to her child, the mother is the dominant figure. She's in the position to stop or start the sex. So mother–son incest is very rare because of the inner psychological taboo."

But the strength of the taboo does not mean that the desire is not there. In fact, the very severity of the laws against incest suggests that such tendencies do exist. One authority, Sir James Frazer, argued early in the century that there is a "natural instinct" for incest. And many psychoanalysts believe to this day that all mothers unconsciously want to sleep with their sons, and all sons want to sleep with their mothers.

Although incest is far from commonplace, a 1972 study indicated that 3.9 percent of the population in the United States had experienced incest, and experts now regard that figure as an underestimate. In the nation's largest incest clinic, the number of cases has been more than doubling each year. One prominent authority on sex in the family, who works with incest victims, maintains that the "prevalence of incestuous relationships is much larger than anyone would acknowledge. We hear a lot about parents who batter their children, but for every parent involved in a physically abusive way, many more are involved in a sexual way."

It is not just father–daughter incest, the most common type, that might be even more widespread than we thought. It is also mother–son incest. Up until 1977, only six cases had been described in contemporary psychiatric literature. But when staff members at one institute became interested in the phenomenon, they discovered that three cases were being treated at their facility alone. Later, they discovered two additional cases of consummated mother–son incest in the vicinity of the institute. Dr. Marvin Margolis of the Detroit Psychiatric Institute suspects that many of the participants in incest feel too much shame or guilt to admit the act. Even when in psychiatric treatment, they may mask their incestuous history. Not only do patients deny it, their therapists may deny it as well because of conflicts about their own incestuous urges, writes the Michigan psychiatrist in the *Annual of Psychoanalysis*.

BREAKING THE TABOO

Just who are these women who break with the taboo and have sex with their sons? The prevailing view has been that they are psychotic in almost every instance, that a healthy or neurotic woman would never give in to such urges. "The barrier between the conscious and the unconscious is broken down when there is a psychosis," explains one expert in family sexuality. "The psychotic is flooded and overwhelmed. Because of insufficient control, the woman will act in relation to her desires. If her desires are for incest, she will perform it. The neurotic, by contrast, inhibits the fantasy of sleeping with her son, a fantasy that every neurotic has. She's unconsciously struggling with these desires all the time. Although she has these wishes, she doesn't know about them on a conscious level." Still another authority on sexuality, Dr. Robert Dickes, maintains that "A mother has to be very emotionally ill to do this to her own child."

What about the son? Must he be psychotic to submit to his mother's incestuous advances? And when he's older, must he be psychotic to initiate the incest himself, or might he be the average boy, the "boy next door"? As to the first question, the answer is definitely no. *All* little boys are vulnerable to their mother's advances, and some will even make advances themselves. Young boys are normally very seductive, very sexual, and once they are seduced they will not put a stop to it. They will constantly be looking for the possibility of more seduction. But for an older boy who initiates incest, the question is more complex. Some authorities believe that a schizophrenic breakdown must occur for the incest to take place. There are many cases to support this view.

One young man in the early stages of a psychotic episode attempted to have intercourse with his widowed mother. He had heard voices telling him to have intercourse with someone; he thought intercourse with anyone but his mother would mean that he was an unfaithful son. Another man, twenty-one years old, suffered a severe breakdown shortly after his father died. One night he entered his mother's bedroom and had intercourse with her. It was a one-time event, but his mother seemed very upset and remorseful about it. She said she had submitted to her son because she thought he was "sick."

While other documented cases indicate that psychosis is not always present in the incestuous son, more often than not mother–son incest comes out of the interaction between an emotionally disturbed mother and an emotionally deprived son. In the son's hunger for contact he may overrespond to the mother's sexual signals. And so he may be chosen above her other children as the recipient, and as the victim, of her incestuous urges.

THE EFFECTS OF INCEST

Whatever the mental condition of the son before the incest has occurred, there is another important question to be asked: What will his mental state be like after the sexual union? In the view of Dr. Alvin Blaustein, a psychiatry professor who is affiliated with the Human Sexuality Program at Mount Sinai Medical Center in New York, "Mother–son incest can have nothing but a disastrous effect on a son's entire future sexual life and on his total emotional development. I've seen letters in men's magazines where sons say they've had a wonderful sex life with their mothers, and it's helped them to love other women. That's nonsense. Incest is a grossly pathological situation from A to Z."

One reason is that the relationship is not an equal one. It is a case of exploiter and exploited. "The parent–child relationship is so uneven that the mother can be a powerful seducer," points out Dr. Rosenbaum. "The relationship involves one partner giving in. It involves the use of power and control. The son does not learn as he is growing up that he owns his own sexuality."

Various outcomes of mother–son incest have been described: self-destructive behavior, physical abuse of women, even psychosis. Many of the problems, not surprisingly, are in the sexual arena—like impotence. Just as the grownup son is being aroused by another woman, he relates back to his earlier incestuous experiences with his mother. Guilt takes over, and his arousal dies. He is *not* a better lover of women for love of his mother, despite what he may claim in a letter to the editor.

It is not hard to find cases of sons who have been psychologically damaged by incest with their mothers. Some of the sons become suicidal later in life, and some even homicidal. In fact in two published cases mother–son incest culminated in the murder of the mother by the son. But there is another, less popular school of thought whose experts contend that incest is not necessarily damaging. As David Lester writes in *The Journal of Sex Research*, "Incest behavior can take place without any special psychological harm to the participants and without disrupting the family." Dr. Rosenbaum offers an example of a supposedly healthy adjustment to incest: "In this case, the mother–son incest started during the boy's adolescence. It became an exclusive sexual relationship. It was a very satisfying relationship, and mother and son were both contented. They lived together for the rest of the mother's life. Some people may conclude that it must have damaged the son, that it stopped his growth by keeping him from relating to other people. But who's to say? It worked for them."

Perhaps it's the age of the son that's the key; perhaps *when* the incest occurs will determine just how damaging it will be. Some experts say that it's most devastating if performed early on, particularly in the first year or two of life. Their reasoning goes like this: "The infant is intensely involved with his caretaker. He depends upon that

person for everything. He is completely helpless. Any seduction that occurs during this early period of development is bound to have a profound and limiting effect on
the child." But other experts believe it is the teenager who
is affected most adversely by an incestuous experience. It is
he who is most aware of transgressing society's strictest
taboo, he who has the most power to stop the act and the
strongest guilt when he does not. Although sons of different ages may be affected in different ways, it is the very
rare child who has developed a strong enough ego and
powerful enough defenses to ward off a psychologically
devastating outcome.

While incest remains a destructive sexual aberration,
sexual attraction in itself is a very normal aspect of the
Oedipal age; if it does not progress to seductiveness or to
sexual acting out, it helps to cement the bond between a
mother and her son. Soon enough, your growing son won't
seem very attracted to you at all, as he wipes away your
kisses and pulls away from your hugs. But the force of the
attraction will recur on different levels throughout your
relationship with him, flavoring your interaction, helping
him to grow into his manhood, helping you to savor your
motherhood.

4

The Turbulent Teens

*H*e needs you but he doesn't. He's a child but he isn't. You want to kiss him but you dare not. Sometimes you think you want to kill him instead. The son you have nurtured for more than a decade is changing before your eyes into a man, into a monster, into that alien creature who is popularly known as a teenage boy.

The lines of battle between mother and teenage son seem clear enough. You want him to take out the garbage, to clean up his room, to look at you without sneering, and to talk to you without cursing. He would just as soon live with the stench of the garbage and the smell of his room. What he can't seem to live with is you. And so the turbulent teens begin. It is a time when you are fighting for your child. It is a time when he is fighting for his life.

Just a few years earlier, there was little sign of what was to be. This now tempestuous teen seemed wonderfully, serenely latent. If that disturbing Oedipal stage had been properly resolved, he was filled with the joys of childhood, and you with the wonder of watching him grow. You could take pride in his intellectual and social progress—and in the fact that he still had time for you. Kiss him, and he might upon occasion kiss you back. Ask him what happened in school, and he might actually tell you more than "nothing." Ask him for a game of Ping-Pong or an evening at the movies, and he might even forgo his homework to be with you. With the hot issues of sex and separation temporarily out of the way, he is free to show you that he loves you as a mother, and sometimes even as a pal. He might not like *other* females so well, banishing them from his after-school athletics and crossing them off his party lists. For these short golden years, you may well be the only permanent soprano to sing him "Happy Birthday."

Sounds wonderful, perhaps too wonderful to be true. Indeed, psychologists now believe there are some ripples in this so-called sea of serenity. During the latency period, which coincides roughly with the elementary school years, children don't just sit around being latent. They sometimes make waves. Their sexual feelings have not entirely disappeared but have just gone underground for a time, safe from their parents' scrutiny. But still, from the parents' perspective, it all seems relatively calm compared with what went before and what will come after. "Children have a more reasonable attitude toward their parents during this time," notes Dr. Harvey Greenberg, associate clinical professor of psychiatry at the Albert Einstein College of Medicine in New York. "They are moving toward the outside world, they are forming relationships with their peers. It is a short rest for mothers."

Grade-school children seem to save up most of their hostility for their teachers. "Little Johnny is the terror of the classroom," his teacher might say as she produces an array of spitballs and graffiti-filled textbooks as evidence. Johnny's astonished, horrified mother may protest, "But he's a perfect angel at home." Johnny is, temporarily, working out his conflicts at school and sparing his mother.

But comes the teenage turnaround, and all that changes. The schoolroom devil may become an angel, but home is not so heavenly. Beth, the mother of fifteen-year-old Noah, got a report from his math teacher that didn't seem to add up: "His work is excellent," she was told. "And it's not just his high intelligence. It helps that he's more stable and emotionally mature than the other students." Beth was stunned. She thought to herself, "Who is she talking about? Could it be the boy whose room is decorated with dirty underwear and fingerprints? The mature young man who deliberately belches at the dinner table? My God, what can the *other* math students be like?"

Most of the other boys are probably not very different. They are going through a developmental stage that is rough on them and rougher on their parents. For much of the time it is the mother who is considered the enemy. Nothing she says seems worth listening to. Nothing she does seems worth doing. Her mere existence is too much to bear. It's not easy to like a son who seems to so dislike you. But if you can understand what he's going through, you can actually help him get through it, to the other side, where he sees you more as a person than as a pain.

TAKING THE FALL

What he is going through in adolescence is something like what he went through before, way back when. Remember his tantrums as a two-year-old? Remember his preschool pledges of undying love? Reruns of both the good times and the bad may be awaiting you right around the adolescent bend. In fact, psychoanalysts say that every conflict of the first five years of life is resurrected and recapitulated during adolescence. And so we come again to the pre-

Oedipal conflict between dependence and independence. In infancy, it is often played out physically. The child moves away from Mother but keeps looking back to make sure she is there. Every once in a while he comes back to her for a reassuring snuggle, the fuel he needs to move away again. In adolescence, the struggle is played out emotionally. It can take a heavy toll on a mother who cannot accept being the heavy.

And the heavy she is. As Dr. Greenberg puts it, "Mother emerges as the witch mother of fairy tales and myths. Because the power of mother is so deep within the boy, he is afraid of being drawn back to dependency on her, to fusion with her. He is afraid of being passive, or being a wimp, of being a mama's boy." And so Mama is pushed away on a wave of negativity ranging from mildly offensive to really tough stuff. She is pushed away with anger and with criticism, with protests of "I can do it myself," "Keep out of my room," and "Keep out of my life." What the son is really telling his mother is that he is not a little boy anymore, that he is a grownup, that she can't tell him what to do. The intensity of the rejection can hit like a physical force. Says one mother of an adolescent son, "I feel it in my bones and in my stomach and all around."

The fight against mother is the fight for autonomy, and in these early years of adolescence, it is directed against all females. Most emerging teenage boys have little use for girls. They turn away from their sisters and any female friends they may have as well as from Mother. A girl seems the incarnation of evil, writes Dr. Peter Blos, a well-known authority on adolescence. Not only is she deemed useless but catty, bitchy, double-crossing, even downright murderous. And so young adolescent males band together with other young adolescent males in groups of gangly boys; they are united by machismo and misogyny.

Up until now, mothers may have felt that they and their sons shared some common ground. But once adolescence strikes, their relationship seems based on nothing more solid than quicksand. Their difference in sex, which had seemed to be a magnetic attraction between them, is now tearing them apart. He is definitely moving off into a masculine orbit. Many mothers feel intimidated by the alien male world he is entering. What's it all about? What will it do to him? What will it do to her?

For the first time in her son's life, a mother may keenly feel the difference in their sex and all it entails. "Adolescence is a time when mothers and sons stop being like each other," notes Dr. Aubrey Metcalf, clinical professor of psychiatry at the University of California at San Francisco. "Their sexual differences are played out." Before puberty, he says, children act and are treated more unisexually. But that changes with the pubertal spurt and the enlargement of secondary sex characteristics. "Mothers and daughters become more like each other in a general physical way. When a girl starts to menstruate, the identification between mother and daughter strengthens. But as a boy starts developing into a man, mothers and sons become less like each other. Even the camaraderie departs. At ten or eleven, he shared a lot with her and imitated her. Now he finds her company uninteresting. He departs for sports and for the gang. She's left behind."

LOVE ME *AND* LEAVE ME?

But she doesn't have much time to resign herself to the loss. Just as she's given him up to the gang, he's back asking when dinner's ready, and where's his other sock, and what do you say to a girl when you call her on the phone? Ironically, just as he insists he wants nothing more to do with his mother, he needs her nurturance and care and protection perhaps more than ever. He is not as eager as he likes to seem to abandon the security of his family. The

gang may be good for some things, but when it comes to a
hot meal and clean laundry and a look of love, it's back to
mother again.

It takes a steady woman to weather these changes, from
the violent storms of rejection to the high-pressure demands of a needy child. It's true, she's already gone
through similar seasons, first at the "terrible two" stage,
then when her son went off, fleet footed but faint hearted,
to first grade. But the swings from dependence to independence, from babyish clinging to defiant bravado, are
never as dramatic as in the teenage boy. One woman who
will attest to that is Susan, mother of thirteen-year-old
Christopher. He is at the beginning of adolescence; she is
at the end of confusion. This is how she describes her son's
baffling behavior:

There are enormous swings between "Oh, God, Mother,
I can do it myself," to "Will you please help me? I can't
find my other sneaker." Sometimes he's really annoyed at
me when I suggest that maybe it's time for him to leave for
an appointment. He'll say "I know what time it is. I know
I have to go. I'm going. See, Mom, I'm putting my keys in
my pocket. Bye, Mom." And then there'll be a terrific re-
gressive swing. It's incredible how one minute he'll do
something astonishingly independent, and the next minute he'll act as he did when he was about six.

Try to do something for him, and he'll bellyache. Ne-
glect to do something for him, and he'll bellyache louder.
It's a no-win situation for mothers who expect the son they
see today to be the son they knew yesterday. There's a
glimmer of hope for mothers who see their adolescent sons
as who they really are: not exactly children, not yet adults,
but flirting with both. Who is it walking through the door
this time? The man-to-be or the baby-who-was? If you
guess right, you may be spared the drop-dead look and the
daily dose of sarcasm. Who knows? You may develop a real
talent as a mind reader.

Of course, switching gears may not be so easy. Why

should you take the abuse and also dish out the affection? And why is this boy who's almost as tall as you are acting like a baby, anyway? Some mothers don't let their sons get away with it. They say, "What's the matter? Cut it out. You'll never grow up." But psychologist Dr. Lydia Seggev, the mother of a teenage boy, stresses the importance of accepting the baby in the boy. "Sometimes the teenager is frightened and dependent and goes back to being a little boy again. If his mother puts him down for it, he will suffer. He learns he has to suppress the child in himself. His creativity and spontaneity will be stifled. But if she understands and accepts the adult and child in him—that within a few hours you can have both—then those feelings can work through more easily."

The teenage boy changes from mood to mood as well as from age to age. He is a true chameleon. To keep some semblance of sanity, his mother must become one, too. Flexibility is an important asset during this mercurial stage; so, too, is the patience to wait it out and sometimes sit it out. As her son sheds his moods more often than his clothes, she cannot always be picking up after him.

Already Susan sees these quick sleights of mind in her adolescent son. "Christopher will be just regular adorable Christopher, and all of a sudden something will happen. I don't know what it is. I don't know what I did. I don't know what anybody else in the room did, but suddenly the room is filled wtih this gigantic black cloud, and his face gets all dark, and he announces that he can't stand it and he's going to his room. And he goes to his room and he slams the door. I don't know what happened. Even when he tells me what happened it doesn't make any sense."

Mothers and their young adolescent sons often don't make much sense to each other. It is perhaps the worst of times in their relationship. The years from twelve to fourteen are colored by the boy's hormonal eruption, his biological changes, his psychological search for autonomy. It is a time when the teenage boy is preoccupied with himself, apparently indifferent to the needs of others. He seems to his parents to be a taker, not a giver, and he takes with a vengeance. He wants it all, and he wants it now. Says one mother of her teenage son, "When there's something he wants, he's got a bee in his bonnet. He is unbelievably tenacious and a terrible nag, just a terrible nag. And he always couches it in terms of how I am ruining his life if I do not accede to these wishes, whatever they are." There is a strong sense of nowness in these years. Gratification must be immediate or someone will pay. It is not hard to guess which person most often doles out the payment.

CHANGING PATTERNS OF POWER

How long must a mother keep on paying? Most expect that the bill will keep getting larger until their son is finally out of the house. Perhaps so, but it may be passed on to someone else. Psychologists have observed that boys from about eleven to thirteen are most aggressive against their mothers. From around ages fourteen to seventeen, Father becomes the enemy. One recent study, conducted by Dr. Laurence Steinberg, developmental psychologist at the University of California, Irvine, looked at twenty-seven boys and their parents to trace the changes in family relations that occur at puberty. (The boys ranged in age from eleven to fourteen at the time they were first observed for the study; the third and final observation took place a year later.) The beginning of puberty was found to be a time of conflict between the adolescent male and his mother. Mother and son frequently interrupted each other during discussions and did not bother to explain to the other the reason for an assertion or an opinion. The patterns of family interaction were rigid—a sign of family conflict. Then, during the latter part of puberty, the adolescent–mother conflict seemed to subside. The reason was not that the boy began to listen to Mother more; his behavior toward her remained about the same. It was that *she* began to back off. She interrupted him less and deferred to him more. His evolving relationship with his father was much different; he became less assertive, and his father became more assertive, during the period of early adolescence. This study, like others, showed that the young male adolescent does not become more influential in his relationship with his father but gains more power over his mother.

Suddenly to be faced with a son with muscles, a son who is taller than she is, a son with hair on face and legs and other places, can be quite unsettling to a mother. She had trouble enough controlling him before, how can she possibly control him now? As he wrests the controls away, how can she stop him? Myra is the mother of a son who is not quite adolescent. She is enjoying the last vestiges of her parental power: "He still fears me. He fears my anger. I can devastate the child. I can say something to really hurt him. I know it and he knows it, so he attempts to please me. I'm still taller than he is. Last night I told him I'm still stronger than him. But it won't be for long. I'd better start watching my tongue."

The physical changes can make a mother feel she has not only lost her power; they confirm she has lost her little boy. One woman prominently displays a picture of her teenage son, but not a current one. It's a picture taken eleven years back, when he was a freckly-faced, loose-toothed five. When she looks at the black-and-white photo she wonders, "Where is my child?" When she looks at her flesh-and-blood son she wonders, "Who is this person?" Another mother told me that she feels the change, and the loss, most vividly when her adolescent son is asleep. She sees his feet sticking out at the bottom of the bed, and his head at the very top. In between, his knees and elbows hang out everywhere in adolescent awkwardness. She remembers the time when all of him took up just half the bed. It doesn't seem so long ago.

A son's lanky limbs and longish whiskers can bring yet another loss to mind—a loss of one's own youth. If he's getting so big, and so mature, what does that make her? If he's reaching his peak, is she over the hill? The mother of a sixteen-year-old with a full-grown beard was not all that delighted that he looked twenty-one. She told him to tell everyone that he was her brother, not her son, so that she wouldn't feel so old. He had other ideas: "Mom," he said, "if it would make you happy, tell them I'm your lover." That did it. His beard could stay. She was charmed by what she considered his good sense of humor. She also felt a sense of pride in his tall good looks despite their reflection on her own fading youth.

THE PRICE OF PEACE

By the time the adolescent has passed puberty and is in the midteen years of fifteen to seventeen, the war between mother and son seems to have quieted down—if she has let him win it. He no longer has to struggle because autonomy is his, at least as much autonomy as he can handle without running home and crying "Help!" For many mothers it is a time of resignation, of getting used to what they no longer have. The battle they've fought with their sons is now a battle they fight with themselves. It is a battle to face the loss of authority.

Diane and Gwen are both mothers of sixteen-year-old boys. Both have seen their authority slip away. Neither likes it. Says Diane, "I'm aware I can no longer manage him. There's a whole sense of responsibility he has taken on himself. I feel much less significant. I'm becoming less and less important in a certain way, and that's hard. But it really has to be." Gwen feels the same frustration, but she is not quite as resigned. "I have a hard time with him because he doesn't do things my way. I lost the ability to say 'I want you to stay home and study.' Even if I made him go to his room, he wouldn't study. I'm responsible for his actions without the control to get what I want. I try to achieve it through good will and diplomacy. Sometimes I feel like a Russian in the Chinese embassy—I have to be so careful."

Some mothers actually welcome the loss of control because it means that their sons have taken over some responsibility. Susan has been a working mother ever since thirteen-year-old Christopher was born. She is relieved that he can get around the city by himself now, that he is responsible enough to do it, that he has taken control over that part of his life. "An enormous burden of constant traffic planning has been lifted. It has freed up time and energy for me to have more fun with him instead of just sweating out the logistics of everything. I have less anxiety, I can enjoy more things with him, and he really responds to that."

Susan is glad for his sake as well as for her own, glad that he's finally "checking into reality," as she puts it. "Christopher has always been a little vague about where things are and when he's supposed to be somewhere and when things are due. As he's getting older, he's beginning to get a grip on what is required and where he is supposed to be, which I really like. I find him gaining control and getting rewarded for it. And I really welcome this change. I much prefer to have the ranting and raving of adolescence if it accompanies his getting control of activities that enhance his self-esteem. The other stuff doesn't really seem like much."

Some mothers are not as hurt about losing control as they are about not knowing what they've lost control over. They can't find out what's going on in their son's head, in his life. The key word is privacy. All adolescent boys want it. Most of their mothers will give it, at least up to a point, but not without a sense of loss, a feeling of rejection. Physically, they are shut out. One mother knows her son is home if his bedroom door is closed. If it's open, she knows he's out. Mentally, mothers are also told to get lost. For Sandy, a mother who was always very involved in her son's life, it was a hard thing to accept, but she had no choice. "I'm not sure of what Wayne is thinking. I used to know everything about this child—how he formed a concept, where he was at, what information he had taken in, what was going on in his entire life. Now I don't know. I recognize I can't." The physical and mental blocks are minor compared with the social ones. Mothers are not supposed to know who is on the other end of the phone, or who is going out with whom, or just which teenage girl wears the shade of lipstick smeared on her son's collar. Asking is futile, as Diane, a mother we met earlier, found out. "He sets limits on me as to his privacy. I no longer know the crowd. I ask him what he thinks of a certain girl. He tells me to bug off. I say that your sister Nicole tells me. He says that he's not Nicole, that he won't tell me. I hear girls call him to invite him to parties, but I don't know what's going on."

When parents *do* get an inkling of what's going on, they may not like what they find out. Drinking, drugs, fast driving, fast girls—what some teenage boys like best—are what their parents dread the most. But even much safer activities may drive these same parents to a bit of their own drinking. They are activities that say, "I'm different from you. I don't want to live the same kind of life you did. I am choosing a different path." Rationally, the parents may accept the differences. But emotionally, it's the most hurtful rejection of all, a rejection of what they are, a rejection of what they stand for.

It would seem that a son's admission to West Point would be a reason for great celebration in many families. But not in Sean's family. His mother, Roberta, is a psychiatrist. When this eldest son chose a military career, it was the final blow to her hopes that he would follow her professionally. It was the seal on their separation, a separation she dates from his thirteenth birthday. "When a boy turns thirteen, he goes off with his peer group," she says with sadness. "He just doesn't want you. It was a confusing time for me. If he's part of me, if I'm part of him, why would he go off like that? Now he's eighteen, and he's going off to West Point. It's not what I intended. How did that happen? I've had a million thoughts on how he came to that, but not the answer. That just isn't me. Yet he's part of me. How could he be doing that which isn't me?"

THE LONG GOODBYE

A child's earlier attempts at separation are draining for a mother, threatening to a mother. But at least there was the knowledge that the child really wasn't going anywhere. He would still be there for her to patch up his scraped knees, to kiss away his tears, to guide him through the pleasures and pains of growing up. But the adolescent separation is for real. The boy is getting ready to physically leave, to pack up and to move out, to find someone else to fill the needs mother used to fill. It's not just a phase. It's forever. Never again will she be mother to him in the way she once was.

Some mothers pay lip service to accepting this separation, but in moments of humor their real feelings may show. Irene is already thinking ahead to when her fifteen-year-old son, a high school sophomore, goes off to college. She jokes about it with him. "I say to him 'I'll go along with you and clean your room and brush your hair. Who's going to do that for you?' I don't even do it now, but we kid about it." Lorraine is closer to the departure stage—her eighteen-year-old son is leaving for college in the fall—and she's really getting worried. "I don't want to lose him. I say to him, 'You're going to college? I don't want to lose you.' He says, 'Ma, I'll be here every time you turn around.' He's really very special to me. I hope he'll come home to me and know I'm here.''

Irene and Lorraine are women who still feel emotionally close to their sons. They are holding on to that closeness, not nearly ready to let go. But for some mothers and sons, the closeness disappeared with his boyish body and high voice. The wrenching away was awful, agonizing, and complete. His leaving for college, or a job, or a woman, is a mere formality. Denise's son is just sixteen, but already she has emotionally kissed him goodbye. Nothing will be as painful as that was. "I have come to terms with the loss of my child. He is another person. I can't count on him to give me a lot of anything. I've learned that he's the type of person who would move to California and call three times a year. I don't think his getting married will be as painful as the pulling away he's already done. That was the initial trauma. It's been so total, I've gotten used to it."

Is it possible for a mother to have a close relationship with a son and still relinquish him to the outside world? It can be done, if she remembers that he is a separate person. She doesn't own him. He doesn't belong to her. But if she treats him with respect when he needs her and respect when he doesn't, the loss will not be total. There will be a bond between mother and son that miles and years cannot break. A son a continent away is still a son.

If she lets him go with love, the last phase of adolescence—beginning at age seventeen or eighteen—can make up for the first two. It is a time when almost-adult boys see their mothers in a new light. Instead of cursing her they are courtly to her. They hold open the door they slammed on her years earlier. Mothers who have all but written off their discourteous, ungainly child see in his place a chivalrous young man. Now she is glad she has let *that* one go and gotten *this* one in return.

Joyce Tretick is a New Jersey psychotherapist who sees

adolescents in all their fascinating phases of development. She compares and summarizes the three main phases in the relationship of mother and teenage son: "In the early phase there is more ambivalence, more vacillation between dependence and independence, more turmoil because of physical and emotional changes. In the second phase the boy shows the beginnings of heterosexual interest. As he becomes more involved with girlfriends, his mother's role lessens. She begins to feel more out of place. If those two phases are worked out, the third phase begins—the reattachment and bonding between mother and son leading to a more normal relationship. She is able to let him leave the nest, and he is able to go." In this scenario of healthy adolescence and healthy motherhood the relationship of mother and son evolves from one of dependency to one of equality, a relationship between adults.

THE RETURN OF OEDIPUS

Tretick talks about yet another aspect of adolescence which you may rather not hear about, especially if you are currently going through it with your teenage son. It is the blossoming, pervasive, rampant sexuality of the teenage boy. It is a sexuality that parents can literally smell as they enter the house, that can knock them over in a roomful of adolescent boys. The entire subject is discomforting enough to most parents without this added element: Some of the boys' deepest sexual desires are directed toward their mothers. Oedipal longings may again come to the surface, this time more heated, more pressing, more based in reality than during their initial emergence.

Your son is a big boy now. At four or five, his idea of sex was quite unclear. At fourteen or fifteen, he knows just what it is he wants to do with his mother. And now, hormonally and physically, he is well equipped to do it.

His fantasies can be quite powerful. In many boys, the

very earliest masturbatory fantasies are about Mother. Although a variety of women may be gradually added, Mother often remains the star of these sexual psychodramas of early adolescence.

So the teenager, consciously or unconsciously, wants it more than he wanted it before. Perhaps that's why society's taboos are so absolute for the adolescent. He is forbidden to do anything about his wishes or even to say anything about them. A four-year-old can get away with telling his mother he wants to marry her or sleep with her. Even the direct approach, "I want to go into your vagina," may earn him just an embarrassed smile and diversion to another, less interesting activity. His mother may even telephone her best friend to relate her son's latest amorous advances. But should a fourteen-year-old use the same line, he might find himself indefinitely grounded, except for the visits to the psychiatrist whom his mother telephoned to relate her son's incestuous invitation.

Some boys will not be deterred. One well-developed ten-year-old expressed a desire to sleep in his mother's bed and to keep his father out. He demanded to be embraced and kissed and to be allowed to sit on her lap. His mother did as he asked. Only through therapeutic intervention was the pattern broken. Another boy tried a slightly subtler approach. He had been very modest in front of his mother from age eight on, never appearing less than fully clothed. But when he turned fifteen, overwhelmed by Oedipus, most of his clothes came off. He routinely walked around in front of her in tight underpants, even kissing her good night in that scant attire. She says she doesn't like it, but she doesn't stop it. "I have to keep my eyes away from his underpants. I make myself focus on his face. I know that he's maturing. That may be one of the reasons he's doing this, to show me that he's becoming a man."

More commonly, a boy has the opposite reaction to this sexual upsurge—an increase in modesty, a shying away from Mother's gaze, from Mother's touch, from any possible stimulation. One mother of a young adolescent senses her son stiffening up at the slightest physical contact. "I find there are times when he doesn't quite know how to hug me anymore. I am aware suddenly that my breasts bother him, that if he hugs me there's no way that my breasts aren't going to hit him in the chest. So that kind of freaks him out."

Teenage boys can also be threatened by mothers who look too sexual, too provocative, too good to resist. On the surface, they may want a glamorous mother, a mother they can show off to their friends. But their real feelings may be quite different. One teenage boy claimed to be proud of his mother's appearance. She is an attractive, single woman in her early forties who has been married several times. But the boy's psychiatrist saw beneath his pride: "He was really very cynical. He told me, 'That's all she has. She'd better make the most of it before she loses her looks.' He sounded very angry at her."

But if the mother is married, her son may see her good looks as a definite plus. They will keep her husband interested, and her husband will keep this teenage rival away. He is safe in his fantasies because his fantasies cannot come true. Ruth Newman, a psychotherapist and mother of three boys, notices how happy her two teenagers seem when she gets dressed up to go out. "They seem to want me to look nice, to look glamorous. It's reassuring for them when Bob and I go out. We dress up and look romantic. It's a big relief for them. I can almost hear them thinking, 'I don't have to worry about these feelings. My dad will take care of her.' They're glad I'm attractive enough to keep my husband's attention."

Glamorous mother or not, all teenage boys face a difficult task, the task of repressing their sexual feelings for mother and turning them outward. It is a task that is harder for boys than for girls, contend many psychiatric experts. For girls, sexual feelings move from Mother to Father and then to other men. But there remains a tie to mother that can continue. It does not have to be withdrawn. There's not the painful pulling away. For boys, however, when the sexualized attention to mother is pulled away, part of the loving, nonsexual attention is also withdrawn. There is less talk as well as less touch, less laughing, and less loving. Only when the sons have their own children, these experts say, do their nonsexual feelings for their mothers fully resurface. Through a baby, their relationship with mother is reborn.

During adolescence, sexual desire between mother and son can be quite mutual. If even an infant male can arouse his mother, just imagine what can happen at puberty's peak. The physical attributes of this man-child become hard for her to ignore and may reactivate her own incestuous adolescent longings—longings that were directed at a brother or a father. It is common, and normal, for mothers to have sexual dreams about their adolescent sons, though even their analysts may not know for sure. The incest taboo is so strong that repression is usually total. But there are mothers who are aware of their feelings, have examined them, and will even talk about them:

"I find the changes in my son's body stimulating at times," admits the mother of a sixteen-year-old boy, her second child but first son. "He's handsome. He has big shoulders. He's six feet two and weighs 170 pounds, and is the hope of his high school's football team. Once in a while I feel attracted to him. It's not abnormal to appreciate a good-looking guy, even if he is your own son. But I feel it's important not to act on it, not to complicate his life by that sort of thing. I get my satisfaction from other areas, and other people."

Some mothers don't. Instead of simply acknowledging and accepting their desires, they act them out in seductive ways. The resulting anger will be as strong in a teenage son as in a younger one, anger at being stimulated without being satisfied. Of course, most seductive mothers are not consciously aware of what they're doing. One woman tried to help her son in the area of sex education. Whatever he asked, she told him. Whatever he *didn't* ask, she told him. Her favorite lesson was about sexual positions. When her therapist asked her why she goes into such detail with her son, she said, "Because he asks. I just want to be honest." One night she became *too* honest with her son. She became so explicit about the sexual act and all its positional possibilities that he screamed, "That's enough!" and slammed out of the house. Her attempts to "inform" him were actually attempts to seduce him, and they finally drove him away.

When honesty turns into seduction, most teenage sons will tune out or run out. Sometimes the man in the mother's life will be the first to notice. One man was so upset about his bride-to-be's behavior that he wrote to an advice column for help. It seems that his betrothed, a thirty-four-year-old divorcée, often walks topless into the room of her eleven- and thirteen-year-old sons to talk to them, and thinks nothing of strolling about the house naked. He has observed that her sons seem somewhat embarrassed and uncomfortable. They are probably trying not to notice how their own budding bodies are responding to their mother's bare body. Yes, sons can be turned on by their mothers. And some mothers try, consciously or unconsciously, to do just that.

In more commonplace situations, mothers and sons handle their sexual feelings for each other by keeping a comfortable distance. Sons wriggle away from kisses. Mothers avert their eyes, and their thoughts, from their sons' enlarging sexual attributes. It is a time for modesty, for clothed bodies and closed doors. A mother who is aware of her feelings and of his will be aware of what has to be done and what has to stop.

Rick is just thirteen, but already his mother, Lise, proceeds with great caution. "I don't press myself on him the way I did when he was little. You know when they're little you just grab them and give them a kiss, whether they like

it or not. I don't do that anymore. I really test the waters
first. Partly it's because of him. I don't know enough about
what's going on with him sexually, and I don't want to
stimulate him. But it's more based on my feelings. As he
has gotten older I have become aware that he is not really
a little boy anymore. I am aware that every now and then
when I give him a hug or when I kiss him good night that
he is really not a baby, that he is getting to be very close
to my size, and I am aware of sexual possibilities. Not that
I would ever force myself on my son, but I am aware of it.
I am alert to the fact, for example, that he no longer smells
like a child. He smells like an adult. And that causes a
whole set of prohibitions to arise immediately in my mind,
which has me leave him alone most of the time."

When mothers and sons are not leaving each other alone,
they are often at each other's throats. They fight about doing dishes and doing homework, about dirty rooms and
dirty words, about coming home too late and about sleeping
too long. They fight with rage. They fight with fury. They
fight with passion. Part of the struggle is over autonomy.
And part is over sex. Their sexual love for each other, pro-
hibited and repressed, finds an outlet in these scenes of
verbal violence.

Mothers who cannot face their sexual feelings for their
sons may develop other feelings—that their sons are dis-
gusting, that their sons are dirty. One mother, a stylish,
well-to-do woman from Manhattan, watched her twelve-
year-old son step out of a shower with his towel on. She
looked at him and realized that she was turned on. She
yelled at him, "Get your dirty feet out of here. Clean up
your feet." She was the one with the "dirty" mind, but she
put it on him.

In some more "action-oriented" families, physical scuffles
may replace, or alternate with, verbal ones. Physical confrontation is not uncommon between teenage sons and their
mothers. Dr. Aubrey Metcalf comes across it frequently in
his practice. "Often a boy of thirteen or fourteen will be

brought in for counseling because he hits his mother. The family will say 'He's awful. He's terrible. In our family no one hits anyone.' Often there's been a building of sexual tension, unconsciously, between mother and son. It's a passion without a positive outlet. It finds an outlet in passionate disagreements, in shouting matches, in physical bouts. For some youngsters pushed past the limits, it precipitates big problems."

Another boy who made the lovelorn columns obviously did have serious problems. Just thirteen, he had already struck his mother with a baseball bat, given her black eyes, and twisted her arms until she thought they were broken. Most recently, he had knocked her against the stove and broken two of her ribs. It probably wouldn't make her feel much better to know that this might just be his very disturbed way of courting her.

In normal families, all of this (minus the really rough stuff) is actually preliminary to the son's courting someone else. He is learning that his sexual desires cannot, must not, be satisfied by his mother, that he needs another person for that, and he starts the search. His mother can help him by not responding to his advances but by showing him, nonsexually, that she still loves him. She can help him by refusing to be a party to verbal or physical abuse. She can help him by accepting that he has to find someone else for sexual fulfillment, that she cannot be his sexual object forever, nor he hers.

THE DATING GAME

When he starts to actually look for that "other woman," some mothers can take it in stride. They see it as a sign that he is sexually "normal" and are relieved that it's girls and not boys who interest him. (For a discussion of boys who prefer boys, see Chapter 7.) These mothers may sigh with relief that their son's lecherous looks are finally directed toward someone else. The mother of one budding Romeo was glad when her son started "collecting" girls. "I am delighted. I am absolutely delighted, because the sooner he discovers them, the sooner he will stop thinking of me as the answer to all his needs." The mother of yet another ardent adolescent said that she's just as happy that he started dating, and feels as secure in their relationship as ever. "He dates this one, he dates that one. The girls go out and give him a good time. I don't mind, because it's nothing I can give him. It's not taking anything away from me." It helps if the mother likes the girls her son goes out with. There's the feeling that she did a good job in raising him, that she was a good model for what females are all about. But if the girlfriend or girlfriends are not up to par, the mother may be jealous, angry, and hurt, and not afraid to let her feelings show.

A summer away from home turned out to be long and hot for Adam's mother, a fashion designer, when he fell for an eighteen-year-old girl. Adam was fifteen at the time, a bright boy with a promising future. As far as his mother was concerned, anything was better than an involvement with this girl. "He had a real crush on her," his mother told me, "but she wasn't too bright, not nearly at his level. We just didn't think she was his cup of tea. Did he know how we felt? Well, we weren't friendly with her entire family, let's put it that way. We left it up to him to see that the relationship was not going anywhere." Would Adam's mother be any happier if he had chosen a brighter girl, a younger girl? At first, she claimed she would be. "I would hope that she'd be pretty, intelligent, that she'd have a little money. Then I wouldn't be a clinging mother or a horrible mother-in-law. I'd leave him alone to grow up and have his own life." But in her next breath she doubted her own intentions. "I want him to have an affair and fall in love. I really do. But if a nice cute dark-haired girl comes along . . . I don't know."

Many mothers who can tolerate their son's casual dating

cannot abide a serious relationship. It threatens the mother's hold on her son. It threatens their future together. It threatens her standing as the most important female in his life. Says Dr. Richard Oberfield, assistant professor of psychiatry at the New York University Medical Center, "This means, to her, that she's going to lose the male–female relationship they have. It means there's another female who is as close or closer to him than she's been." Some mothers try to insert themselves into the relationship to keep from being left out and left behind. They may seem to be good sports when they buddy up to the girl, even going shopping with her or knitting her sweaters. The mother's actions may be based on genuine feelings of affection—or on a genuine desire to keep her son her own. One mother grilled her teenage son after each date: "How did you two get along? Could you talk to her? Could it become serious?" She sometimes went through his little black book to see who was crossed out and who wasn't. That way she knew at whom to aim her ammunition.

The sabotage can be subtle or heavy-handed. Either way, the son rarely guesses his mother's true intentions. When she finds out who his Saturday night date is, she might say, "Oh, is that the girl from down the block? The one who's a little fat?" She may even do her best to see that that Saturday-night date never happens. Say her unsuspecting son doesn't clean up his room the way he's supposed to. Or he comes home with a bad report card. Or he belches in her face once too often. Instead of the usual round of punishments—mowing the lawn, or not getting double desserts, or a week's banishment from the video arcade— she has a new one up her sleeve. "Just for that, you can't go out with Joanne."

The mother's fear in all this is that she will lose her son. The fear is that she will be replaced by someone better— if not smarter, at least younger; if not sophisticated, at least cuter. This teenage girl can be an unpleasant reminder that she's not so young herself anymore, not so cute, not so perky. She is what she is, a middle-aged woman. How can she compete? Some women fear that their sons will look at them with new eyes now and won't like what they see. One mother of sons put it plainly and painfully: "At ten, they say they'll love you forever. At seventeen, they compare you with their girlfriends." Dating may be a game for sons, but it can be serious business for their mothers.

SEX AND THE SINGLE MOTHER

What if mother and son are *both* in the dating game, both available socially, both available sexually? In today's high-divorce society there are more and more mothers and sons in that position, living without a grown man in the house to come between them. It's a difficult spot for a boy to be in. Mom is not just old married Mom anymore, the Mom he can't possibly envision having sex with paunchy old Dad. Now she's a sexy single lady, a lady who's available for dates and for what comes after. He may fantasize about being *the* man in her life, living with her forever, having her all to himself. Frightened by those fantasies, he may try to transform her back into old married Mom, in appearance if not in reality. One adolescent son told his single mother that she looked too young for her age, that she should wear only "old lady" clothes.

If his mother plays into his fantasies, turning him into her little boyfriend, he may be painfully jealous when an older boyfriend comes along. According to psychotherapist Joyce Tretick, "Oedipal jealousy used to be worse in girls. Now, with the high divorce rate, with more mothers living alone with teenage sons, it's as bad in boys." In one family, she told me, the newly divorced mother took her teenaged son into bed with her to watch television. It was a sexually charged situation, no matter how boring the TV fare. Now the mother is back dating the father. Where does that turn of events leave the son? "He's angry and rebellious," says Tretick. "He doesn't know where he is, whether he's fish or fowl. His mother is beautiful and artistic. They joked around together, they shared an interest in art. It was like two people dating. Now suddenly they're not dating. Part of him wants his parents to get back together. He wants to be able to identify with his father. But part of him is frightened, and jealous. He had his mother to himself until his father came back into the picture. He's so confused, it's more than he can handle."

The sons are not the only ones with fantasies. A single mother may visualize this teenage boy of hers as staying with her always, loving her more than anyone else ever has, certainly more than his father did. She may tell him, "You're the man of the house" as she tries to make her fantasy come true. Some single mothers transform their sons into little husbands, turning to them for advice, sharing their lives in inappropriate ways.

Other mothers are so threatened by their own feelings, so threatened by their son's sexuality, that they turn their sons into babies instead of into boyfriends. Dr. Oberfield worked with a group of lower-income single mothers of preadolescent boys. He found a common link: "Many of these women tried, unconsciously, to keep their sons asexual and immature. The idea of their sons' maturing sexually made them extremely uncomfortable and was hardly ever talked about freely. Yet many of the boys were still in the same bed as their mothers." It took one mother eight months in the group before she revealed that intimate sleeping arrangement. Another mother was more forthright. She said, with no sign of embarrassment, that she and her fourteen-year-old son slept together in a big double bed. She made sure to emphasize how big the bed was, as she told the group (with elaborate hand motions), "I start over here, all the way over on one side. By early morning, he ends up right under me." Dr. Oberfield was impressed with the woman's unabashed honesty. He at-

tributed it to her image of her son. "She was seemingly unaware of the sexual implications or she wouldn't have
admitted the arrangement openly. She was denying the
fact that her son was physically mature."

What happens to the sons of these mothers, mothers who
won't let their sons become men? In extreme cases, nothing
good. Says Dr. Oberfield, "They fear becoming adult males
because of their mothers' derogatory attitudes toward men.
They've learned that men are no good, they're not worth
much, they're just around temporarily, and then they leave.
The message is that *you're* okay, you're my son, you're part
of me. But don't become a man like *that* one. It's an impossible bind for the boy. The way that he resolves it is
that he doesn't resolve it. He becomes aggressive, surly,
nasty, and gets into trouble. These boys are actually angry
at their mothers. Some of them may express the anger
through violence toward women."

The problems of being a single mother are not just sexual. Without a father at home to rail against, your teenage boy has only one target—you. And he'll aim for the
bull's-eye every time, even if you're innocent of all the
transgressions discussed above. Ordinarily, teenage boys
complain that their mothers are overprotective, that they
"won't leave me alone." They complain that their fathers
are too domineering, that they think they're "so strong and
so smart," that they think they "know everything." In
single-parent families where mother is the single, she often
gets it both ways. She is criticized as being too protective
and too competitive and too strict and too bossy, all at the
same time.

YOUR SON AND YOUR MARRIAGE

If there's a man in the house, adolescence can be easier for
all concerned—if the man and the mother are getting
along. Fathers are crucial in the lives of teenage boys. They

provide role models of what a man should be. They provide a buffer between mother and son, a protection against their incestuous impulses. They provide the competition that spurs a son on to greater achievements and to finally stop being a boy and grow into a man himself. If father and mother are happily married, so much the better. Their life together provides an example for the son of how much a man and a woman can share; with such a positive model of a male–female relationship in view, he is more likely to one day achieve it for himself.

But if the relationship between his parents is not going so well, if it is filled with antagonism, the boy may be torn: Should he identify with his father or side with his mother? He may be used as a pawn, fought over by his parents in their battles with each other. A common reaction of the boy is to get into trouble. He will take drugs or drink too much or run away. The parents may bring him in for psychological help, thinking that *he* has the problem, not realizing or owning up to its true source. His acting up is actually a way to distract them from their fighting, a way to keep them together. If the parents can understand what's going on, perhaps they will be motivated to help themselves, and so help him.

Ironically, adolescence is a crucial time for parents to have a good marriage, yet it's a time that can blast marriages apart. There are so many different issues that come up and so many different ways to handle them that the situation is ripe for marital mayhem.

Ruth, the mother of three boys, felt bad enough when her adolescent son turned away from her; she was really devastated when her husband was not supportive of her, either. She blamed her son's intransigence for the double desertion: "I found Michael's adolescence horrible. It turned my life upside down, and I was unprepared for it. He seemed to get perverse pleasure in never doing anything I wanted him to do. He wouldn't study. He wouldn't do papers. I would get on him to do them. But my husband would say that there's nothing we can do about it, that I should just leave Michael alone. My husband tended to ignore things more than I did. We dealt with things differently. We reacted in our own separate ways. It was a very stressful time in our marriage. If we didn't make sure to get away on vacations together, I don't know what would have happened." When the issues become more serious than whether a son is studying, when they involve drugs or sex or delinquency, the strains on a marriage may be too much for even vacations to cure.

Marriages can be torn apart in different ways, often by jealousy. A mother may not be able to tolerate her son's temporary abandonment of her to become buddy-buddy with his father. How could this be, she may wonder, bitterly? I've put fifteen good years into him while his father's been out working, barely managing a "good morning" and hardly ever being around for a "good night." Why is my husband getting all the good stuff now while I'm being told to get lost?

If the father doesn't respond to the good stuff, that's yet another reason for marital discord in some families. A mother may see how badly her son needs his father, wanting him for a talk, for a catch, for a friend. Because she understands the importance of it, she may not feel left out. But she does feel angry if the father does not respond to the boy's needs—if he is too busy to pay attention to them, if he is too closed off emotionally to develop an intimacy with his son.

But there are marriages that blossom during this period, despite the stresses of parenting an adolescent. It is a time when many parents can rejoice in their relative freedom. As their children are letting go, they are letting go too, and they have more time for each other. As psychologist Lydia Seggev points out, "Until now, the parents were involved with their children. But that role is slowing down. It doesn't require all their attention anymore. They can direct their attention to other things. They can spend more time with each other, redeveloping the relationship they had before the children came along. They can look forward to doing things they always wanted to do, and to growing together."

SMOOTH SAILING, ROUGH RIDING

So far this chapter has emphasized the more challenging aspects of living with a teenage boy. But for every mother I interviewed who thought this period was a nightmare, the worst time in her life and his, there was another who was surprised at how easy it went, how good he was, how grateful she was. Certainly there were rough spots, these mothers acknowledged, but infancy was infinitely worse, age four more frightful, age six more savage. Adolescence was just not as awful as it was made out to be.

Psychologists are divided on just how awful adolescence must be in order to accomplish the transition to adulthood. Some contend that it is, by definition, a terrible time, a time of deep conflicts, and if the conflicts are not worked through in an emotionally wracking way, they will show up later in life in an even more devastating form. A quiet adolescence, they say, is a sign of trouble ahead. Dr. Seggev gives an example of a boy who was apparently too quiet for too long. As a teenager he was the "ideal" son—very bright, athletic, musical, the prototypical all-American boy who gave nothing but pleasure to his parents. He was accepted to a prestigious university in a prelaw program, yet another feather in his parents' cap. But then the trouble started. He dropped out after the second year of school and went on to marry a woman who hadn't finished high school, a woman who wasn't nearly as bright as he was. As Dr. Seggev saw it, "He was finally rebelling against the values given to him by his parents." Had he rebelled during adolescence, he might have gotten over it sooner and gone on to fulfill his potential. Instead he was rebelling at a time when, professionally and personally, his future was truly at stake.

There are other psychologists who take a different view of the necessity for teenage turmoil. They assert that a noisy adolescence is just one possibility, that many young-sters get through their teens with a minimum of external uproar, and are none the worse for it. Whichever view-point is valid, it is true that adolescence is different for every teenager and every family. Some households sail right through it, business as usual; some households are shaken to their very foundations. Generally, it is the child who has been the most difficult for the mother all along who will be hardest for her to handle in the teenage years. And the goody-goody will stay that way, aside from a few flashes of adolescent anger. In most cases, adolescence is an intensification of the old ways of relating.

Amanda, the mother of two postteen sons, was not sur-prised that her first son staggered through adolescence while her second son simply sauntered. The signs were there from the start: "The hospital nurses told me that my older son slept twenty-two hours a day when he was a new-born," Amanda recalls. "But when we brought him home, the sleeping stopped. Whenever we had guests he'd wake up and cry and not go back to sleep. But my second child was always easy, even as a baby. If we had company, we'd bring them into his room and wake him up. He'd go goo-goo, we went bye-bye, and he went back to sleep. He was just never the problem his brother was."

Amanda's situation tells another story I have heard many times: The first son had a horrendous adolescence; the others were no match in misery. Apparently, mothers gain some valuable insights the first time around. They learn how to roll with the punches and, if need be, when to stay down for the count.

What if the family's first adolescent contender is a girl? Even then the boy coming up behind may benefit from being the second teenager in the family, and so may his mother. For one thing, he may work out a lot of conflicts with his older sister rather than with his mother, reserving for his sibling his most loathsome language, his dirtiest looks, his most deliciously erotic fantasies. For another, his mother may be happy enough to put up with his adolescent shenanigans, relieved she doesn't have to go through it all again with a girl. Adolescent girls present challenges all their own. It used to be that daughters looked up to their mothers as role models. A mother could take pride in seeing her daughter trying to look the way she looks, act the way she acts, be what she is. But in this time of rapidly changing roles, more often the mother is a model of what *not* to be. "I don't want to have the same kind of life *she* has," is the adolescent daughter's refrain. If mother is a housewife, "That's so boring, I'll go out and have a career." If mother is a career woman, "How could she leave us kids like that? I'm going to stay home with my children." Anything to be unlike mother. But boys don't have to be their mother's opposite to be unlike her. They do not have to reject her very being to be themselves. And their mothers do not have to sting from that rejection.

There is a certain something between mothers and sons that transcends the difficulties of the adolescent years. There is an element of attraction, a softness between the sexes, that helps them get through even the worst of times. Psychotherapist Ruth Newman has experienced it many times with her three boys. "A mother has a bond with a son that she can always reach and get to. There's always the basis for kissing and affection. You can always use your softness with a boy. It's harder with girls because they're very ambivalent to their mothers. That relationship is so competitive." The mother of two teenagers, a son and a daughter, put it even more succinctly: "There's one thing about a son—if he gives you a hug and a kiss, you're ready to give him the world."

FROM PAST TO PRESENT

To understand a boy's adolescence, it is not enough to look at his past, at what he was like as a young child. It is also important to know what his mother was like as a child and as a teenager. As we saw earlier, her relationship with other men in her life, especially with her father and brothers, helps determine her reaction to this newest young man. Those early relationships take on even greater significance as her son grows into an adolescent and into a man, as he looks, sounds, and acts more like the males from way back when. Now it is especially likely that she will tune into her feelings, both good and bad, toward the important males of her childhood and of her own adolescence.

A problem can arise if she has never properly resolved her Oedipal conflicts with her father. If she hasn't let go of this first male in her life in the way a grown daughter should, she will likely now have trouble letting go of her adolescent son—a symbol of her father. She will fight against his attempts to separate from her, try to keep him from going the way of her father. As Joyce Tretick asserts, "This relationship between mother and son will be imitative of her own unresolved conflicts. She hasn't grown up herself, so it's hard to let her child do so."

There's yet another way her past relationship with her father can influence her present relationship with her son. For fear of losing her father's love, a daughter may forgo the common rebellion of adolescence and continue to be the dutiful daughter. But the rebellion may well be expressed, later on, through their sons. These women may encourage their sons to be defiant in a way they never dared. For example, a mother may tell her teenage son that he must be home by ten o'clock. But when he comes home at midnight and her husband wants to discipline him, she'll say, "Give him another chance." In that way, she's not only allowing him to break the rules but egging him on. After all, when she was a teenager, *she* wasn't allowed to, and she didn't have the courage to. She wants her son to act out her own inner rebellion.

A mother's relationship with her brothers can also influence her relationship with her son. Noreen is a mother who sees a lot of her brother in her middle child, and it helps her to understand both her positive and negative feelings toward her fifteen-year-old son. "I adored my brother," she relates. "Whenever I think of him, I see him as an adolescent. Whenever I look at an adolescent boy, especially my own sons, I'm reminded of him. But my brother was so mean and obnoxious. It makes me more attuned to my son Cory's meanness. He is mean, especially to his younger brother. I know it makes me identify with my youngest son. There's a positive aspect, too—my feelings of admiration for my brother that I've carried over to my sons. I love the energy of adolescence. I love it. I love to be a witness to it. It's an exciting time to be with a child." It is a time that brings a mother back, in mind but not in body, to her own adolescence. The trap is that she can be sucked back into her old feelings of conflict and chaos, of rebellion expressed or suppressed, of incestuous longings. The trick is to use those feelings to help a new generation of adolescents cope with the confusion.

THE MIDDLESCENT MOTHER

Although the mothers of adolescents all come from different pasts, they all share a present reality: They are middle-aged women in a world of the young. It is a time of change, of challenge, even of crisis. Sound familiar? Indeed, it is so similar to what their teenage children are going through, it has been dubbed "middlescence." Both adolescent son and middlescent mother are undergoing the rigors of transition.

Hormonally and biologically, they are both in flux, one puzzled by puberty's changes, the other perhaps melan-

choly about menopause's approach. Psychologically they
are both experiencing the pain of separation. The mother
may have to deal with the permanent loss of her own
mother or father or other loved ones. The boy is also sepa-
rating, moving away from his parents. It is not as abrupt
as his mother's losses, but he needs to adjust, and to cope,
in much the same way. They are also both faced with questions of identity. As the mother's children leave home, as
she may be confronted with long stretches of empty time,
she may wonder what to do with the rest of her life. As one
of her major roles ends, what new role should she begin?
It is the same "Who am I?" question asked by every adolescent who faces, and fears, adulthood, her own son included.
Both mother and son are also faced with sexual issues, the
son wondering what all his new-found sexuality will
amount to, the mother wondering if her sexuality still
amounts to anything much. "The similarity of concerns is
staggering," says Miriam Seltzer, professor at the University of Minnesota Center for Youth Development and Research. "Almost every area of growth that the adolescent
is experiencing, the middlescent is experiencing also."

The major difference is that the mother has already been
through it all at least once before. She has gone through
a biological transformation at her own puberty; she has,
most likely, left her parental home long ago; she has pon-
dered who she is and, presumably, found out; she has confronted the sexuality of her adolescent awakening. Now
there are more changes to be faced of similar magnitude.
But for her child, this is all new. This is the first time
around. This is really scary stuff. The danger is that his
mother, more experienced, perhaps able to take it more in
stride, won't understand his anguish. She'll say, "My God,
get with it, it's all so obvious." From her vantage point, it
may be. But from his, it's far from obvious. It can be
frightening, terrifying, and her dismissal of his feelings
may only add to his terror.

There are other dangers in the adolescent–middlescent

clash. The child's feelings may be so close to her own, the mother simply cannot deal with them without feeling vulnerable. And so she leaves him to sort them out himself, a task he may not be up to. She may even secretly relish seeing him struggle a bit. After all, from her perspective, he has everything going for him: He's on the upswing, she's on the downslide; he's getting in touch with his sexuality, she fears losing touch with hers; he's becoming the young adult male whom society reveres, she sees herself becoming the used-up old woman whom society discards. And so envy may get in the way of a normal maternal response to a troubled child.

Although a woman should in no way use her son as an emotional crutch, mothers and sons can use their concurrent crises to help one another. They can empathize with each other in their struggles, understand each other better for their mutual miseries and their shared opportunities. They are both on the brink of something big. They can help each other reach for it.

THE TERRIFIC TEENS

No matter how many doors he slams in your face, no matter how many words he shouts at you that aren't in the dictionary, your son *does* need you during this confusing time in both your lives. You'd be surprised how much. A wealth of research documents the importance of a mother to a teenage boy. She is seen as more understanding, more receptive, more comforting, less distant, and less punishing than his father is. She is favored over Father as an adviser, two to one, according to a study of ninety-three adolescent boys. Other research indicates that boys who are faced with a complicated life situation would seek out their mothers first, their fathers second. Despite their turning to gangs for group support, teenage boys are more likely to turn to their parents for emotional support. It is girls, actually, who become more emotionally dependent on peers, boys who don't stray far from the fold.

A mother who deserts her son in anger, in resentment, in retaliation for his apparent rejection of her, is doing more harm than she knows. Dr. Britt Rosenbaum is mother to four teenage boys. She realizes the importance of her role in their lives. "The mother still provides a sense of safety, of nurturance, of being there. She is a steady person in a teenage boy's life, a person he can cling to. She also provides a loving, safe, female model, and a person who mirrors back his masculinity. He gets from her the sense, 'You're doing well,' 'You're a nice man.' "

As the adolescent begins to deal with other females, he may turn to his mother for her inside information on the subject—if she has been available to him without being intrusive. One mother who has achieved the right balance describes her role as a social resource to her fifteen-year-old son: "He asks me how to ask a girl to the movies. He wants to know what to say. He asks what combinations of clothes go together. Once he told me a story and wanted to know if he had done the right thing. He had brought a girl in his class a rose with a note attached calling her his special friend. She made it clear that she was *just* a friend, scratch the special. I talked with him. I said that girls are afraid of too much romance in a relationship. I told him how gallant he had been, how well he had handled it. And I asked him if there were any *other* girls he liked. He seemed less dejected after our talk." Still, it may be a while before he'll risk a rose again.

Not only do adolescent boys turn to their mothers for advice; they also turn to them as examples. It has long been thought that children rely mainly on the parent of the same sex as a model of how to act now, of what to be in the future. Recent research belies that concept. In a study of one hundred college students and their parents, it was found that daughters were as much like their fathers in personality as they were like their mothers; more pertinent to this discussion, sons were as much like their mothers as like their fathers. In fact, in such personality traits as gregariousness, spontaneity, passivity, cognitive complexity, and stereotyped sex-role behavior, there was more similarity between mother and son than between father and son. Another study looked at the political and religious orientations of 653 teenagers and their parents. The researchers, Alan Acock and Vern Bengtson, summarized their findings in the *Journal of Marriage and the Family:* "In short, contrary to much previous commentary and research, mothers are more predictive of the child's orientations than are fathers." Additional research shows that mothers have a role in their sons' future as well as their present, influencing their aspirations, their educational goals, and their vocational choices.

So while a mother may not feel wanted, she certainly is needed. Dr. Harvey Greenberg stresses her importance: "It may seem as if her role diminishes compared with the father's as the son becomes interested in more masculine pursuits. Mothers sometimes despair. They withdraw. They leave their sons in a vacuum. But they should just accept that it's a tough time, that good things can come of it. A boy needs to look at his mother, and at the relationship between his parents, as prefiguring his relationship with women. Although many mothers feel abandoned, they should not disappear. These sons need their mothers."

As the son matures, the nurturance and support may begin to flow in both directions, with mother sometimes on the receiving end. It can come as quite a surprise. Pamela, the mother of sixteen-year-old Steven, is still recovering from the shock. Before she started her crash French course she would never have guessed who her tutor would be. She planned a trip to France, but with the way she was failing to master the French language, she didn't think she'd get past a *parlez-vous.* "I just couldn't learn it. I was absolutely blocked. I sat in my room and cried. Steven passed my room to go out and saw me upset. He put his face in my neck and kind of moved me back and forth and said, 'It'll be better when you stop being so scared.' I was amazed. And he backed up his words with real help. I said to him, 'Steve, I don't want to fail. My four young classmates are all doing well. I'm an old lady. I don't want to look bad. It's humiliating not to know anything.' So every night now he drills me in verbs for half an hour, and he doesn't mind at all."

If a mother is open to her son's insights, she can learn a new way of looking at the world, the way he looks at it. A perspective that may seem strange at first may actually be creative, and inventive, filled with the freshness of youth. Teenagers can help their parents reevaluate their previous beliefs about the world, perhaps even inspire them to try to make some changes.

Some mothers see, in the son who leans on them today, the man they will lean on tomorrow. One mother had a strange vision of such a time. It happened at her father-in-law's funeral, when her eldest son was still a teenager. "My husband was a pallbearer," she recalls. "I had my hand through my son's arm. I had a horrible flash ahead. I thought that this will happen when my husband dies. I will walk with my son behind my husband's coffin. My son will be the man I'll have to lean on." The imagery may have been bleak but not so the idea behind it: One day she will be able to count on her son, to draw from his strength. He will be there for her in her time of greatest need.

The outrages of adolescence pass. But its excitement can linger to flavor the future relationship of mother and son. It is the excitement of seeing a boy become a man, a man you never imagined, a man bursting forth from the child you love. It is the excitement of the unknown, of having no idea what manner of boy or beast (or so it sometimes seems) will be with you this day. It is the excitement of forming a new relationship, a more equal relationship, with the man who stands in place of the boy. It is the good sheer fun of watching your son grow up. For women who refuse to just sit back and wither with the years, it is the exhilarating joy of growing along with him.

5

That Other Woman—
Your Daughter-in-Law,
His Wife

*T*he band seems too loud, the food too bland, the room too small. To make matters worse, these cramped quarters are overflowing with flowers you weren't asked to choose, with colors you don't like, with people you mostly don't know. You feel like escaping. Perhaps if anyone would notice you would make a dramatic exit in a huff of hurt feelings. But you suspect your presence or absence counts for little to these inebriated celebrants. So you stoically stick it out on this most wonderful and awful of nights, the night your son is getting married.

Some mothers of grooms feel that theirs is a peripheral position, that the night belongs to the bride and groom and the bride's parents. Such a mother may focus her discontent on the trappings of the event: the fact that she wasn't properly consulted about the flowers, or the band, or the guest list. But the wedding is only a metaphor for her real fear: that she will lose her son to this woman he is marrying.

In one sense, she is right. Just as the adolescent passage changed, in some basic ways, the relationship between mother and son, so does the son's commitment to marriage and to forming a family of his own. His vision, and his energies, turn in large measure from his family of origin— including his mother—to the family he hopes to create. And yet his mother has not lost her importance in his life, nor the mother–son bond its power. The unique relationship they formed in childhood is not totally undone by his marital vows. Dr. Norman Kelman, a psychiatrist, emphasizes the strength and the continuity of the bond, even after a son weds. "It is a relationship that is powerfully involving and continues to be so into adulthood. A mother is always a mother, no matter the age of her son." Dr. Kelman goes on, "The caricature is of a mother who always carefully measures her daughter-in-law. She's portrayed as always complaining that her son isn't being treated right or fed right. That's the substance of humor and comedy. In that way the mother-in-law is made to seem almost pathological. But there's a natural possessiveness which mothers have toward what came out of their bodies. You can't avoid that. It is simply one of the qualities and characteristics of humanity."

But the jokes about such normal possessiveness can hurt. Stung by the comedic routines that portray mothers-in-law as meddlesome and mean, as talking too much and staying too long, many mothers of married sons feel awkward in their new role. And so they choose to relinquish any meaningful part in their son's life rather than risk being labeled as interfering. The so-called recipe for being a good mother-in-law is to "keep your mouth shut and your pocketbook open." It's a "recipe" that really reduces the mothers of sons to nonpersons, not entitled to express any of their thoughts or opinions or feelings. Women who follow it are probably so fearful of rejection by their newly married sons that they cut themselves off emotionally to avoid the hurt.

But the truth is that a married son usually does *not* reject his mother. In fact, this can be the best of times in their relationship because they can interact more out of want than out of need. The mother no longer has to prove that she's a good mother, often subordinating her own needs to the needs of her child. If she's willing to admit it to herself, she may actually be relieved—relieved that he has enough emotional maturity to make this important step, relieved at her release from responsibility, relieved that there's another woman on the scene to take on some of her role. As for the son, his marriage is an important symbol of his manhood. No longer must he rebel to prove that he is independent of his mother. No longer must he cut her down to build himself up. He has shown that he can live his own life. He can now return to an emotional closeness with her as a married man, as an adult, without the fear of being drawn back into childlike dependency.

But while the mother–son relationship can be easier in some ways, it becomes more complex in others because of the enlarged family picture. Now there's also a new daughter-in-law to consider and the relationship to her, and the daughter-in-law's parents and the relationship to them. It's certainly not easy being a good mother-in-law, knowing when to speak up and when to keep quiet, when to visit and when to stay home. It's a sensitive relationship, but one that more and more women are negotiating successfully. According to studies cited in the book *Marriage and Family Interaction,* 75 percent of women rate their relationship with their mother-in-law as good or as very good. In a 1980 poll conducted by *Redbook* magazine, more than 80 percent of women said that their mother-in-law is not "interfering." This chapter will take a look at that in-law relationship, along with the continuing relationship of mothers with their married sons. And it will look at the triangle that often develops between a mother, her son, and his wife. Some of the stories it will tell are lessons in failure; others are guides to success.

SETTING THE SCENE

One night a friend and I got to talking about our relationships with our sons, and what it would be like for us when they grew up and got married. And what it would be like to have a daughter-in-law, the closest either of us would ever get to having a daughter. And my friend said, with a smile on her lips but a hardness to her voice, "I just know I'm going to hate my daughter-in-law."

Another mother of another son, an older boy who already started dating, had a much different attitude toward her son's future wife: "I think of the woman my son will marry as being my friend." It seems that each of these women saw the future clearly, a future foretold in their earliest reactions to their sons. The woman who predicted the worst was well aware of her response to each of her son's moves toward independence—her hidden fury at his first steps away from her, her sense of panic at the sight of the school bus rounding the driveway on his first day of nursery school. The ambivalence we all feel at such times became a shock of sadness for her, a sadness she projected into the future as she mourned even now the marriage of her son, a son not yet seven.

But for the other mother, each such step toward independence was more of a reason for triumph than regret. She could greet each girl her son introduced to her as an interesting addition to both of their lives, not as a rival for control over him, nor as a threat to her very reason for existence. And there the difference lies. One mother needed her son to validate herself emotionally; the other felt complete within herself. Dr. Lorelle Saretsky, a psychoanalyst, explains the psychology of the woman who will not mind being mother of the groom: "She is the one who recognizes her son as an individual. She doesn't need him for something inside her, so she is able to separate from him. For these mothers, the son's new marriage will not be a loss." The natural feelings of possessiveness all mothers have for their children will be matched by a feeling of pride.

This is not to say that an uncomfortable twinge of envy is not a normal maternal response to a son's new-found love. Just as his adolescence may have come at a bad time for her, so may his courtship and marriage. Here she is, the groom's mother, perhaps past middlescence now, perhaps still not comfortable with the physical and emotional facts of getting older. And here she comes, the bride-to-be, at an age that seems so enviable once you're long past it. Full of the optimism and vitality of youth, the fresh beauty that is this society's standard of good looks, she may serve as a painful contrast to the older woman's view of herself. That contrast can be most hurtful if the groom's father notices it as well, and acts on the differences. He may dress in a way designed to please the family's newest female and act in a way intended to impress her, with elements that are more seductive than fatherly. His intention is not to actually win her over from his son, but to bolster his own self-image, to inhale the heady fragrance of youth.

So what may be viewed as a threat to the mother may seem like an opportunity to her husband, a development that only intensifies her threatened feeling. She may be tempted to get rid of the threat, to persuade her son that this is not the girl for him, and in that way to keep the men of the family her own. Most mothers don't act on that temptation, either because they don't think their interference would be right, or, more practically, because they don't think it would work. Why would their sons listen to them about this most personal subject, anyway, when they seem to toss off their advice about everything else? But some mothers *do* try to sabotage the courtship of their sons, and with it the fantasies of their husbands. Often they do it in an offhand way, but the intent comes through. "My," said one nervous mother of her future daughter-in-law, "she's the shortest girl I've ever seen." Interestingly enough, when this mother took off her high heels, she was no taller than the girl she had tried to bring down to size. Then there's the comment passed through someone else. One woman, horrified that her son was dating a non-Catholic, gave the word to her daughter to give the word to her son. He got the message.

Some mothers, however, risk the direct approach. Michael is a son who remembers it well. He didn't need any prodding to recall the days of his young manhood, more than twenty years back, and his mother's undermining attitude. "There was always some fault my mother was able to find in whomever I dated, always dissatisfactions and criticism. She'd criticize not so much looks, but that the girl's not smart enough, or she didn't like the parents, or she didn't like the way the girl acted. She made me feel that my selections were somehow poor or misguided, that I just couldn't make the right choice."

What is the effect of such maternal opposition? Studies show that it can do what it's apparently designed to do. There is some evidence that the parents' disapproval of a marriage is an important factor in broken engagements. But if a mother's critical attitude is really designed for something else entirely, to hold on to a son who is struggling to let go, it can only be self-defeating. "It's like a self-fulfilling prophecy," says Dr. Saretsky, who works with many mothers of sons and with the problems they face at times of separation. "To the mother, it's as if this new woman is going to take her son away. And in some way it begins to happen, because the son has to have a strong reaction against his mother. His mother doesn't even have to say anything. But by a look, or a gesture, or a movement, something is communicated, that the mother disapproves, that she's not happy about this, that the son is doing something wrong, something bad. And if the son has been a 'good' son who's always tried to please his mother, he doesn't want to be seen as bad. It's a new place for him to be, with this disapproving mother, the mother who used to appreciate him and need him. So he has to push her away, to turn his back on her."

WHEN MOTHER KNOWS BEST

Does that mean that you must be silent for fear of losing your son? Must you accept, unquestioningly, a relationship you don't think is going to work? One woman who found herself in that dilemma is herself a marital therapist and the mother of two sons and a daughter. She had no problem when her daughter married, or her elder son. She remembers no feeling of rejection or of being replaced by her son's wife. She attributes her relaxed attitude largely to her professional knowledge. "I was especially aware that if you don't let your son grow away from you, you're in for a problem. My husband and I both just watched what was going on in the boys' love lives, and were very pleased when they found girls." But they were not so pleased at the particular girl their younger son found and wanted to marry. She was not of the family's religion, she seemed too young, too headstrong, and they didn't think the marriage would work. "I voiced that to him. But I also saw that he was in a rebellion and that he would do it anyway. When the wedding came about, we all made peace. It was our decision not to lose a son but to gain a daughter. We accepted his choice, and we still do."

Interestingly enough, though the son is still married, there is one major problem area in the marriage: the difference in religion. Specifically, in what religion should the children be raised? His mother had sensed that the couple wasn't mature enough to handle the difference in a way that would satisfy them both; she felt that it was the combination of lack of maturity and religious issues that might cause difficulty. "It's exactly what I said," she told me, though she makes sure not to tell it to her son or daughter-in-law. Meanwhile, the marriage goes on, and so does her relationship with her son.

This story illustrates the wisdom of not blocking a son's marriage despite misgivings—but it also illustrates the wisdom of many mothers in assessing the choices of their children. Sometimes a mother sees what her son does not, that this woman does not have the qualities that will make him happy, that this marriage will just not work out. If she is low-keyed about her objections, she may help her son eventually see things more clearly and work his way out of the relationship. In some cases it may take a failed marriage to do it, but he may finally learn to at least consider what his mother has to say.

It's not easy to find a man who will admit that his mother was right, but the husband of a friend of mine was willing to share his own experiences with me. Kevin, as I'll refer to him here, was feeling lonely and vulnerable when he entered into his first marriage. He was away at graduate school at the time, and was very anxious about his work and about his general ability to function. As he remembers it, "I just felt as if I was falling apart. I felt totally isolated. There were married students out there at the time, and to me they seemed less lonely. At least they had someone to warm their beds at night and to cook their meals. That is the level on which I was operating at the time. So it seemed to me that the solution to my problems was to marry someone who could meet my dependency needs, someone familiar, someone who could bring home closer to me. That's where Andrea, my hometown girlfriend, came in."

Kevin's mother tried to talk him out of the marriage. She was not so much against the particular woman as against his reasons for marrying at the time. She realized that he was grabbing for the first available crutch, and she didn't think that that was a sound basis for an enduring relationship. Kevin said that he listened to her, silently, "knowing full well inside that she was right" but going ahead and marrying anyway. The marriage lasted little more than a year. As Kevin tells it, "Once we were married, my mother stood back, and just waited and watched to see what would happen. Once we broke up, she didn't go, 'I told you so' or rub it in or anything like that. She was really decent about it. She had been right all along, but I had to find out for myself."

The key for the mother, in such cases, is to just say her piece and stand by. She can't make her son's decisions for him; she can't substitute her knowledge for his needs. But she can be a source of experience and wisdom, even when her son is an adult, even when he's married.

Of course, mothers are not always the naysayers. Most mothers are glad to see their sons take this important step toward a more fulfilling life. Most will accept their son's choice of bride, trusting his judgment, or at least trusting to luck. If it's a second marriage for him, they may trust that he's learned something from the first experience and chosen more wisely this time. Some mothers even give nature a nudge. One woman, firmly opposed to the bachelor way of life, told her two happily single sons, "If you're not married by twenty-five, that means you're homosexual." Each of her sons was married at age twenty-four.

LIKE MOTHER, LIKE MATE?

Whether you approve or disapprove of your son's choice, there is an interesting sidelight to your view of the woman he wants to marry. You may well be measuring her up to yourself and to your values. If she reminds you a lot of yourself, physically or temperamentally, it may bode well for your opinion of her. After all, isn't it a compliment to you, proof that your son is following the musical maxim and searching out a girl just like the girl who married dear old Dad? Aren't you the ideal your son should be measuring every woman against? You were, indeed, your son's introduction to womanhood, his first model of what femaleness is all about. But that does not mean that you will look at his mate and see yourself. You may see reminders, something in the way she smiles, or in the way she walks, but most likely not the whole picture. According to one line of psychological thought, the differences are based on your son's experiences with *other* women in his life, women through whom he filters your image, step by step, until he comes out with his own ideal. For example, he may be attracted to a grade-school teacher because of her resemblance to you. In developing his next crush, he then incorporates some attributes of this teacher as well as your qualities. And so it goes, with you as a starting point, until he meets the woman he wants to marry.

Actually, as psychologists look more deeply into it, they see even greater complexities in the choice of spouse, complexities rooted in childhood experience. It seems that the father plays a role here too, and that elements of both parents are incorporated into the mate a man searches for, and the mate he settles for. Rarely does a son choose a mate just like his mother. Where that does seem to happen, it is generally anything but a compliment to the mother. It may mean that the son did not have enough mothering as a child, and is trying to make up for it in his marriage. Or it could signify that he is still dealing with Oedipal issues that he hasn't worked through in childhood or adolescence. With a wife so like his mother, he can finally win the elusive Oedipal victory, in appearance if not in reality.

Some men take the opposite course, choosing a wife as unlike Mother as possible. Again, different sons do it for different reasons. Most obviously, it is a rejection of Mother and everything she stands for, a message to her that she is not what a woman should be. But it can also send her a very different message: In choosing someone so unlike her, he is not replacing her. He is telling her that no one can fill her role in his life, that she is still the first and foremost female for him. True, he is somebody's husband, but he is still *her* little boy.

The age of a man's mate, as well as her other qualities, may be influenced by his relationship with his mother and the role he saw her playing in the family. A man who marries a much younger woman often wants to be looked up to. "He sees himself as taking care of his wife. He wants to be in charge," points out Dr. Robert Sherman, family counselor and associate professor at Queens College. "This can signify a rebellion against his mother, whom he saw dominating his father. Or it can signify the opposite. The role of the females in his family may have been to be taken care of, to lean on the men. And so he chooses a mate to fit into that role."

If a man chooses a bride who is considerably older than himself, he is most likely looking for someone comfortable and safe, someone who can take care of him, mother him. The reason may be found in his relationship with his mother, but again the possibilities are complex: "It may be that he didn't get enough mothering, or that he got a lot of it and likes it, and wants to perpetuate it," says Dr. Sherman. "Still another possibility is that his role, while growing up, had been to take care of his mother. As a result he chooses as a mate a woman who's older but weaker than him, and who behaves less adequately. He then moves into the role he is familiar with—taking care of an older woman."

Some psychologists have begun to look at the question of marital choice from yet another angle. The son's selection, they contend, may be his way of getting out from under the thumb of a domineering or overprotective mother. Says Miriam Seltzer, of the University of Minnesota's Center for Youth Development and Research, "Men often marry women who will give them the courage to walk away from their mothers. The wife is in conflict with the mother and forces the separation that the son really wants but that the mother, and son, have not allowed to happen." According to this view, it is not that the son has "married" his mother; it is that he has married a woman who is able to take his mother on.

But a healthy man from a healthy family is not chained to the past, determined to duplicate his mother in his wife, or to seek out her opposite, or to find someone who can fight her off. He is free to choose a woman who will complement his own personality, a woman he respects and loves for her own special qualities, a woman who is herself emotionally healthy. If a man is able to make such a choice—a choice that bodes well for his future happiness—that is the real tribute to his mother.

MOTHER OF THE GROOM

Once the wife, and date, are settled upon, family relationships and loyalties are really put to the test. The mother-son relationship may be threatened in a very new way—jeopardized by the family the son is marrying into. I could see it happening in the case of a close friend of mine during the planning for her wedding. The reception was going to be a gala affair, and her parents were following tradition closely. As the parents of the bride, they would pay for the party, and they would largely run the show. They had most of the say in deciding where it would be and how big it would be, who would provide the music and the flowers, who would take the pictures. My friend went along with them unquestioningly. She was still more daughter than wife and defended each of their decisions. Since she was busy on an important work project at the time, she left most of the planning to them.

But she found out, from her fiancé, that things were not going so smoothly in his family. His parents were unhappy about some of the plans and feeling frustrated about their relative lack of input. His mother would give him the word, who would then give it to the bride-to-be. My friend

didn't take it all that seriously at the time, but she can see
now the strain it caused between mother and son. The
older woman didn't want to spoil things for her son, to
make it awkward between him and his fiancée, yet she
wanted to be consulted more often and to feel that her
opinion carried weight. And the groom was caught in the
middle, sympathizing with his mother's position but not
wanting to make waves with his new bride and new in-
laws. He was slowly but surely moving over to the bride's
side, resisting his mother's efforts to keep him on theirs.

Wedding time is often crisis time; just as the young man
and woman are planning a life together, their families may
be facing off against each other, testing the loyalties of the
engaged couple, threatening to break the newly formed
bond of love and devotion. Many families are not quite
ready to give up son or daughter to matrimony. If they
must, they want it done *their* way. Often, the mother of
the groom is seen as central to the crisis. In some cases, her
instigating role is clear-cut. One South African mother, for
example, used extreme but effective measures to prevent
the marriage she dreaded—she locked her son up in the
shower and hid his suit and ring. By the time he escaped,
everyone at the church, bride included, had gone home.
The newspaper account of the incident did not describe
the next meeting of mother and son. The verbal and physical interchange was probably not fit to print.

But in other cases, the mother's guilt is more a matter
of perspective. Sari and Jay, a couple married more than a
decade now, each remember their wedding very well. To
hear them tell it, though, they might each have been at a
different wedding. For Sari, a computer programmer, it
was an affair ruined by her mother-in-law. The woman
tried to control everything, Sari relates, from how many
people should be invited, to who should walk down the
aisle, down to the color of the tablecloths and napkins.
"She butted in where it was none of her business," recalls
Sari with spirit and anger. "She wasn't paying very much

for the wedding, but she was going to tell everyone how to do everything. I remember we brought her with us when we took the hall. The man said the place held 250 people comfortably. She had a guest list herself of 185 people. She kept saying they wouldn't all come. I said, 'What if they come? What if they come?' I didn't want 300 people at my wedding, 185 of whom I didn't know. But she kept at it. She acted like the expert, and treated everyone else as if they'd never done anything and couldn't make a rational decision." Sari resented, perhaps most of all, that Jay was on his mother's side. Or that's how Sari perceived it. "He just kept defending his mother. It got so bad that one day I just slammed out of the car and walked away from him."

But Jay, a stockbroker, did not consider his mother the root of the problem. It was Sari's father, he contends, who was the *real* troublemaker: "He offered to pay just a fixed amount for the wedding, and that was only half of what it would cost. His attitude was pick a place, pick anything you want, this is what I'm putting in. He was so unemotional about it all, so cold." As for Jay's mother, she just felt left out, her son said, and well within her rights to complain. "She wasn't consulted. She was told. Sari decided what the colors would be. Sari decided what the wedding party would be. My mother wasn't brought into the decision-making process, and she resented it."

To Sari, it was Jay's mother who had made a mockery of the wedding she had dreamed of. And Jay had only made matters worse. To Jay, his mother had been pushed out of the limelight by Sari and her unfeeling father. The conflict did not end with the exchange of vows and the cutting of the cake. As we will see later in this chapter, Jay's mother remained something of a sore point in her son's marriage; only when she moved across the country did the wounds begin to heal.

If the groom's mother is often seen as troublemaker and wedding wrecker, it may be because our traditions have set her up for that role. They are traditions that usually exclude her from an important role in planning her son's wedding. She often has little control over the conduct of the ceremony and little say about the reception; even her place in the wedding party is not a given. At best, she may feel like an honored guest; at worst, like an unwanted outsider.

It certainly can be a frustrating time for the mother and father of the groom, a time when they don't seem to matter much. Some may withdraw in hurt, thinking no one cares. But others make sure they are not left out. They are asserting their rights, and finding, more and more, that the bride's parents are respecting them. The key is to strive for open communication in which differences in viewpoint between "his" side and "her" side are recognized, accepted and negotiated. If both sets of parents co-operate during this stressful time—either in helping to plan the wedding together, or in stepping aside for a young couple who want to take charge of the planning themselves—they can help make it as lovely and memorable as it should be. The wedding can truly be a joyous occasion for everyone, as one woman, Rise, remembers hers was: "My in-laws were thrilled at our engagement. Their son was already thirty-three, and they were delighted he finally found someone he wanted to marry. We were both older, and so much in love. We met in September, were engaged in December, and married in March. Nobody wanted to cause waves, neither set of parents. So the wedding was a happy event for everyone." Words of contentment are not as dramatic as words of jealousy and outrage, but they show how it *can* be for parents who accept their new place in their children's lives.

AFTER THE AFFAIR

Once her son is married, and the wedding safely over, a mother's relationship with her son is very much influenced by this new person in both their lives, his wife. Usually all parties start out on their best behavior, gradually letting down their guard and really getting to know one another. When each person is confident of his or her place in the new pattern of things, everyone can relate to each other with honesty and respect. There is enough love to go around—no need to fight over it. In such a situation, the mother–son relationship can continue to be a rewarding one. True, there is probably no longer the day-to-day proximity the mother may have been used to, but the emotional bond is sustained. In some ways, it can even be strengthened, as her son lives more of the family-style life she is used to, leaving behind his flighty bachelor ways. As he adopts a more familiar pattern of living, their lives may touch in new kinds of ways.

That may be the most common pattern, but it is not the most publicized. More often we hear about all kinds of terrible in-law problems, problems frequently laid at the mother-in-law's door. As you approach this stage in your life, and your son's, it is helpful to be aware of what *can* go wrong, so you can avoid the traps.

One type of problem is common fare in advice-to-the-lovelorn columns. To cite just a few examples, one daughter-in-law bemoaned the "infantile dependency" of her husband upon his mother, while another accused her husband's mother of pushing for a divorce, and "fixing him up" with another woman. Sometimes financial revenge is resorted to. One mother-in-law asked how she could keep her daughter-in-law out of her will. In one newspaper column, there was a running commentary on whether the wife or the mother should sit next to the son in the front seat of the car. The women were not so much interested in the roominess or the view as in the symbolic show of who's important and who's not.

The one who probably wishes he could curl up in the trunk to get away from it all is the coveted male, son to one, husband to the other, prize to both. He is at the

center of this triangle. Both wife and mother want him for
their own; they each think the other is out to get him; they
each guard jealously their piece of him, hoping it is the
bigger piece. What he does for one of the women is resented by the other. What he gives to one is coveted by the
other. He is told by his wife that he calls his mother too
often, treats her too extravagantly, loves her too much. He
is told by his mother that he is being henpecked by his
wife, blinded to her faults, poisoned against the woman
who *really* loves him.

We saw the beginnings of such a triangle earlier in this
chapter in the story of Sari and Jay. As their marriage continued, and they became the parents of three children, Jay
became even more entrenched in his position in the middle, and only recently has he begun to break out. Sari, not
surprisingly, sees the problem as being between Jay and
his mother, and she sees it as longstanding. "Jay was always
exalted by his mother. He was the cutest boy, he was the
smartest boy, he was so good in school, that kind of thing.
When he got engaged she acted as if I had gotten the greatest prize in the world, and I was chopped liver."

In Sari's view, Jay still acts like a little boy around his
mother, wanting everything to be just right for her. He
gets flustered if dinner isn't ready when she visits, he gets
angry if Sari isn't acting the perfect hostess. Sari traces
their severest marital problems to the relationship between Jay and his mother, and the way they seem to team
up against her. There's one particular instance she just
can't forget, perhaps because it lasted so long. She talks
about it with the same animation, and anger, she had dis-
played in describing her wedding:

"There was about a year and a half when Jay's mother
wasn't talking to me. Even though Jay knew she was
wrong, he couldn't bring himself to confront her. And he
kept in contact with her, which I resented. His parents
would come to our house. They'd say hello to me and that
was it. If I walked into a room the conversation would

stop. In our old apartment, we had a table against the wall with three seats around it. I'd come in from shopping. Nobody, including him, made a move to pull the table out so I could sit down with them. I'm serving coffee, and no one is moving this table. I really felt as if I was an outsider. I felt it more from him. 'How dare he?' I thought. He was so afraid of what their reaction would be. As always, he was more on their side than mine.

"I was not included in the decision to end that lengthy feud. It was just presented to me as a fait accompli as we were driving out to a party his parents would be attending. Ten minutes before we got to the exit, Jay said, 'My parents said they don't want to be mad anymore.' That was supposed to be the end of it. They were moving to Arizona, and they didn't want to be mad anymore. 'Tell Sari.' "

Jay was not blind to what was happening in his marriage, nor his mother's contribution to it. He saw clearly how his mother took his side, always looking out for him, but he had to admit that he kind of liked it. For example, his mother was forever expressing concern about whether Sari was feeding him right and taking care of him. She'd ask him, "What'd you have for dinner tonight? Pizza again? Ohhhh!" Jay recalls that she didn't approve of that at all. In Jay's view, "My mother was looking out for her little boy."

What Jay didn't like was the uncomfortable feeling of being the man in the middle. He felt the tension of the rivalry for him, the strain of keeping such an incendiary situation from blowing up. And he saw it more as Sari's fault than as his mother's. He blamed his wife for not handling his mother with the same caution, and deference, as he did. "We see my parents less often now that they've moved away, but still, whenever Sari is with my mother, I feel tension. I'm always afraid something's not going as smoothly as it might. Both ways. And the pressure's on me to make sure that nothing's going to happen. I feel in between. I've told Sari that it would be easier if she accepted my mother for what she is, and dealt with her on that basis, rather than expressing differences of opinion. My mother just doesn't care about differences of opinion. Sari should say 'Yes' and do what she wants rather than say 'No' and cause friction. I don't think it's necessary to argue over things that can't be resolved. So if we're in Arizona, and my mother cooks with a lot of salt, so you eat it for the three days you're there and then you don't eat it anymore, instead of arguing over it or discussing it, or something on as stupid a level as that." Sari and Jay's situation has improved somewhat over the years, thanks to marriage counseling and his parents' fortuitous move. But improvement in such instances is generally hard-won because the problem is often deep-rooted.

Where such triangles form, it is not so much that the wife minds what her husband gives to his mother; it is more that she minds what her husband is not giving to her. In some cases, the wife feels insecure about her ability to be loved and needs constant proof of her husband's devotion. In other cases, the deprivation is real; the man is too preoccupied with his mother to be giving to his wife. A basic element of these triangles is the skewed relationship between mother and son, a relationship that often sets the daughter-in-law up for trouble. What commonly has been happening is that the son has been passive with his mother, acquiescent to her demands, always the "good son." He is very comfortable in that role—but he has other needs, needs to tell his mother off, to fight back her demands, to finally be her equal. So his wife is thrust into that role, the role of troublemaker. Dr. Anna Leifer, a psychoanalyst, explains the dynamics and dangers of such a situation: "If the son is subservient, if he's not able to talk up to his mother the way a son needs to do, the daughter-in-law may well express the hostility to the mother that the son can't. She may be nasty in a veiled kind of way. She is the designated bitch, so to speak, and in a sense everybody is satisfied."

Mothers-in-law and daughters-in-law are not always destined to be enemies, with all kinds of intrigues and infighting going on. What happens between them largely depends on what happened between mother and son before the marriage. For a mother who has had a healthy relationship with her son, one that's become more equal as the son has grown older, his marriage is not likely to provide grounds for battle.

BATTLE OF THE SEXES

Where the relationship has not been so healthy, another type of triangle can form. In this configuration, the mother and wife are not enemies, fighting over the "man in the middle," but allies against him. They share jokes about his weaknesses and support each other in their complaints against him. In some situations it is the wife who initiates such an alliance. She may feel overwhelmed in her marriage, unable to stand up to her husband, and so she tries to get her mother-in-law on her side. But surprisingly it is often the mother who tries to team up with her daughter-in-law against her own son. And her efforts can start early on, even before the marriage. "If you can live with him, all the luck to you," the future mother-in-law may say. After the marriage, such disparagement becomes all the more pointed: "Well, you have to live with him. I told you all along he was a good-for-nothing no-good bum, but you have to live with him."

What can motivate a mother to put down her own child, and even try to turn his wife against him? Some mothers really do believe the words they are saying. They are disenchanted with their sons, disappointed in what they've done or in what they've failed to do. And so they can't

understand what anybody sees in such a "loser." Or
maybe, to such women, this wife can be the child they wish
they had with the qualities they admire; maybe they can
push their own son aside and claim their daughter-in-law
for their own.

But in most cases, the alliance with the daughter-in-law
is really an attempt to get closer to the son. His mother
doesn't want to be direct about it; she doesn't want to
seem the overpossessive mother. So she will seemingly let
go of her son, at the same time grabbing on to her daughter-in-law and perhaps her grandchildren as well. To all
appearances, she leaves her son alone—but she really
doesn't. She is still very well entrenched in her son's
family.

Some mothers are not entirely satisfied with that arrangement. They want to make things better with their
sons, but they have long since lost the ability to communicate with them. The troubles in the relationship are deep,
and go way back. These women hope that through their
son's wife they can make contact with the son, and finally
establish with him the relationship they want.

That's what Claire was trying to accomplish, but it
didn't work out the way she intended. Claire is the mother
of three sons. The younger two have moved out of town,
partly to achieve a measure of freedom from her. She is
getting along with them better now that their relationship
is a long-distance one. But the older son still lives nearby,
and their relationship, a love–hate tug-of-war, has grown
progressively worse. Claire is a woman who needs to control; her son Ivan is a man who has been trying with increasing success to get out from under her dominance.
Their battles are ferocious ones, and Claire won't admit
that she is losing them. Instead, she tries a diversionary
maneuver, trying to hook in her daughter-in-law as a nego-
tiator for peace. The morning after a battle she'll call up
Terri, her son's wife, full of indignation and hurt feelings.
"Did you hear how Ivan talked to me last night? How

could a son treat a mother like that? Please talk to him for me. Please tell him that I'm his mother and he's got to respect me." She's sending her messages through her daughter-in-law, hoping to somehow win her son back, hoping that he won't leave town too. But Terri won't be the messenger. She understands her husband's reaction to his mother, and she realizes how she herself can be hurt by playing the part of go-between. She would rather risk her mother-in-law's wrath than get caught in the emotional crossfire that started long before she was on the scene—a crossfire that could shoot her down if she doesn't stay out of the battle. Claire is finally beginning to catch on and making fewer of those frantic phone calls. She is learning that to use her daughter-in-law is *not* to get what she wants.

Using a daughter-in-law to win back a son is dangerous business. Most likely it will alienate both the son and his wife, and leave a mother isolated with her feelings of rage and hurt. That's not to say that it's too late to try to repair a mother–son relationship that has somehow gone awry. But the efforts must be made directly, between mother and son, or with the help of an outside professional. To involve a son's wife is only to lose her as well.

THE END OF A MARRIAGE

Just as a son's marriage can mean a shift in the mother–son relationship, so can a son's divorce. Mother and son may resume more of their old relationship as he turns to her for emotional solace and support and some of the comforts of home. If she is sympathetic to his pain, and withholds accusations of blame, she may find a strengthening of their relationship—a strength that will help him face his life again.

But she may find it hard to be sympathetic if *she* is the one who is blamed for the breakup. And that is not an unusual position for the husband's mother to be placed in. According to a recent report in *Redbook* magazine, in-laws were cited as the number five cause of marital difficulties among couples in their twenties. And the in-laws who were accused most often of causing conflict were those on the husband's side of the family. But such an accusation is often just an easy way out for the couple, a smoke screen for their real problems. Most often, the marital difficulty lies mainly between the husband and wife. Yet the mother-in-law may be blamed because it's easier to say it's "she" than "we." It is more palatable to claim the problem is from without than to admit it's from within. And because the reputation of mothers-in-law is bad to begin with, they make convenient scapegoats.

Even when the finger of blame is not pointed her way, the mother of the husband may still feel she's at fault. It may be for no rational reason; it may be just a feeling. Helen, an energetic woman who looks much younger than her sixty years, felt that way when her son's seven-year marriage dissolved in divorce. She hadn't seen it coming. She saw no one to blame but herself. "I remember being terribly hurt when they broke up, as if I had failed. And I just couldn't understand why I had that feeling. It was as if I had failed terribly, that it was because of something I did that this marriage didn't hold together. It wasn't that *he* was no good or *she* was no good. It was me. They had seemed so happy together for such a long time. But maybe I just didn't see all the things that were happening." Ironically, though, the mothers who really contribute to a divorce are the ones most likely to deny their role; the guiltless ones feel the failure the most.

Sometimes, the mother is involved in a marital breakup in an indirect way. She is simply too attractive a figure in her son's life, and he cannot truly leave her for another woman. It may not be anything she does but simply what she is to him. Even when he marries, he is still more comfortable as son than spouse, not quite ready to give up the privileges of childhood for the responsibilities of adulthood. He has not fully entered the new relationship and may find it over almost before it's begun. "Family loyalties are very powerful," points out Dr. Robert Sherman, "and they often function unconsciously. Loyalty to the nuclear family may require that a man create tension with his partner. He may do it to please family members who dislike her or some things about her, or to force her to conform to his family's rules."

Whatever the reason for a son's divorce, this is a time when he may ask from his mother the things she used to give him. He may need his ego soothed, his emotional stores replenished, before he can risk another deep emotional involvement. It is a time of crisis for him, and another clue to her that sons never do, entirely, outgrow their mothers.

A BOND BETWEEN WOMEN

Something unexpected can happen after a divorce. While a husband and wife are steeped in hostility, determined never to see each other again, the wife may go right on seeing her mother-in-law. Their relationship may last long after the end of the marriage, especially if grandchildren are involved, but even if they're not. Helen's son and daughter-in-law, for example, had no children, but the two women continued to communicate. In fact, when the daughter-in-law had a baby later by another man, she named the child after her former mother-in-law.

So far in this chapter, I've emphasized the daughter-in-law's role as it affects the mother–son relationship. But because a daughter-in-law can become such an important figure in a woman's life, it might be interesting to take a brief look at that relationship by itself. Most of what we hear about it are the negatives, the difficulties, what can and sometimes does go wrong. But when it goes wrong it is because the women expect it to be something it isn't. Often it's the older woman who wants to forget about the "in-law" part and have a real daughter in her son's wife. Perhaps she doesn't have a daughter of her own, or is disappointed in the daughter she does have, and hopes that her daughter-in-law will make up for what she's missing. But the odds are that this new daughter-in-law will have no intention of doing so. She may refuse to be the daughter who wasn't born, or the "good" daughter to the "bad" daughter. She will find her mother-in-law too intrusive, too demanding. In turn, her mother-in-law will find her too distant, too indifferent. This is perhaps most likely to happen if the daughter-in-law is the son's second wife, and too independent and mature to play into such fantasies.

The reverse situation is less common, but it can happen. Some young women crave maternal warmth and closeness, perhaps because their own mothers weren't maternal enough, or are no longer available to them. They would like their mothers-in-law to be like mothers to them—but the older woman may want no part of it. Again, it's a case of mismatched expectations.

The best relationship can develop where the expectations on both sides are realistic. Dr. Saretsky advises the mothers of sons not to expect too much from their daughters-in-law: "I think you have to really know that you're not going to be your daughter-in-law's mother, nor are you her contemporary, her best friend. You can be helpful, you can be warm toward each other, you can like each other, even love each other. But if you're expecting to be a mother or a close friend, it usually doesn't happen in a healthy relationship. There's something else. You can be a mother-in-law to a daughter-in-law, and have a good relationship there."

It can be a comfortable relationship, one that's satisfying to both women. Its benefits to the younger woman are perhaps most obvious. Her mother-in-law can be a source of strength and wisdom, of insight into the man they both love, and last but not least, one fine baby-sitter. Remember Rise, the woman who felt she had a gem of a wedding? She also feels she has a gem of a mother-in-law. As she describes her husband's mother: "She doesn't believe in making trouble. If we're happy, fine. She believes in allowing us to live the way we like. Sure, she corrects me sometimes, but she helps me a lot too. My mother-in-law and I really love each other. A lot of the good relationship is from her. She created it, she worked at it, and she taught me how to work at it."

The benefits a woman can derive from her son's wife are less tangible, but there are benefits nonetheless—benefits of being included in a larger, loving family, of sharing in a network of mutual assistance and emotional support, of transmitting one's values to another generation. There is the opportunity to form an intimate relationship with this woman of another era—an opportunity that is rare in this age-stratified society. It is a relationship that can, in some ways, be easier than one between mother and child, easier because there is no past friction between them. So mother-in-law and daughter-in-law can start anew, looking at what can be, not at what was.

True, in the beginning, what with the tensions of the wedding and the adjustment of everyone to his or her new role, the role of in-law can be a hard one to fit into. But, as studies show, it gets easier all the time. The longer the marriage goes on, the less troublesome the in-law "problem" and the likelier a woman is to compare her mother-in-law favorably with her own mother. Changes in our society are making it easier still. For one thing, as women become more fulfilled in their own lives with work and activities, they are depending less on their children for fulfillment, and are less likely to be disappointed. The woman who goes out with friends on Saturday night is not the one moping around on Sunday morning waiting for the "kids" to come over, bitter if they don't. Now mothers-in-law and daughters-in-law can relate more out of choice than out of duty, out of a desire to truly get to know this new woman in their lives, and maybe even get to love her. In this era of awakening sisterhood, they can relate more as women than as rivals for the affection of a man.

A good relationship with a daughter-in-law is worth striving for for its own rewards, as well as for what it means for the mother and son. A man will only appreciate his mother more for accepting the woman he has chosen. Her positive attitude shows him that she thinks highly of him and of his choices, that she feels confident enough in him to let him go, confident enough in their relationship to embrace the woman who is his wife. And he will reciprocate with a son's love, a love that is for her alone.

So when a son gets married, it may be appropriate for his mother to cry over what's past, the little boy who is no more, the child who tugged at her skirt and at her heart. But if she avoids the traps of the triangle, there is no need for her to cry over what's ahead, for mother or for son. Nor is there reason for her to wish him anything but well in his marriage. His new relationship need not take anything away from their longstanding bond of care and devotion. In fact, the more solid his marital relationship becomes, the more confident his mother can be of an important place in his life. Dr. Cynthia Deutsch, a Connecticut psychologist and professor at New York University, explains the connection between the relationship between husband and wife, and mother and son: "The healthier one relationship is, the better the other is. If the husband–wife relationship improves, so will the mother and son's. These relationships are all different, and not competitive. They can exist side by side." Just because a man has found the love of his life doesn't mean he's given up his first love. A contented husband is likely to be a contented son as well.

6

Why Some Mothers
Lose Sons

Just as a son's marriage puts a new face on the mother–son relationship, so do other aspects of his adult life—his moving away, his moving into new social and business circles, the consolidation of his identity as he finds his own special way of facing the world. His world has expanded beyond that of his mother and his childhood home, and he may seem at times to turn his back on his origins. Some mothers resist this seeming abandonment; they make every effort to keep their son within the circle of his childhood and to remain at the center of his life. Others will let their sons go, confident that the mother–son bond will outlive the passions and professional pursuits of his adult years.

The fear of somehow "losing" an adult son—whether single or married—is very real to many mothers. It is something we were taught by our own mothers, who cautioned us to enjoy our sons as children because they won't be ours for long. It is something we may have even learned from our religion, as a Biblical text prophesies a falling-out between mothers and sons. More secular readings may have also underscored our fear: A survey published in *New York* magazine indicated that the parents most likely to feel neglected by their adult children are the mothers of sons; more than half were reported to be dissatisfied with the current amount of contact, wanting to see their sons more often.

But if we look beyond the limited research, we can see that mothers and sons have every chance to maintain warm, meaningful relationships throughout adulthood. In some ways the mothers of sons are at an advantage over the mothers of daughters, whose adult relationships may look wonderful from the outside but are all too often steeped in dependency and guilt. In contrast, a son's independence can be a virtue for the man and his mother alike; as they relate to each other from their strengths, they are free to meet each other as equals, and to develop a relationship better than the uneven one of his childhood. As we'll see in this chapter, there is no reason a mother *has* to lose her son. As we'll also see, some mothers manage to do it anyway. Although such mothers are often beyond consolation, at least others can learn from their losses.

The first lesson was hinted at in this chapter's first paragraph. There we talked about two kinds of mothers, the first of whom holds on to her son for dear life. It is the hold of a desperate woman who cannot imagine life without her son. Strangely enough, this same woman might let a daughter go without any difficulty. Dr. Joseph Newirth, a psychologist at Adelphi University's Institute of Advanced Psychological Studies, explains why some women find their sons, in particular, so hard to give up: "It's easier for these women to idealize their sons than their daughters. That's because their son is less familiar in a lot of ways. He does things that the mother would have liked to do if she had been a man. In that way, he represents her unconscious wishes and her unfulfilled dreams. Also, he may represent his father, as he plays substitute for a husband who's absent or unsatisfying." For her to lose this son is to lose a lot—the embodiment of her innermost desires, the substitute for a missing mate.

But if she acts on her instincts, she will most likely find that her son will be missing as well. She will learn that to hold on too tight is to squeeze the life out of their relationship. Dr. Newirth predicts that such a relationship will deteriorate rapidly. There will be subtle disagreements, then more forceful fights, reasons for the son to keep away from his mother until he can't find reason enough to come back. His absence may eventually deepen into total estrangement. So in the end his mother has made her own worst fear come true, shattering her connection to her most secret ambitions.

INDEPENDENCE AND INTIMACY

What about the other type of mother depicted in the first paragraph? Is she justified in thinking that giving her son his freedom will keep their relationship alive? Before answering that, let's go back to the way sons are raised in our society, and the place of men in various societies throughout history. Says psychiatrist Norman Kelman, "The male is an outsider who enters. Sexually, he comes into a woman. Historically, he is the one who stands guard at the periphery of the community, or goes out and comes back, who does the hunting. Distance is one of the dimensions that man, as man, lives with, much more than a woman does. Men tend to be much more discrete, much more separate."

Their separateness is encouraged by the way they are brought up. From the beginning, sons are trained to leave. From babyhood, as discussed in Chapter 2, they are programmed for freedom, for making it on their own, for leaving their first family and forming their own. They are

schooled in independence and learn the lesson well. And
as we've seen, the more fiercely the mother tries to hold on,
the more fiercely the son struggles to be free.

But the woman who dares to set her son free has most
likely trained him in something else as well. That something else is intimacy. True intimacy is not something that
is immediately obvious. It has nothing to do with the apparently devoted son who calls his mother every morning,
or the daughter who just can't do enough for her perfectly
healthy and able mother. Those are demonstrations of dependency, not of a satisfying, intimate relationship between parent and grown child. Intimacy actually has a lot
more to do with independence; a boy's independence
training is an excellent basis for a future relationship of
intimacy with his mother, as well as with other important
people in his life. What ideally happens, in the beginning,
is that there is some give and take between mother and
child, a sharing that benefits them both, a nurturance of
one for the other. According to Dr. Martin Fisher, an expert in the subject of intimacy, "In infancy, the child
should be giving to the mother as much as the mother is
giving to the child. That's a notion that a lot of people
have a very hard time with: How could the infant give in
any way, degree or proportion to what the mother is giving? The equality doesn't have to do with quantity, or with
time, but with psychological giving. And ideally that flows
both ways." Dr. Fisher stresses that there are no more
barriers to intimacy between mothers and sons than between mothers and daughters. In fact, a son who has
learned to develop his own stores of self-reliance has more
to share than a daughter who has been trained to always
rely on others.

The idea of a mother and adult son being intimate may
be uncomfortable for people who do not truly understand
the term. It does not mean a sexual closeness. It does not
mean constantly checking in with each other, or living in
each other's lives. What it does mean is an awareness of

each other's needs and wishes and goals, and sharing those, without being in each other's way. A mother and son can be intimate without living in the same house or town or state. An outsider would probably never even guess what a good relationship they have. Says Dr. Fisher, "A mother and son can live very separate lives, personally and professionally, and still be very caring and intimate and involved with each other. Sometimes we get caught in the trap of saying that a good relationship or a bad relationship looks like the following. What I'm trying to say is that it doesn't look like anything. It feels. And what feels good for the mother and for the son, what encourages them to be separate and independent, is the relationship that's right for them both." A woman who is wise enough to let her son go would also be wise enough not to wait for professions of love on Mother's Day, or for ritual visits on Friday nights. She will know when her son has emotionally returned to her without such outward trappings of devotion. A mother like that can be quite sure that her son won't be gone for long.

A QUESTION OF GUILT

While the potential for a rewarding mother–son relationship is very much alive, the psychologists I questioned noticed in their practices more cases of estrangement between mothers and sons than between mothers and daughters. It would appear, from that observation, that a bad relationship is worse when a son is involved. But again, appearances can be deceiving. A temporary absence of contact may be less hurtful than a relationship filled with recriminations and based on nothing more solid than guilt. Daughters may be more likely than sons to stick it out with their mothers not because they love them any more but because they are simply too guilt-stricken to leave. It is guilt born out of their earlier Oedipal conflicts with their mothers (somewhat like a boy's Oedipal conflicts with his father), guilt at having wanted her out of the way, guilt that keeps them from leaving a mother they no longer love.

When I raised this issue with one New York psychoanalyst, she surprised herself by her immediate recall of four cases in which the son got away from a difficult mother, but the daughter didn't, or couldn't. One involved a woman in her fifties who was very subservient to her mother. She was bitter toward the now elderly woman, whom she considered to be cold and critical, but she continued to do her mother's bidding. Her brother, by contrast, has almost no contact with the mother, visiting her maybe twice a year, keeping his children away from her. The other three cases described to me were similar. Each mother–daughter pair, bonded by guilt, lived in New York. One of the sons left for Boston, one moved to Arizona, one made it all the way to California. Says the psychoanalyst, "The different responses seem to be because the daughter's resentment of the mother in the Oedipus complex is so much stronger. So out of guilt she stays. And the son is not as guilty and can move away." For mothers who want their children nearby, the responses of the daughters may seem preferable. But for those who are more interested in a genuine relationship, not one born of a childhood complex, it is comforting to know that most sons who stay emotionally close do it out of love, not out of guilt.

SEXUAL ESTRANGEMENT

As Dr. Fisher noted, mothers and sons can be every bit as loving, every bit as intimate, as mothers and daughters. But many mothers and sons let something get in the way of their closeness—the taboo against their sexual interaction. It is a taboo that is stronger than ever for the adult son and his mother, making any physical intimacy between them seem dangerous, even emotional intimacy suspect.

The son may internalize the taboo even more than the mother does, turning away from her to keep the barriers up. He can, and most often does, seek his satisfaction elsewhere, escaping the sexual anxieties he experiences with his mother. On her part, the mother may feel rejected and frustrated by her son's distancing, and resentful of the person who satisfies his desires. Says Dr. Joseph Newirth, "This is why a daughter-in-law can be a threat. She's perceived as stealing the son away. And the mother may wonder, 'What kind of goodies does *she* have that I don't have?' "

The incest taboo keeps some mothers and sons apart emotionally as well as sexually. They may become so used to tiptoeing around a subject that affects them both—sexuality—that they also learn to skirt other important, and intimate, issues. As long as they refuse to see each other as sexual beings, their images of each other will be distorted, and their relationship based more in fantasy than reality. But their sexuality can be a bond, not a barrier. That doesn't mean acting out the sexuality but simply recognizing each other as sexual people and accepting each other's sexual lives. In that way, the difference in sex that exists between mother and son can flavor their relationship but not dominate it.

On a more practical, day-to-day level, some mothers complain that they can't do with their sons what they do with their daughters. Their sons won't help them choose a fabric for the couch, or go to the health spa with them, or join the same book club. They always seem to be doing something else, somewhere else, with someone else. This is a situation that largely has been set up by society. The roles that men have traditionally been given—of going out and establishing a family, of going out and earning a living, of going out on their own—have not been compatible with staying close to the hearth. They *have* been compatible with some oft-heard excuses of sons to mothers: "I'm just too busy to see you." How can she dare to compete with his worldly pursuits, with the world of men? But daughters have been encouraged, generation after generation, to stay close to home, to enmesh themselves in family—in short, to do what their mothers have done. It is a question of "social fields," according to Dr. Newirth. Mothers and daughters have been playing the same game in the same field, while mothers and sons have been fields apart.

CHANGING TIMES

But that is something which is changing with the times, as the rigid dichotomy between men's and women's roles narrows. The easing of those roles works on several levels to bring mothers and sons together. For one thing, young mothers are beginning to complement the independence training of their sons with training in nurturance. A boy who is allowed, even encouraged, to kiss a doll now may not be as reluctant to kiss his mother later. As the behavioral boundaries of each sex expand, sons and mothers are more likely to meet on common ground, to share interests and experiences. In this freer environment, a son may be interested enough in interior design to help his mother with her couch, or conversant enough in literature to become a member of her book club. For her part, she may be as enthusiastic about sports or as interested in business as he is, so they'll have more than enough to do together and plenty of conversational topics. As men and women begin to occupy more of the same space, personally and professionally, there will be less space to separate mothers from sons.

The future of mothers and sons seems more promising than ever, but there are mothers who don't see it that way. They view their son's evolving manhood in itself as a loss. They can't face the fact that a relationship with an adult son cannot, should not, be the same as it was when he was a child. They refuse to settle for anything other than dependency. Dr. Martin Fisher looks at these mothers: "They want their sons to call all the time. But that's not intimacy. That's dependency. That's the confusion. In order to feel more like a mother, she wants the son to act more like a son. It's because her own needs of being a mother have not been fulfilled, her perception of motherhood not been met. Such a woman can be gratified only by a son who relates to her like a needy little boy. She'll then tell you that she and her son have a wonderful relationship. But it's really quite neurotic, and not wonderful at all."

As we saw earlier, there can be intimacy without dependency. In fact, dependency most often subverts the development of a truly close relationship. The goal of the mother should be to let go of the dependent little boy and to rejoice in the independent man, to get past the parent–child relationship and to accept the new relationship between equal adults. In a physical way, the relationship will not be as close as it has been. There won't be the same daily contact, nor the same primacy in each other's lives. But there can still be caring and emotional sharing. For a mother to let go of what was and accept what is is her first and most important step to true emotional intimacy with her adult son.

WHEN THINGS GO WRONG

Even when there isn't intimacy, most mothers do manage to maintain decent relationships with their adult sons. As one therapist put it, "A reasonably good mother will generally have a reasonable relationship with her children." But some mothers are not "good enough," and they sometimes lose their sons.

In some cases, the reason is clear-cut: The mother has abused her son as a child, and now he will have none of her. That's what happened to Paul, a divorced artist in his midthirties who remembers the physical and emotional torment he suffered at the hands of his mother. She's not the one who actually hit him—his father did that—but he sees his mother as the instigator. As Paul tells it, his father would come home after a long hot subway ride, after a day's work at a job he didn't like. And he would be greeted by a long list of Paul's alleged mischief-making. "She told him about it before he showered, and he'd go crazy, just lose total control. He'd hit me with a belt, shoes, whatever was in his hand. After the beating, my mother would call him an animal, and they'd scream at each other. Later she'd come into my room and say, 'See, if it wasn't for you, we'd never fight.' At the time I didn't realize she was an accomplice, but I do now." And now, Paul's mother doesn't see much of her son. He stays away out of fear of what he would do to her should they meet.

That story is an extreme one, and Paul's rejection of his mother is certainly understandable. But just to balance the picture, it's important to note here that mothers are not always the ones to blame. If they tend to feel like perennial scapegoats, they have good reason. Mothers have been psychological scapegoats since at least the World War II era, when a book entitled *Generation of Vipers* coined the phrase "momism," and berated mothers for ruining a generation of men. Mothers may be blamed by their sons for all sorts of things, such as loving a husband too much at their expense, or daring to have another baby. Psychoanalyst Milton Kapit explains how such normal occurrences can seem like abandonment to a son and cause a long-lasting rift in the mother–son relationship: "Her love for her husband, her desire to have another child, are normal parts of life. But they can still alienate her son. He may think, 'My mother already has a child. Am I not good enough? Why did she have another child?' " And his confusion may turn to anger as he sees his world threatened. "The son is really self-centered, still geared to his own self-importance. It's 'Look what she's done to *me,* look what she's done to my life.' Later in life, if he can come to understand how his own self-importance has clouded his vision of his mother, he may begin to see her more objectively." He may realize that she really did love him, despite her feelings for others; he may also realize that her love seemed inadequate because he needed more love than *anyone* could give him.

The need for boundless, endless love is one reason for blaming a mother; the other is the need for an excuse. Whatever a son's dissatisfaction with his life, he can trace it to something his mother did, or didn't do, or did too late. For Keith, a 42-year-old high school teacher living in a Detroit suburb, both those needs were intense. He blames his mother for his personal problems; if she had only loved him more, he'd be a better husband and father. He also blames her for his professional problems; if only she hadn't made him lazy, he'd be something other than a teacher by now. The irony is that he blames her both for doing too much and for doing too little. On the one hand, she was always "bragging" about him, always "bailing him out." What others might interpret as signs of love, he says, made him nervous, unmotivated, and irresponsible: "Because she always fought my battles, I became lazy. I chose teaching as an easy way out. I tried business school for a year, but I was too interested in playing ball and lying in the sun to finish it out. I keep saying I'm going to get out of teaching, but I don't. And it bugs me. If she had only been different, I wouldn't be at a professional dead end now." But the one time she wasn't there for him, he can't forgive her for either. It happened thirty-five years ago, on the day he had his tonsils out: "My grandmother was there, not my mother. She claims she couldn't take a day off from the office without losing pay. But goddamn it, her own son was being operated on, and she wasn't there at the end of the operation. It was wrong, and it affected me." But had she been there, would she have been blamed for overprotecting him? Or perhaps for making him fearful of doctors? There seemed to be no way she could win.

There's even further irony in this story. Keith's father was a gambler and a womanizer, and withheld neither fact from his son. He often took Keith to the race track with him, and they'd pick up the tickets off the ground together. Then at night, they'd look through the stack to see if there was a forgotten winner in the bunch. The father's lechery was not a well-kept secret, either. As Keith puts it, "He was a philanderer. He had a lot of women. My mother knew it, and I knew it." Keith is well aware of the similarities between father and son. "I learned gambling at his knees. Now I find it hard to stay away from the track. I also learned about women from him. I was always looking, and even though I'm married, I'm still looking today. Sometimes I do more than look." Although these are qualities considered undesirable by society—much more so than that of being a teacher—Keith does not condemn his father for passing them down. In fact, he considers his father a positive influence on his personality and his character. It is his mother whom he condemns, both for loving him too much and for loving him too little.

In most cases of emotional estrangement between mother and son, the mother is probably both villain and scapegoat, and the son also contributes to the split. To learn more about the roots of estrangement, I interviewed a number of grown men who are not on good terms with their mothers. Three of those men offered especially poignant stories—stories with pointed lessons for mothers who don't want to lose their sons. There are certain common themes that emerge from these accounts as well as some individual variations. Each of them illustrates that the anguish of losing a son may be matched by the anguish of being a lost son.

A word of caution: These stories are told solely from the sons' perspective. They reflect the feelings of the sons, not necessarily what actually went on. These mothers may not be quite as malevolent as they are made out to be. Yet the sons' feelings are very real. What they voice is what they truly experienced, if not externally, then internally. Something was going on in their childhoods that did not mesh with their emerging personalities, something they blamed mostly on their mothers.

The Seduced Son

Vincent is a married man in his midthirties, an apparent success in the banking world, the father of a young son and newborn daughter. He seems to have mastered both his professional and personal lives, yet he doesn't feel secure in his accomplishments. He traces his difficulties back to his childhood, and to how he was used and abused by his mother.

As Vincent remembers it, his mother was the major force in the household. She ruled the lives of each of the family members—her husband and two sons. Part of her power game was to keep the males of the family apart, to play relentlessly on the sibling rivalry between her older son and Vincent. From Vincent's perspective, he was always the loser, displeasing his mother with his active nature. It was his brother she preferred, his quiet, placid older brother who was her eternal favorite. And nothing Vincent could do could change that.

Vincent's mother split the family in yet another way, turning her sons against her husband. In Vincent's view she was very intentional about it, and very manipulative: "She wanted my brother and me all for herself, and at the same time she wanted to cancel out my father. So she gave us reasons to hate him and to fear him. I remember her telling me that he had wanted me to be a girl—that she was satisfied with my sex but that he wasn't. That really hurt. It underscores the way she tried to alienate my father and me. She set me up so strongly that I always felt I had absolutely no feelings for my father. In fact I had a lot of feelings for my father. They were just masked because of the way in which she positioned me against him."

When Vincent was about eight years old, his father experienced severe emotional problems. That was difficult enough for Vincent to cope with, without his mother's reaction. She turned to a family friend for comfort, and eventually she turned to him for love as well. Vincent was directly exposed to her infidelity, as he was used as an alibi for her absences. She would purportedly be going off with him for a mother–son "outing." He would be left "out" all right, out at a playground, or park, or ball field, while she met her lover for their sessions of afternoon ardor. Then she would pick up her son, rush home with him, and tell her husband what a lovely day they had spent together. And Vincent was not to tell him anything different. He was forced to go along with his mother in betraying his father.

Vincent was not all that shocked at his mother's behavior. He was already quite aware of his mother's sexual side. As he recalls only too well, she had used her sexuality on him: "I felt it in the way she fondled me and rocked me to sleep when I was a little boy. There was definitely a seductive element to it. She used her body in a way that was much more sexual than maternal. When I got a little older, she would drink a lot. Once when she tried to teach me the facts of life she got very vulgar and graphic. I was just horrified at the fact that she would do something like that. I didn't think the graphic details were necessary."

Although he was bathed in his mother's sexual love, Vincent didn't feel he was really loved by her at all: "She was never really there for me, or interested in my interests. I'm sure she loved me as a child because that's the thing Italian mothers do. And if anything would have ever happened to me she would have lugubriously mourned my death. But I don't think she had a genuine interest in my well-being. She was much more enraptured with herself, and with the love affair she was having, and with my brother. I was too strong-willed for her. She couldn't manipulate me and so she didn't really love me for myself."

Vincent traces many of the troubles of his adult life back to the seductive love of his childhood, the only love he knew. In his view, it emasculated him, making him less confident of his manliness and his ability to shape the forces of his life. Perhaps its most direct effect has been on his relationship with women. He says that he can't tolerate any "shallowness" in women, that he easily becomes hostile toward them and thinks of them as "bitches." Much of that hostility is directed toward his wife, a hostility he is trying to control through therapy.

Although Vincent has done very well professionally, he still feels there is something holding him back, something also related to his mother's past behavior. The problem, as he sees it, is that she made him so fearful of his father that he is petrified of other authority figures. For a long time he couldn't deal well with people in high-powered positions and felt in conflict: He had a compelling drive to succeed and yet was desperately afraid of success. Therapy has helped him to face the conflict, and to at least partially overcome the fear.

With all this anger toward his mother, you would think that he would turn his back on her. And yet the ties that bound him as a child continue to bind. He is *still* in competition with his brother for her favor, *still* trying to be the good son. "In dealing with her I'm subservient and obsequious, playing the role she wants me to play. I try to please her, but it's not easy. Her love definitely has strings. She cares about me only so far as I am performing the way she wants me to perform. Right now I'm relatively successful in my career and stable in my family life. So she's accepting of me because I've fulfilled her requirements. It's conditional. I think if I decided to run off and be a ne'er-do-well, she wouldn't accept me. She wouldn't welcome me into her household and say, 'Oh, you're my son, and whatever you want is fine.' She would worry about what people would say. If I wanted to get a divorce or if I wanted to quit my job and just hang out and take my family and live on a commune, she wouldn't understand. And I think she would be very angry. She certainly wouldn't display the positive feelings she displays today."

It would seem, from what Vincent has said, that things are still going his mother's way. Her children are still vying for her love, and she's getting what she wants. If someone asked her about her current relationship with her sons, she would probably still say it was wonderful. But Vincent is understanding more now about his past. And the more he knows about himself, the less he wants to know her: "Since I've gotten in touch with my intense hostility to her, I sometimes act out my resentments. She may say, for example, that she doesn't like something I'm doing with my son. So I say, 'Well, if you don't like what I do with him, can you imagine what you did with me?' I think she feels a lot of guilt about what she's done, and she gets very defensive. I've hit below the belt like that a couple of times. It's probably that I have this subconscious desire to get back at her. My rage and my hostility are coming out through these little digs."

So what does Vincent's mother have now? She has, more or less, the same thing she gave her son—the look of love, with little real love behind it. And he feels that there's so much more she could have had, so much more he could have given her, if she had only been different.

If Vincent's memories are based more in truth than in fantasy, he was clearly an exploited child. It was the exploitation of a woman unsatisfied in her marriage, a woman looking for gratification through sons and lovers. The former gratification is more destructive than the latter, as vulnerable children are victimized by a mother's misplaced needs. What brought Vincent and his mother together physically in the early years is driving them apart emotionally now.

With Vincent, something else is going on as well. He is trying to develop more of a relationship with his father, while at the same time moving away from his mother. His mother doesn't like it. She is still trying to sabotage the father–son relationship by telling her son, "So now he's trying to be a father to you. Where was he all these years? *I'm* the one who raised you." She tries to beat her husband to the phone in an effort to prevent the very thing she has always feared: her husband taking her sons away from her. She needs to be first, and she doesn't want him to be second.

This move toward the father is not a unique happening, notes a prominent family therapist, Dr. James Framo of Philadelphia. "A common theme is that the adult son tries to reach his father. It may be because he believes he has his mother in his back pocket, so to speak. He can count on her. She's reliable. He knows he won't lose her love, even if he murders someone. But he doesn't have his father in that way, and he tries to win him over." The move toward the father can happen for a different reason, as it did in Vincent's case. "It may be because the relationship between mother and son has been too close, and that between father and son too distant. So the son tries to break the shackles of an overprotective mother and reach the father. But the mother may try to block it. The son then has to ask her to get out of the way if he's to find his father."

There is yet another aspect to Vincent's story, the sense of a mother who takes more than she gives, and who gives only for her own purposes. There is a sense of love given because it is supposed to be given, not in the spontaneous free-flowing way that nurtures a child, that helps him grow, and that cements an eternal bond of love between mother and son. But the grown son, almost invariably, gives the exploitative mother back her own, playing at the dutiful son as she played at the dutiful mother.

The Rejected Son

Michael is a forty-year-old psychotherapist, twice married, and the father of two girls. He credits his mother for his professional achievements but blames her for his personal failings. Most of all, he blames her for not being Mother enough. It seems to him that there was always someone else she loved more. Perhaps the person she loved most was her father, as her son remembers: "According to her he was gorgeous, handsome, a great success in everything. She would talk about how he used to bounce her on his knees when she was a child. Memories like that, memories that showed she deeply loved him. Perhaps no one else could ever fill her father's shoes. I remember when he died. I was about ten or eleven. My mother and I embraced for a long time. I remember it so vividly because it was such a unique, outstanding experience of my life. We embraced for a very long time, trying to console one another. That was the only closeness I ever felt with my mother."

Before that time and since, Michael has felt only rejection from his mother. To him, it was as if she didn't want to be a mother at all, as if child rearing was just too much of a burden for her. And so she pushed Michael away, too soon and too fast. And so he clung all the harder.

Just as Michael felt surpassed by her father, he also felt secondary to her career. She was an ambitious businesswoman, thriving on a hectic schedule that often meant baby-sitters for Michael, a steady stream of them. As he recalls, "In one situation I peed in my pants constantly because I was so frightened and so unhappy. In another, the baby-sitter had a kid of my age who was very competitive with me, and that created problems of another sort. Whatever my problems were, my mother just wasn't there for me. She was never one I felt I could approach."

Venturing out was never easy for Michael, whether it was to spend the afternoon in a baby-sitter's care or, when he was older, to spend the evening with a woman. Again, he places the blame with his mother. On the one hand, she pushed him out and away from her; on the other, she almost invariably disapproved of whomever he went out with. Michael saw this as one more way in which she put him down and devalued his choices. "Her main message to me was that I really didn't know what I was doing, and I would basically fumble through life making mistake after mistake." After a while, he stopped trying to win her approval; in fact, he chose women she was sure to criticize, women who were in many ways her opposite. He says he didn't do it consciously, but he did it anyway: "The thing that would turn me on more than anything else would be someone who had none of the cultural features that the people I grew up with had. There was something about the people I grew up with that turned me off. So my history is one of rebellion, against many things, but mostly against my mother. My first experience, sexually and otherwise, was with a woman who was close to twenty years older than I was. Then I got involved with a blond, blue-eyed Minnesotan, and then I lived for four years with a black woman. It was as if I was paying my mother back for being so stiff. Sure, I enjoyed dating those women, but it was also a good kick in her teeth."

Predictably, his mother disapproved of his first marriage, but since his second marriage came soon after his affair with the black woman, she was so relieved that she gave it her blessing. But still, the relationship between mother and son continued as always. And he sees its stamp on his own character, and on his current marriage. For one thing, he sees his wife as being like his mother in a number of ways, none of them especially good. He sees her as critical and judgmental, almost impossible to please. And so he feels he is reenduring what he went through in his childhood, and his marriage has suffered for it. At the same time, he admits that he exhibits some of the other negative qualities he sees in his mother—the tendency to be opinionated and negative, to feel that nothing is worthwhile, that there's no reason to put oneself out to do things. It took him many years of therapy to come to the realization that he is definitely his mother's child. It took him more years to try to reverse those aspects that he doesn't like, so as "not to infect the next generation in quite the same way."

As a man in his forties, he still feels his mother's continued rejection of him and preference for others. He's jealous that she's closer with his wife than she is with him. He's jealous that she's even closer with her neighbors than she is with him. He feels that his thoughts and opinions are still scorned by her. The rejection is still there— but now it's flowing in both directions: "She gets very little from me, and I know that it bothers her. She would like to have a demonstrative loving son who calls up once in a while and is willing to take her around. But I have absolutely no ability to do it and very little interest in doing it. What she gets from me is a taste of her own medicine. A kind of cool, aloof, uncommunicative thing. I don't do it purposely. It's just become such a part of my character. And she's taught me how to do it. I cut my teeth on it as my basic training."

Michael acknowledges that his mother has also influenced him in some positive ways—she's passed on to him her passion for hard work, her stability, her honesty— qualities he has generally taken for granted. He also credits her for his choice of profession, though she certainly wouldn't consider the reasons a credit to her. In his work as a psychotherapist, he is seeking the intimacy he didn't have with her, the warm personal relationships, the richness of experience. He is trying to make up for lost time.

Will Michael and his mother ever make up for *their* lost time? He doesn't think so, and it is one of the deepest regrets of his life. "I don't think our relationship is going to get any better. She's not going to change at this point. We've never had a close relationship. We never will. It's as much my responsibility as it is hers, and I never sought to turn back to her and try to make it anything better. I just don't think we can get beyond certain hurdles. I will always feel a resentment and stiffness with my mother, and I think she will always see me as disappointing in many, many ways. I'm sorry to say that we're going to carry this to the grave. She will die, and then I guess I will feel very profoundly what I might have had and never did have. I'll feel terribly sad and probably terribly cheated."

Although Michael has managed to salvage something positive out of his pain—his career in psychotherapy—his words are still shaped in sadness, his tale almost too terrible for him to tell. Despite all the times he's gone over it before, including his years in therapy, talking about it just one more time was difficult for him, a reminder that he would never have the mother he wants. Even in adulthood sons need mothers and want mothers; giving up on their own mothers is too devastating, too final, for most men to do, and it is never easy. Even Michael keeps the door slightly ajar: "The only thing that would get me back to her now would be a major turnaround in graciousness and generosity." Although he has said repeatedly that a good relationship between them is impossible, he has left her this smallest of openings, an opening he is sure she won't use, but then, who knows?

In Michael's story, we also see the effect a mother can have on a marriage. His mother may not be alive and well in his affections, but her specter is certainly alive in his marriage, and an ever-present threat.

Throughout Michael's narrative is a strong sense of rejection, of a son not feeling truly wanted by his mother. As he sees it, she preferred her father to him; she prefers his own wife to him; she has even preferred her job to him. The last may have been the hardest to take, as his memory burns with her daily leaving of him. But it is not simply that she was a working mother that made her son turn off and turn away; it is that she apparently did not work hard enough at being a mother.

The Favored Son

Warren cannot complain that he wasn't wanted. His mother wanted him so much that she couldn't let him go, and that's just why he left. Warren is close to fifty now, a second-time husband, the father of two sons, and a successful accountant despite a chronic illness. His father died about fifteen years ago. His mother is still alive, but only on the outskirts of his life. Warren told me how it came to be the way it is.

To be favored by his mother was no favor, he recalls. It just meant that she interfered even more in his life than in his sister's, and tried to chart out his future. He didn't see this as a sign of love but of her need to control. In fact, like the other sons in this section of the chapter, he didn't feel loved at all: "She didn't understand my sister or me, and she didn't have time for us. She'd spend more time worrying about someone popping in on her and finding a cushion out of place than really caring about what my sister's feelings were and what my feelings were. She was also very devoted to the business, and to making money. She spent more time in the luncheonette we owned than on us. When my mother did have time for me and listened to my problems, it was more as an obligation of a mother to a child than as really being there for me the way I'm there for my kids. That's also the way she loved me, because it's the thing to do, because you *should* love your children."

Neither Warren nor his sister stayed at home longer than they had to. He joined the army when he was just nineteen, and she got married at the same age. They were driven away, he said, by the constricting environment of their home. He considers his enlistment the best move he ever made. It took the control away from his mother and allowed him to shape his own life. "The army was a good experience for me. It did for me in eight weeks what my parents couldn't do in nineteen years—make a man out of me. I learned to be totally responsible for myself, to be totally independent without having to ask anybody what I should do. I knew what I had to do. It was my decision to make."

Since his enlistment, Warren never really psychologically returned to his mother. He stayed home for two years to go to school, but his twenties and thirties were largely spent wandering—traveling around the country, settling for a while in California, spending a stint in Las Vegas, and briefly marrying a showgirl. During those years he stayed in touch with his mother, and even lived with her for a while after his father died. But he kept the relationship on as superficial a level as he could. Her desire for control had not abated, nor had his intention of having no part of it.

When he returned to his hometown and remarried, his relationship with his mother hit an all-time low. She refused to accept his wife, and so he would no longer accept his mother. According to Warren, the only reason she had accepted his first wife was because of the glamour of her profession. But she saw this second marriage as an infringement on what was rightfully hers. "It was as if my wife had stolen me away. My mother just couldn't accept or adjust to the idea that the kids do fly from the nest, that there is a time for a mother to cut the cord and let you be your own person. My mother lost me then, she lost me when she didn't accept my wife for who she was. I was very angry at her, and for six years I hardly spoke to her or had anything to do with her."

That total estrangement has ended, but Warren and his mother are still not getting along well at all. From his perspective, it's because she still demands her "rights" as a mother, but he refuses to pay her eternal homage: "She feels because she's my mother I should do what she wants me to do. She still wants control over me, and she hasn't had it for a long long time, since I'm nineteen, and she

can't accept it. But I refuse to get an ulcer, to feel uncomfortable, just to make her comfortable. So if I have
something to say, I say it."

Warren is not fully satisfied with the situation, and yet
he has accepted it. On the one hand, he's convinced that she
won't change. He compares her to a house that's hardened
into its foundation: The concrete is settled, the creaks are
out, and all the cracks have been plastered over. On the
other hand, his illness has made him aware of the fragility
of life and the value of human relationships: "Sometimes
I'm really sad that my relationship with my mother is
what it is. I realize now how short life is, so why can't we
have a relationship that's fruitful and meaningful? Why
have all these ill feelings toward one another, that you
didn't do enough for me, and I haven't done enough for
you? But that's how it is between my mother and me. I feel
sad about it, but at least I don't feel guilty about it. It's
true, I probably could have been a better son to her. I
probably could have been a *much* better son. But she could
have been a much better mother."

In this son's story, as in the others, you can hear the
tremendous ambivalence—the feeling that the relationship
can't change, it just can't change; it *must* change, but it
can't change. The emotion conveyed in the words of these
men was clear on their faces as they spoke, and obvious
in the breaking of their voices. No one likes to be a lost
son.

But no one likes to be a son without an identity, either.
And that's what Warren feared was happening to him before he picked up and moved out, moved across the world
to Korea, then across a continent to California, to become
his own person. What Warren's mother did, other mothers
sometimes do, and their sons often react the way Warren
did—to get the hell out. This is how Dr. Joseph Newirth
explains what's happening: "It's not exactly smothering
that the mother is doing, which means trying to swallow
the person up. Instead, it's a lack of differentiation, a lack

of awareness of what the son's life is about apart from her own. It's not knowing the other person, not accepting him for who he is, not acknowledging that the son is separate. It's as if the son doesn't exist outside of the mother's head."

Dr. Robert Sherman of Queens College stresses the lack of boundaries in such a situation: "There is a confusion of feeling, where what you experience becomes my experience. Where do I leave off and you begin? You have a pain in the back, but it hurts me. Because of the lack of boundaries there are constant intrusions into the other person's life, a constant invasion of privacy so there is no privacy." Either the son gets out, as Warren did, or the son remains a child, never to grow into an autonomous adult.

In Warren's view, his mother has always clung to the role of the authority figure, trying to cast him in the role of obedient little boy. When he stands his ground she calls him "stubborn"; when he speaks up for himself she says he's got a "big mouth." She appears to be the woman Dr. Fisher described earlier in this chapter, the woman who has not felt fulfilled as a mother, and so plays the role to the hilt. She refuses to acknowledge her son as an adult, as an equal, and so he refuses to acknowledge her as an important person in his life. And so they go along, playing out their mother–son relationship until the end, but not really living it.

Out of these men's stories come a myriad of reasons why some mothers lose their sons: they seduce them, or infantilize them, or devaluate them, or exploit them, or abuse them, or some combination of the above. Or at least that's how the sons see it. But there is an underlying factor common to these mother–son pairs. The sons do not feel loved for who they are. They are loved because they are *supposed* to be loved, or not at all. In turn, they love their mothers because they are *supposed* to, or not at all. It is a mutual process that causes these mothers and sons to be emotionally estranged.

But estrangement does not mean indifference. Far from it. These men were more than willing to talk about their mothers, eager to go over their pasts again, their hurts again, to try to understand and to communicate just what went wrong. They are men who are still very much involved with their mothers, and the deeper the anger, the deeper the involvement. If they *really* didn't care, the rage and the anguish would have given way to casual indifference, and the mention of mother would not be so painful. Dr. Fisher puts it like this: "Where there is estrangement, there is usually intense involvement at the same time. It's only people whom you have some investment in who are capable of pushing your buttons because you are concerned about their reactions and their feelings." Dr. Fisher also explains the ambivalence that has turned each of these men's stories into almost a contradiction of itself: "On the one hand, the son wants very much the closeness and the intimacy with his mother. On the other hand, as he gets closer, the anxiety level builds up because the intimacy, the closeness, is frightening. And then he begins to bail out."

Remember Keith, the man who used his mother as a scapegoat? When I interviewed him, he seemed overcome with anger toward her. He told me how he resented her, how furious he was with her. Yet several weeks later, he seemed disturbed at what he had revealed, almost guilty at his "betrayal" of her. He told me, "I was just a little miffed about something she had done. But everything's all right between us now." Quite a turnaround! And quite a reflection of how these "lost" sons still long for their mothers. What they seem to want is not estrangement but a different relationship with their mothers than they currently have, one that's more genuine and more equal. Their minds may be closed to the possibility, as they each maintain that "she just can't change." But their hearts are another story.

HOW TO KEEP YOUR SON

Sons don't really want to be lost to their mothers, and
there are countless ways for their mothers to "keep" them.
Some of the ways are good, and some not so good, as
psychotherapist Ted Dubinsky describes: "One way to
keep a son is to refuse to let him go. You do such a number
on his head that he can't go. He tries over and over, but
he can't get away. He'll be so disturbed, he'll be yours
forever. The other way is to be a lovely, nice parent and
respect the child for himself. If you see him as an individual, if you appreciate his autonomy, there's a good chance
he won't disappear into the wilderness never to return."

The "good" mother who won't lose her son is the one
who has admired his masculinity and other attributes from
the time he was a boy and now appreciates the manly part
of his nature as one important facet of him. She is the
mother who is willing to relinquish some of the mothering
part of her role and become more of a friend instead. If
she has a good sense of herself and a life for herself, she
can more gracefully give up the life she has known as
mother to a child.

For a mother to be separate is to allow a son to be
separate, and yet to give him the incentive to return and
learn about his mother in a new way. She is no longer the
mother who lives only in the house and only for him,
doing his cooking and cleaning and the rest of his bidding.
Through her classes, or her career, or whatever new interests she has, she has become more a woman of the world,
or at least of the community, and a more interesting person
for him to know. She has more things to offer him than
what he no longer needs. And so mother and son meet as
adults, as interesting people with ideas and experiences
and whole new worlds to share.

That is definitely the way it was for Miriam Seltzer, a
professor at the University of Minnesota and the mother

of four grown sons. She was able to let her sons go as she pursued her own interests, and was surprised when they didn't go as far away as she had expected:

"My husband and I had a lot of fun raising our children. It was the best thing that ever happened to us. But we didn't have them in order to hold on to them. We just assumed that independence would come early for them. When they reached eighteen and went off to college, I separated from them in the sense of no longer being responsible for them. I expected the intimate relationship I had with them when they were growing up to end. I just assumed they were launched on their way. Then when they graduated college they were really on their own, really gone. At least I expected them to be gone. I never thought they'd live in our town, but two of them are here. I never expected to see or talk to them as much as we do, but we do. We genuinely like each other's company. We look forward to seeing them as friends, not to demand or require or to tell them what to do. To have dinner with them on Sunday is like icing on the cake."

Seltzer stresses the change from relating to a child to relating to an adult. "I had no expectations of what an adult relationship with adult children would be like. It can click or not click. You meet them in a different way than as children, especially if you've been apart. You see them as people with wants and faults and God knows what else. The nice thing is to wake up and find, 'I like these people. They're really neat.'"

One of the tricks to enjoying an adult relationship with a son is to not get caught in the trappings. Too many mothers judge their sons on the number of calls they get a week, the number of visits a month, the number of flowers on Mother's Day. But those formalities are no real measure of a son's feelings. If calls are made and flowers sent out of a sense of obligation or guilt or overdependence, they are no measure at all. The mothers who don't do the counting are the ones who can truly count on their sons' affection.

They are also the mothers who do not give or withhold love based on what their sons have done for them lately— or who their sons have married, or the size of their house, or the size of their paycheck. One of the major regrets of the "lost" sons I spoke with was the seemingly conditional nature of their mother's love. That was stated most explicitly by Vincent, the seduced son, who felt that were he to divorce or be demoted, his mother would not be thrilled to see him. Since these sons had to meet certain standards to keep their mothers' love, they sensed that it wasn't real. A mother who loves her son truly, without smothering him, will have little chance of losing him.

Craig is a man in his early thirties who is not doing spectacularly well in business; he was divorced and is living with a friend; his romantic life is sporadic and his bank account low. His is not exactly the American success story, at least not at this juncture of his life. But he is as confident as ever of his mother's total love: "I have the secure feeling of knowing that she loves me for who I am, not for what I might become, or how much money I have in my pocket, or what kind of car I drive. Her love doesn't have to be proven. It's there. It's a constant." And so is their relationship. Craig really loves the woman who loves him. "She's fifty-two but she's young, young at heart. It's funny. I enjoy her company more now than I ever did. I won't hesitate to invite her to a movie, or out for dinner with me. Sometimes we even confide in each other. I won't go to her *first* with a problem. First I'll ask a friend. But sometimes I will bounce something off her. And recently she started confiding in me about a lot of things, especially things involving the family. We really do have each other, and I really feel her love."

Most mothers and sons do maintain ties of affection and devotion throughout the adult years. Although the story of a satisfied son is not as compelling as the story of a forlorn one, I'm offering one here about a man who has unusual insight into his relationship with his mother, both the good and the bad of it, a story that illustrates how deep the feelings of love can run and just how close mothers and sons can be.

THE SECURE SON

Jared is in his late twenties, studying psychology, the field both his mother and father are in. He lives with a woman in an apartment not far from his parents' home. His relationship with his mother is not quite where he wants it to be yet, but he envisions great things ahead.

Jared remembers always having a very warm, affectionate relationship with his mother. It's not that she was always physically warm or even physically present—she was often away at work, leaving him with two older sisters and a maid to care for him. It was more her warm voice, her warm manner, along with the atmosphere she created of freedom. As Jared recalls, she was responsive to whatever he was concerned with, and allowed him to explore whatever he was interested in. What made Jared feel even more loved was the love he saw between his parents. They were each in a second marriage and seemed to be the model couple. Jared recalls that the two or three fights his parents did have seemed "earth shattering" to him because everything always seemed so peaceful and understanding between them. As he sees it, "Their marriage could last indefinitely. If they lived forever I think their marriage would last forever because they reached very early that incredible understanding that's so rare."

Having parents like that made Jared feel very secure—perhaps even *too* secure, he says. "It was the kind of security that somebody was *always* there to take care of me. It was the house I could always go home to. There was a sort of magic all the time. No matter what trouble I got into, no matter how serious the trouble was, I would always be gotten out of it. On the one hand, that didn't help me grow up. But on the other, if they hadn't bailed me out, my life wouldn't be where it is now. I am at a point where I can step off and the world is almost mine."

When Jared was old enough to go out on dates, he didn't feel reined in by his mother. She never tried to control or manipulate his relationships. In fact, she rarely commented on the women he dated. All he recalls her saying is, "Jared, I don't care who you're with, just as long as they care for you and you care for them." He remembers her interfering only once. He says that she was distraught over a situation that had arisen between him and a girl, and she told him what was bothering her about it. He admitted that she was right. In fact, "I knew it before she said it," and he didn't mind her saying it.

The time came when Jared and his parents decided that he should be moving out of their apartment. He was twenty-three, earning something of a living, and ready to live an independent life—at least he thought he was. The day he moved wasn't so bad, and the first month of setting up his own household was kind of exciting. But then something happened that made him realize just what this move really meant to him. It happened on the night he saw the movie *Ordinary People.* "That movie was the catalyst. It just blew me away. I'm basically very stable, but that night when I got to my apartment I felt as if I was going crazy. I was smacked in the face with an anxiety attack I had never experienced before. I was frozen. I was immobilized. Basically it was leaving home. It was declaring independence. It was looking back on my life and saying 'All this time I've been playing being a son and being a child without being an adult.' That was my rite of passage that night. All that pain, just to move out, to move on, to be my own person."

Although Jared had moved away from home, and managed to adjust well to the move after that night, he didn't move away from his relationship with his mother. He sees how profoundly that relationship has affected him in every area of his life. For one thing, it guided him in his choice of profession—working as a child psychologist. He says that he learned thought patterns from his mother, and an empathetic stance, that have made him want to work with children. "At an early age she helped to tune me in to my own maternal needs as well as my maternal drives. That's why I'm so clear in my professional goal. She gave me that desire to nurture. As a man, that makes me different from many other men." He also feels that she has affected him positively in his personal life—that her energy, her smiles, her warmth, are carried along with him. Even his relationships with women are better for his relationship with his mother. He considers them less stormy, more giving, and warmer than many of the male–female relationships he sees around him.

Jared sees problem spots in his relationship with his mother, along with the strong positives. Here he assesses their current relationship eloquently:

"I think that what I have with my mother, though it's not perfect, is really quite rare. We have a very deep understanding about each other, and we share what we both consider is most important in life. Even if we disagree, it will hurt, but the love is still so clear. Yes, there is a negative aspect to the relationship in that my mother is extremely maternal and desires that maternal instinct to survive forever. And that's how she gives to people, no matter who they are. She is an extremely warm, loving person. Growing up has been hard for me because it means saying goodbye to that part of my mother, which means letting my girlfriend be more of my mother, letting me be more of my own parent, not needing parents anymore. When it's this close, when it's this warm and loving, there is guilt associated with leaving also, because I know it will hurt her. But after the real growing up I can come back again, and I think deep down inside my mother knows all this.

"My mother's is the selfishness of wanting to be loved, and wanting to be needed, and I'm glad she is the way she is. It's delayed some processes, but once these processes are finished I'll be better off than if she'd been different. In a way it's like any fueling technique. I was given so much fuel, and it was so rich and so warm, that I couldn't cut myself off from it. When I do cut myself off from it, and start going on my own fuel, I will have more than people who didn't have this close relationship with their parents.

"The immediate future won't be easy. I think there will be a period when my mother will be very lonely for a little while, and she'll have to turn to my father for solace. There's that period in growth that's so fragile, where the bond is being pulled to its limit, and it's stretching, and it's really thin. That's not pain, that's not argument, it's not anything negative. It's just me saying, 'These things I've got to do by myself for a while.' And that will make my mother feel a little less needed, a little more alone. But once I've stretched the bond, I'll be able to turn to her as an equal rather than as a child.

"There will still be intimacy between us. I know there will be. I have no doubt about it. But it will be more of an equal relationship because I have been able to accept the fact that even some ultrapositive aspects of my mother are negative for me. And when I was able to accept that, and not be angry at her for it, it allowed me to see her as a full human being, rather than as just my mother. When you see your mother there's a split, the good mother and the bad mother. Well I put mine together and I came up with my mother again."

The good mother and the bad mother. This man could merge them, but the "lost" sons of this chapter could not, perhaps because for them the "bad" part seemed so overwhelming. But perhaps, for some sons, it is easier to see the bad, to dwell on it, to use it as an excuse for what they have or have not done with their own lives. And it is easier to be "lost" than to find the courage to change their lives. Jared has taken on the responsibility for his own life, though he sees its connectedness with his mother's. He has grown into a man who can forgive his mother for not being perfect.

In Jared's story, we see what we have not seen in the other stories, a stable, loving marriage between parents that gave him the security to grow and finally to go. Warmth between a husband and wife spreads naturally to their sons and daughters, enveloping them with the good feeling of being loved. And their grown children can then use that feeling in their professional lives and personal lives to build bonds of love with others.

MAKING AMENDS

As we see in Jared's story, a mother can be the recipient of the deepest love of a caring son. And that can happen at any point in their relationship, even if she has made mistakes in the past. It's true, a mother cannot go back and undo what she did twenty years ago, but she can change what she is doing now. She can take the time to truly know her son, to accept him and be there for him, first as a parent, and then as a friend. She cannot obliterate the damage of the past, but if she is willing to make the necessary repairs in the present, she can win her son back.

Some mothers and sons seek psychological help to heal the wounds and to reach a new understanding. That can be an effective way to regenerate a troubled relationship. Both mother and son can look at the issues that have caused them problems and work on ways to resolve them while they are both willing and able to make the effort. If successful, that effort will make them not only happier with each other, but happier in every aspect of their individual lives.

More typically, only the son goes for help, and the mother feels threatened by it. She is fearful that she will be made the scapegoat of all his ills, terrified that he will decide to make a clean break. In some of the stories related to me by the "lost" sons, that would seem to have been the case. Superficially, everything was going well in the relationship until *after* the son entered therapy. Then he started acting hostile toward his mother, and she may have felt for the first time that something was wrong. And she may have blamed the therapy for turning her son against her. But therapy only uncovers resentments that have been there all along, and continued therapy may help sons better accept their mothers for who they are. The desired outcome of therapy is *not* to blame Mother, or Father, but for the son to take responsibility for his own life, to see how his own personality can get in his way. A New York psychoanalyst, Dr. Hanna Kapit, explains it like this: "It's hoped that the son will learn to look at his parents objectively, and not expect perfection because perfection doesn't exist. It's hoped that he'll accept the fact that his parents have both weaknesses and strengths. The idea is not to overidealize them, not to blame them, but to see what they are all about. If a son finds, after a good, true, honest exploration, that his mother is totally sadistic, in the end he may not want to have anything to do with her. But most likely he's going to find out that his mother had her own problems, and that's why she couldn't be there for him all the time, as he would have liked." And finding that out may help mother and son to find each other.

But what if a mother finds that her son, with or without therapy, is leaving her, calling it quits on their relationship? She feels abandoned, rejected. What should she do? Psychoanalyst Milton Kapit, Hanna Kapit's husband, gives this advice: "She should take it with composure, because if she's going to fuss over it, she's going to make it worse. She'd do best if she could be objective about it, realize that her son has to move away from her now, and not make him feel guilty about it or torment him over it. If she can take it in stride, he's most likely going to come back. But if she pesters him and makes him feel guilty, then he may never return."

Dr. Martin Fisher also advises patience, as well as some self-examination, in the face of "abandonment." "The mother has two possibilities," he points out. "One is to recognize that there may be something that's been going on in the relationship that wasn't all that terrific to begin with. Otherwise why all of this behavior to undermine closeness? It has to be coming from someplace." Once she comes to that realization, she can look for the source of the difficulty and try to make the relationship right again. "The second possibility is that the mother may feel that this is okay, that this is necessary, and that if she waits around long enough, the struggle, the wrestling, the static will disappear and they can then both go to a real relationship. I think what often happens, though, is that mothers get frightened that their sons will be so angry, so full of hate, that they'll never have a relationship with them again. So they begin to maneuver and do things that will undermine it even further. They may berate the son, 'How can you talk to me like that?' instead of saying, 'Okay, you're angry,' and then waiting a couple of days and sitting down again and saying, 'Did I make you angry? I'm not aware of how I did it. Is there something you can tell me? Maybe I can learn. Maybe I can do it differently next time.'" And maybe, if she approaches her son's moving away with compassion instead of criticism, she won't lose him after all.

WHEN SONS LOSE MOTHERS

In this day and age, some mothers would like to learn just *how* to lose a son. Their grownup son has not yet left home, or having left, returns again and again, filling up the nest that would best be left empty. As more women are filling up their lives in other ways than with children, they may simply no longer need their sons as much as their sons still need them. And a son may find himself asking, "Ma, I never get to see you anymore. Where have you been?" And she may find herself answering, "Oh, I've been around, doing my thing." More and more parents are picking themselves up from the empty nest and enjoying life without the children, and the children are doing more of the missing. It is not that these mothers love their sons any less, it is just that they need them less, and once they have brought them up to be independent, healthy adults, they feel free to lead their own full lives. Free at last.

7

That Other Man: When His Lover Is Not a Lady

*A*s a journalist, I am very comfortable in the role of asking questions but am not always at ease being interviewed myself. Yet that's just what happened to me while doing research for this chapter. Many of the mothers of gay sons I contacted agreed to talk to me only after I answered some of *their* questions first. They wanted to know whether I had sons of my own, and how I would react if they were to grow up gay. My liberal instincts provided the answer that went something like this: "It would probably upset me at first, but I would come to accept it. My only concern is my sons' happiness. If that's what would make them happy, fine." When I spoke them, they were just empty words, perhaps even exploitive ones, but by the time I completed researching this chapter, and learned as well as an "outsider" can the experience of being Mother to a gay son, I could voice them as the truth.

It may seem strange that a mother of young sons would even think of the possibility of their one day being gay, but it is actually a very common thought, and for some mothers even a preoccupation. Many women size up their sons, very early on, for the stereotypical signs of femininity. A son may be suspect if he prefers playing the flute to playing football, or likes to experiment with his mother's cosmetics, or spends more time with the neighborhood girls than with the boys. If he is small and delicate and good-looking, his mother may see men in his future. One mother was upset that her seven-year-old son was so handsome. She was afraid that his striking looks would one day draw homosexuals to him, and turn him into one of "them."

The fear of homosexuality—a fear now mixed with hysteria because of the AIDS epidemic—is often translated into a deliberate plan of action in bringing up a son. The plan goes like this: Teach the boy to throw a ball the way a boy should throw a ball, keep him away from dolls and other cuddly objects, and he will be well on his way to a life of healthy heterosexuality. That is, of course, if his mother keeps a low profile, careful not to be too domineering or too physically affectionate. There are those who still believe that it's all the mother's fault; that if she doesn't smother her son with too much affection, if her mothering is not too overpowering, he'll grow up to be a lover of women and not a seducer of men.

Fear and prejudice die hard, but scientific investigations are beginning to disprove some of the myths that surround the subject of homosexuality. In particular, Mother is being exonerated from blame as studies show no significant difference in the mothering of homosexuals and heterosexuals. A large-scale study by the Alfred C. Kinsey Institute for Sex Research looked into the origins of homosexuality and found the significance of boys' relationships with their mothers to be "hardly worth mentioning" as a cause of homosexual orientation. The report, pub-

lished in 1981, didn't identify any definitive cause of homosexuality but suggested that a biological predisposition
might be the controlling factor, a factor that has *nothing*
to do with the quality of mothering. An earlier study, conducted by Dr. Marvin Siegelman of the City College of
New York, led to essentially the same conclusion: The
mothers of homosexual men were no more dominant, or
demanding, or close, or protective, than the mothers of
heterosexual men. The role of fathers was somewhat more
telling, but not much. In all, the findings "seriously question the existence of *any* association between family relations and homosexuality *vs.* heterosexuality," concluded
Dr. Siegelman.

An estimated one of every ten males grows up gay, and
one of four families is thought to have a gay member. So
watchful mothers continue to look for signs: Is little
Johnny developing a girlish gait? Is little Christopher
spending too much time behind closed doors with little
Anthony? But such "signs" often reveal very little. While
it is true that many male homosexuals are somewhat effeminate as children, others are not, and can enjoy a good
brawl as well as any bully on the block. And many of those
labeled "sissy" by their classmates grow up as straight as
any mother could wish.

Most mothers see nothing good at all about having a gay
son. In their view, if a son grows up gay, he is condemned
to a life as society's outlaw, performing his dirty deeds in a
frenzy of promiscuous couplings, bound to become a
lonely, frustrated, pathetic old man. It is not a pretty picture, but one that is finally being obliterated by a recent
round of scientific studies. Homosexuals in general are no
less psychologically well-adjusted than heterosexuals, these
studies conclude, no more neurotic, and no less masculine.
Neither the American Psychological Association nor the
American Psychiatric Association classifies homosexuality
as a mental illness any longer, or use the label of "perversion" that has so long haunted the lives of gay people.

Homosexuals can be fulfilled within themselves and find fulfillment with others in intimate and satisfying relationships. Theirs is not necessarily a lonely lot, even as they grow old. In fact, research shows that many gay men age in a positive and healthy manner, and even cope better than their heterosexual counterparts because of their lifelong experience in doing things for themselves.

Of course, even a knowledge of the facts—that homosexuality is a normal variation of human sexual behavior, that it is not a sign of perversion or decadence—does not relieve the gut feeling of many mothers: that this is the worst thing that can happen to my son; that my son is no longer my son, at least not the son I wanted him to be; that my son is a woman-hater, and so on some level must hate me; that my son is lost to an underworld of gay fellowship, a world I can never enter, a world of darkness that has stolen him from me forever.

The world of darkness seems to descend early, often at the beginning of adolescence. The boy who was once so open and so enthusiastic has closed himself off in an uncommunicative shell, moving away from mother and into himself. The mother may experience it as a rejection even more total and hurtful than the average adolescent visits upon his unprepared mother. But for the gay adolescent, it is something much different. It is self-protection of those feelings he may have just recently identified. (Although many of these boys feel "different" even earlier in life, as early as five or six, they generally don't know what to make of it or call it before adolescence.) It is the fear that if his parents were to learn what he feels, and what he is, they would turn him out of their hearts, and maybe even their home. And so he becomes very quiet, and if necessary, very deceitful. Sometimes, he lies about where he's going at night and makes up inventive tales about where he's been. He doesn't do it to be mean. He does it to survive.

The attempt to deceive may extend to actually going out on dates with girls. Arnold, a gay man, remembers having had wonderful times on his almost-weekly dates. That's probably because they were actually double dates. Arnold and his friend Kenny would take out two girls to the movies or to a game, go out for sodas, and then walk the girls home. After kissing their dates good night, the fun would really begin, as Arnold and Kenny would find a secluded spot and have sex with each other. In spending their evenings that way, the boys hoped to satisfy their parents and their dates, and certainly to satisfy each other.

Whether gay teenagers are active sexually or not, there is often a lot they are hiding from their parents. But the deception is not malicious, and the withdrawal not really a rejection. Instead, what is going on is the difficult process that the boy must work through alone, a process of exploring and accepting just who he is before he can hope to face his parents and win their acceptance.

TO TELL OR NOT

In some families, the protective shell of gay adolescence remains; the boy never grows into the man who can reveal himself to his parents for who he is, and the lie he lives cuts through the fabric of their relationship. On many levels, the son *is* lost to the mother, lost because he cannot, or will not, share his true nature with her. It is a struggle that every gay man goes through: Should he or shouldn't he "come out" to his parents? It is never a decision made lightly, and it is sometimes not even made consciously. Instead, the son may leave clues around, hoping on some level that his parents will find out, hoping that they will know without his telling them. One son, during the summer before he went away to college, left some magazines under his mattress, magazines that had obviously made for some interesting bedtime reading. Most of them featured pictures of nude men with stories of their homosexual exploits. There were also some "girlie" magazines, but they were fewer in number and obviously not as well perused. Since this boy's mother was known to turn his mattress upon occasion, he couldn't have been surprised when she discovered the cache. Apparently he wanted her to know about him. His sexual orientation was a secret he could no longer keep. Another gay son, who had spent an unhappy year away at college and was now back home, said he didn't want his parents to know about his life-style, that they wouldn't understand and wouldn't be able to take it. Yet he often had his mother drop him off at a gay bar. And he continued frequenting the same bar even after he found out that a colleague of his mother's worked there. The colleague eventually told his mother about her son's "friends," confirming what she really knew already and what her son had tried in many ways to tell her.

Even when a son decides to tell his parents, there is often a long wait for the opportune moment. Sometimes the revelation comes out in a torrent of anger. It's as if the man is girding himself for the anger that he fears will be coming back his way. That's how it was for a gay man who had moved from Cleveland to Greenwich Village and was visited one Christmas by his mother. Even twenty years later, he remembers well the anger that gave him the courage to finally face her with the truth: "I had wanted to tell her, but I didn't know how. Over the holidays, I remember, we were drying the dishes. We started talking about the Village, and she warned me to be careful because of all the queers living there. Well I turned to her, fire-eyed, and said, 'Don't you ever use that word around me again. I'm one of those people you're talking about.' That's how it happened. I remember it distinctly."

Other men cover the revelation with a veneer of humor. One young man, who now works in a gay bookstore, had been "telling" his mother without words, and she had begun to get the idea. Whenever he visited home, he'd bring along one or two of his male friends, some of them gay, some of them not. She finally asked him, "Why are you al-

ways traveling around with guys all the time? Are you
turning into a homosexual?" He kept denying it, until he
was almost ready for her to know the truth. Only through
humor could he take that final step. As he tells it, this is
how he broke the news to his mother: "I had just moved
to the city, and found a roommate through a gay roommate service. My mother called up and asked how my
apartment was. I told her that it was nice. She asked me
how my roommate was. I said, he's all right. She asked,
'But is he okay?' I said, 'What do you mean, okay?' She
said, 'You know, is he straight?' I said, 'No.' So she said,
'What are you doing with someone who's not straight?' I
said, 'Take three guesses.' She said, 'You're gay?' I said, 'You
got it. You got it on the first guess.' "

But some men find that neither humor nor anger can
motivate them to break the shocking news. In fact, nothing can. They just can't face the anger that may be returned. They won't risk disappointing their parents. Although they don't like the endless deception, they're afraid
that the truth will rock their world. Jonathan is a man
who wants his parents to know. It is a subject that obsesses
him but a subject he cannot come to terms with. He is a
physician in his late thirties; he himself has known for
more than thirty of those years that his sexual feelings are
reserved for men. But for his parents to know—particularly for his mother to know—just seems too big a risk.

As he told me about his family life, the roots of his reluctance became clear. He described his mother as a person
who holds grudges: "If she gets angry at someone, she
doesn't talk to them forever, the rest of her life, that kind
of thing. There are many people on her list whom she
doesn't talk to." He described both his parents as unap-
proachable on sexual topics: "I could talk to my parents
about a lot of things—about problems with school, about
feelings of being hurt, and they could be very understanding. But as for sex, or relationships with sexual connota-

tions, I could not share that with them. I could never ask them anything personal in the erotic sense."

Jonathan had his first homosexual experience when he was twenty, but he didn't come out to friends and colleagues until his midthirties. Now he wants to come out to his parents, but he feels that he can't. "I want them to know me as I am now. I want them to know that I'm happy, and have a good social life, and a lot of friends. I would like them to know that I'm okay even though I'm gay. But something stops me from telling. Part of it is that I think my mother would become hysterical and put her head in the oven. The other part is that I don't want to look bad in their eyes. I always wanted them to be proud of me, to think of me as a success. But telling them this might make me a failure in their eyes, and it might make them think that they've failed, too."

Jonathan's story is unusual in the sense that he seems more fearful of his mother's reaction than of his father's. It is more often the other way around. Research published in the *Journal of Consulting and Clinical Psychology* indicates that young gay men tend to come out to their mothers first—or only to their mothers. And father is left to believe what he wishes to believe. There are several reasons why this is so. Researchers of this study on disclosure suggest that it is because of the closeness these men feel to their mothers; the revelation is an outgrowth of their natural intimacy. But it may also be because mother is reputed to be the provider of unconditional love, and the gay son who reveals himself to her hopes that she will live up to her reputation, that she will love him anyway. He may not have the same hopes for his father. After all, won't his father take it as a reflection on his own masculinity, and a rejection of his model of manhood? And won't he reject the son who is rejecting his manly example? At least that's the fear of many gay sons.

But personalities also come into play, and Jonathan

doesn't believe his mother has the personality to take it. Perhaps his hesitancy to tell her is based on the anger she has trouble getting over. Will he end up on her permanent grudge list? But his hesitancy may be based on something else. Sexuality was a hidden issue in his household, making it even harder to open up about this form of sexuality that many people still consider deviant. Where communication is open on this most sensitive of subjects, a variation in sexuality is both easier to reveal and easier to accept. In Jonathan's case, yet another factor comes in—his own difficulty in accepting his sexual orientation. Only in the past few years has he been comfortable enough with it to begin to tell others.

TO KNOW OR NOT

But who wants to know, anyway? Wouldn't it be better to just ignore the clues and to let your son turn his own mattress and drive himself to the bar that may be on the seedy side but certainly can't be gay? It is indeed tempting not to know, and to make it clear that you don't want to be told. And so the mother–son relationship can move serenely along, unrocked by this devastating revelation. But the cost of ignorance can be high, both to the son and to the relationship. The sense, for the gay man, is that there is something very wrong with him, that some part of him is so bad that he must hide it. So he lives a lie, while his mother tries to ignore the truth. But if the truth is imparted in a loving manner and accepted that way, it will help to improve communication and make possible an honest adult relationship.

Some mothers fear that learning about their son's homosexuality will mean the loss of their son, but it is *not* knowing that may truly take him away. Scott Hatley, a New York psychotherapist who sees many gay men in his practice, and is gay himself, does not consider ignorance bliss. "The gap between parents and children will always broaden if they don't know about your life, not just that you're gay, but how you live your life, the lover or lovers you're interested in, your experiences day to day. Sometimes the gap in communications can't be bridged, for example, where parents are adamantly religious in a particular form. But if it's possible to bridge the gap, this piece of information must be made known. Otherwise parents and children will drift further and further apart."

FROM GRIEF TO ACCEPTANCE

Just as the son goes through stages to reach the point where he can reveal himself to his parents, his parents go through stages before they can accept the truth about their son. They will pass through stages of shock, and anger, and denial—though not necessarily in that order—before they can truly feel at peace with what they now know. Those emotions may be so intense that they are hard to bear, and they may be long-lived. The mother who discovered her son's male magazines found that her own reaction was worse than she would have expected. For her, the anger came first. She directed it at the outward changes she saw in her son. He had lost weight and was dressing differently, and she didn't like any of it. "I just became hysterical. To me he was wearing crazy clothes, like red pants and a purple shirt, and I couldn't stand it. I said some pretty awful things, like 'Are you trying to be gay or are you trying to be a transvestite?' I was cruel, not deliberately, but it came out like that. And we had some very rough times. I'd beg him, 'Can't you dress normally?' He would spend hours standing in the bathroom and fixing his hair. I was angry because he was flaunting it at me."

The anger didn't last long, but the shock did. As she described it, it was as if she had a constant pain every time she thought about her son being gay, as if someone had socked her in the stomach. That feeling of shock lasted for more than a year. And then came the feeling of bitterness. She had taken such pleasure in her son. And now he was gone, taken from her. Or so she believed at the time.

Denial can also be a potent way of dealing with the pain of the disclosure. It can operate, on some levels, for many, many years and even for a lifetime. As one mother–son pair visited together in the son's Greenwich Village apartment, they reviewed for me the progress of their relationship since she learned of his gayness. Their relationship had obviously come a long way since the time of the disclosure, twenty-five years ago. Both mother and son, a magazine editor, felt that they had lost each other then, and they had only recently renewed the bonds between them. And yet the mother's acceptance of her son was based at least partly on denial, denial that only grew stronger with the years. She kept emphasizing that her son had never been "swooshy" or effeminate. When her son briefly left the room, she said, "I still can't feature him as gay because he seems to like women. I just don't think of him as gay. It's true, I see him with other gay men, but I think of them as being friends, not really as lovers." She then went on to express her dislike for that term "lovers"; in her view, the word "companions" should be used instead. While this woman appears, on the surface, to accept her son, it seems that denial is still blinding her to the reality of his life, and his loves.

The stages that have been described here may sound strangely familiar, even if you've never confronted this situation in your own life. They closely parallel the common pattern of response to another life crisis—the death of a loved one. In facing such a death, there is often shock at the realization of the loss, denial that it has truly happened, anger at someone, the doctor perhaps, and then finally acceptance. Death is inevitable, and peace must be made with it. To learn that a child is gay is in many ways akin to learning that a child is dying. To move through the stages that will ideally culminate in acceptance of his sexuality is truly a form of mourning. It is a mourning of lost dreams, of the vision of who the child is and who he will be. Finally, it is an acceptance of who he really is. This process is also similar, in many ways, to what the gay son went through in accepting his own sexuality, in coming out as gay in a straight world. It is a coming out for parents too, when they can truly accept their child as gay. As Sarah Montgomery, one of the old-timers in the Parents of Gays movement, has announced on placards at Gay Pride parades, "I will never be a closet mother."

Just what does it mean, psychologically, for a mother to have a gay son? On one level, it is the ultimate devastation, a devastation to her feelings as both a mother and a woman. As a mother, it is to blame herself for failing to bring up a "normal" child, for having done something to bring about so terrible a result. As a woman, it may mean to her that she is not woman enough. If she were truly womanly, wouldn't her son love women and not men? Wouldn't she have awakened him to the beauty and allure of the female sex? Instead it may seem to her that she has turned him off to women. With her as a rather poor example of the opposite sex, he has turned for sex and love to his own kind.

The sense of loss can be particularly acute for the mother of a gay son. Susan Frankel, a psychotherapist at the Institute for Human Identity in New York, explains why: "From before the son was born, perhaps even from the time the mother was herself a child, she's carried this ideal with her of what she wants her son to be, or to do. The ideal may be high, reflecting the special relationship that a mother and son share. She carries this ideal with her, and then all of a sudden the son comes out as gay, and she's confronted with the reality that he will never be the way her ideal was. She's confronted with the loss of this ideal son."

For certain women, especially insecure women, having

a gay son can be an actual relief. They will never have to deal with that daughter-in-law who may steal their son away. They will remain, always, the most important woman in their son's life. Few, if any, women will admit it, but the feeling is very real for many. Says New York psychotherapist Ted Dubinsky, "The mother may *say* she feels guilty when she hears the news, but she may be secretly gratified. She is the unique woman in her son's life, a woman without rival."

In some ways, it is easier for a mother to deal with a gay son than for a parent to deal with a gay child of the same sex. In cases of a mother facing a lesbian daughter, or a father coming to terms with his gay son, there is often the feeling of being not only a failed role model but a failed heterosexual as well. Any homosexual feelings or fantasies may come painfully to mind. The father of a gay son may recall that uncomfortable but exhilarating feeling of the body contact of high school football, a feeling that went beyond that of sportsmanlike camaraderie. The mother of a lesbian may remember the not-so-innocent bedtime romps of her own girlhood sleep-overs. Will their child's homosexuality lay bare their own repressed feelings of long ago, or for some parents, their own real feelings of today? If my son's a "pantywaist" or my daughter's a "dyke," will people think I am too? And worse yet, might those people be right?

Whatever the sex of parent or child, some parents simply find it easier to accept their child's gayness than others do. These are the parents who can accept that their children are separate individuals, that they are not here to meet parental expectations, that the dreams parents have for their children are not necessarily the dreams their children have for themselves. These are also the parents who tolerate differences, perhaps even rejoice in differences. They do not force their children to conform to their way of doing things, of eating the foods they like, of dressing the way they dress, and most significantly, of dating the kind of people they dated. If their child's girlfriend or boyfriend is of another religion, even another race, they may not like it, but they will allow it. The most accepting parents are those who positively enjoy differences, who find differences good and exciting and exhilarating. They are the most likely to accept their gay child with open arms and an open heart.

Michael Shernoff, a psychotherapist who works with gays and their families, is gay himself. He got a clue to his parents' likely reaction to his sexuality from his sister's earlier dating experience. "My parents went through a very strong trauma when my sister was going out with a non–Jewish man. But they wouldn't have eighty-sixed her from the house. They would not have taken the risk of losing their daughter. No way. So I knew they weren't going to reject me. Their acceptance has not been total, but it's as much as it will ever be. My mother has made it clear that she doesn't approve, but she does accept."

An acknowledging son and an accepting mother can have a better relationship than they have ever known. As honesty replaces secrecy, mother and son can share their loving feelings without being tied up too tightly in each other's lives. Psychotherapist Scott Hatley sees his relationship with his mother, since he's given her the news, to be the ideal blend of intimacy and space. "When I was twenty-nine I sat down with my mother and said that it's long past time for beating around the bush, let's get down to the technicalities of things. What's happened since then is that some of the discomfort between us, and some of the thinking it ought to be otherwise, has lifted. I relate to her to the extent that I want to or don't want to, and I know that she relates to me to the extent that she wants to or doesn't want to. Our relationship has found its own level. I don't think my mother and I are inordinately close, yet I don't feel at all distant from her.

"One of the big bonuses of my disclosure is that both of us have gotten to discuss the past honestly, to go through the family album, to look at pictures and say, 'I was really miserable that Christmas.' And have the other one say, 'I know you were. I was too, and I didn't know how to do anything about it. Wasn't it awful to have to pretend to be so happy that Christmas?' Then we also got to acknowledge some of the positive things. You fail to acknowledge those if you're concentrating on how miserable things were. So it got to be a great sorting out."

GUESS WHO'S COMING TO DINNER?

But Scott and his mother did have one falling-out, over his breaking off with a long-term lover. She couldn't understand why her son left him. Says Scott, "She knew him. She liked him. She saw how we lived. She's never forgiven me for leaving him. She felt he was such a treasure, such a wonderful man. Since then, she's shown little interest in my more casual relationships. Her attitude is she doesn't want to hear about it unless it's serious. She only wants to know if I'm settling down again."

If it sounds like a mother devastated by a son's divorce, hoping to marry him off again, there are some similarities. Once a mother has accepted her son's gayness, and is concerned that he be happy just the way he is, she may hope he finds the happiness of an enduring, intimate relationship. And she may check out the prospective "spouse" as any mother would: Is he smart enough? sensible enough? attractive enough? Can he make a living? If he doesn't meet those criteria, she may still take the loving attitude: "Well, as long as he makes my son happy." Or she may find herself with the same feelings of disappointment, and of rivalry, that a mother-in-law can feel toward a daughter-in-law—that this man who's not even worthy of my son is taking my son away. Or that they see *his* parents more than they see us. And who are they going to spend the holidays with, anyway? No matter the sex, or the sexual orientation, in-laws are in-laws, and they can be a cause of conflict.

But there are a number of differences too, differences from the start. There may be an extra criterion that a man's male lover must meet—he must not look like a lover of men. In other words, he must not be effeminate, or people might suspect the son's sexuality. So he must keep pinky in, hips still, ears free of earrings and speech free of affectations. Only when he proves he can "pass" will he be a welcome member at family gatherings.

But even "passing" may not win the approval of a lover's mother. His very existence may earn him her everlasting enmity. Some mothers labor under the misconception that if this man would only fade from the scene, then their son would give up this nonsense and lead the straight life. After all, their son would not be gay if not for the evil influence and seductiveness of this horrid man. After all, their son is just the unwitting victim of someone else's homosexual lust. Or so many parents wish to believe. And so the lover becomes the hated one, and nothing he can do can alter his image from satyr to son-in-law.

But on the positive side, some of the stickier in-law situations are avoided when a son is mate to a man. One reason is that their relationship tends not to be as explicit as a marital one, and so it is less vulnerable to grabs for power, to jealousy, and to destructive triangular setups. Another important difference is that this in-law relationship is between a man and a woman, not between two women. Scott Hatley sees that as very significant: "The fact that it's a man and a woman puts a whole other coloration on it. With a daughter-in-law, it may be an out-and-out power struggle. But with a man, the mother would use different approaches to get her way, perhaps seductive approaches, where she's going to try to wrap him around her little finger. It's going to be a woman relating to a man, and so it can't be the same."

But can it be as good as a mother-in-law–daughter-in-law relationship can sometimes be? That depends a lot on how the mother-in-law sees her son, and the value she places on his happiness. Sarah Montgomery, that pioneer in the Parents of Gays movement, explained her attitude toward her son's lover most beautifully, and most movingly: "I loved John, too. He was like my other son. I loved him because of the way he loved my son. Anyone who loves my children, I love."

THE MOTHERS' STORY

To hear the mothers tell it themselves is to get a good idea of what the experience of having a gay son is really all about. In this part of the chapter, two mothers of gay sons tell what it has been like for them. Theirs are the stories of individual women who have faced a crisis in their relationship with their sons, a crisis that many mothers of sons fear from the time their son is born. The theme they address is becoming more universal as more gay sons tell their mothers just who they are.

The first mother, Yvette, a music teacher, has two sons and a daughter, but it was her younger son who played a special role in her life, and her younger son who grew up gay. Peter, she says, was always different from the rest of the family, much more open and expressive. His joy in life was like a revelation to her, and helped to release her own inhibitions.

But she remembers well the time he took some of that joy away from her. "It happened while he was home from college for some holiday, the night before he was going back. We were having dinner, just the two of us, and somehow Women's Lib came up. He got terribly terribly upset about it, and said, 'Why does that cause get all the attention? It's stupid. And why do they have to be so important?' And I said, 'Peter, what's wrong? Why not?' And he said that gay rights are just as important as women's rights. And I said, 'Fine, right, I agree, but why get so excited about it?' He said, 'Because I'm gay.' And I said, 'Is this a confession or a revelation?' or I forget what word I used. And he said, 'Yes.' " And that's how Yvette found out about Peter.

For the next two weeks she tried to convince herself that it wasn't true. But a friend made her realize that she was just kidding herself, that her son would never tell her something like that if he weren't really gay. So her period of denial was short-lived.

But then another strong emotion came over her, an emotion she couldn't identify. She knew that it wasn't guilt, but that it was something terrible, nevertheless. She's still not sure what it was, but she thinks it might have had something to do with the special place Peter had in her life. "Peter was the only person in the family I could get emotion from. I thought I could continue to get joy out of everything he did. I thought I would watch him be a big hero with women, and marry somebody, and show all his feelings, and have all these children. I thought he would fulfill all the things I never did. And I just had to realize that that wouldn't happen. It was really cutting the cord. That's really what it was. The other part of it, I think, was a feeling that now he is going off into a place where I can't follow. My older son is married, and he'll have children, and I can be part of his life. And of course daughters are different for mothers. My daughter is just part of my life. But with Peter I felt there's just going to be part of his life I won't be part of ever. I really think now that's what bothered me the most."

Yvette has come a long way since that time of pain and confusion, though she says it hasn't been easy. She joined a Parents of Gays group to meet others in her situation, and she started listening and reading, finding out all she could about the world her son had entered. Perhaps most important of all, she learned that her fear of losing her son was totally unfounded. In fact, she came to see that quite the opposite was taking place. It started a few weeks after his disclosure, when she watched a three-hour television program about homosexuality and called him to discuss it. He was relieved at her positive interest at the time, and later glad to see her increasing visibility as the mother of a gay child. He comes to the Gay Pride March every year and watches her march, and points her out to his friends. It's hard to tell who is prouder of the other, mother or son. Yvette no longer sees her son's gayness as a loss to her. Instead, she views his words, "I'm gay," as the truth that brought them together: "Before his revelation, from the time he was fourteen, there was a screen. I couldn't reach him. He was very nice and sweet and lovely, but I couldn't reach him. Now, the barrier is broken. Peter so appreciated my involvement, he just came open to me. That was just the wonderful thing. Since he's told me, I've seen the real Peter. I feel I know him, not half of him, but all of him.

"When I first found out he was gay I thought that Peter needed love more than my other children. Once I got past that I realized how silly it was, that my other children need love because they have their own problems. So I went from denying the whole thing, from saying, 'This is my gay son, and I love him because he needs this love since he has this burden,' to saying, 'This is my son, and I love him.' It takes time."

Yvette was able to take that last important step—to realize that gayness is not all a gay person is about, that there is more to a gay son than his sexual orientation. Only when a mother can do that—relate to her child as a complete human being, not as her "special" son, or as her "gay" son—has she truly accepted him.

The second mother, Natalie, had to go through the acceptance process twice. The middle two of her four sons are gay. As they were growing up, she doesn't remember seeing any great differences between the boys that would suggest the future differences. So when she learned that her second son—just sixteen at the time—was gay, it came as a great shock. "My husband and I had a very rough time with it," she recalls. "We thought, we've got to send Gary someplace so this won't be. Our reaction was to try to change it, erase it, and if he goes to the right person, he'll fix it. And no matter what that costs, that's something we're going to do." After they moved past that stage, they went through the guilt, the question of "Why?" Perhaps they did something to cause this, they thought. Perhaps if *they* had been different, their son wouldn't be so different. "The beginning was terrible, where you just can't get it off your mind, where you can't even say the word 'homosexual' and you choke on the word 'gay.' We did a lot of crying."

What helped Natalie and her family was that she didn't take out her shock or her guilt on her son. She was able to see that what she was going through was *her* problem, not *his* problem, and that it was up to her to do something about her feelings. She started by trying to learn about homosexuality, to understand what it's all about. But it wasn't an easy process. She says that she and her husband went through many different stages before arriving where they are now, that there were many different levels of acceptance. After a while they felt a little better and weren't quite as anguished. But then something would happen that would throw it back in their faces. And they would step back a minute and know they were still hurting.

The two of them finally did come around. In fact, like Yvette, Natalie found she had a better relationship with her son after the revelation than she had had before. There was an openness between mother and son, a communication, a sharing of problems and feelings. She was at *such* a good place with Gary that she couldn't understand why she reacted so badly when she found out that Jeremy was gay too. If anything, she was more surprised about Jeremy than she had been about Gary. Gary had never been in-

volved with girls at all, but Jeremy had seemed almost a
ladies' man, never lacking for a date. In fact, he had a
steady girlfriend through most of high school. But during
his first year in college he broke up with her and started
spending time with a lot of different people. When Natalie
noticed that some of them were males, she began to wonder, "Could this be the same thing? Do I have another gay
son?" She was baffled. Jeremy was an experimental, daring
kind of person, so perhaps he was just dabbling in bi-
sexuality. When she finally brought it up to him, he first
denied that he was gay but later confirmed her suspicions.
He told her that despite his previous relationships with
women, this was what felt right for him, and he'd never
been happier.

But Natalie had been a *lot* happier. The knowledge
about her second son floored her emotionally, and the
thought of getting up in front of the Parents of Gays group
and announcing, "Now I have two gay sons, not just one,"
was difficult for her to face. "No matter how good I was
about one, it was a little hard having two. I couldn't figure
out why, because I had settled the issue of guilt, not believing it had anything to do with me. That's just the way
they are, that's all. Just a different way. So why was I so
upset?"

After exploring her feelings with a therapist, she realized
what was troubling her, and it wasn't that Jeremy was gay.
"It was his promiscuity. I wouldn't have liked that even if
he had been promiscuous with women. When I realized
that was it, that it wasn't the gayness, but the style in which
he was conducting himself that upset me, that was helpful
in my accepting the fact that he was gay, that now I had
two gay sons. Looking back, I can see that what started out
as a heartache has turned out to be a positive part of my
life. I've fully accepted that that's the way two of my children are, and it's okay with me."

Was Natalie twice blessed, or twice cursed? She would

now consider herself four-times blessed, with four loving, happy children who each know who they are. But that is not to minimize the trauma she went through upon learning that first one, then another of her sons was gay. The first revelation seemed to mark her child; the second revelation to mark her. What kind of mother is she, anyway, to raise two gay sons? That question can be turned on its head: What kind of mother is she to raise two *straight* sons? Try to answer both questions, and you'll begin to understand why the cause of homosexuality—and indeed, the cause of heterosexuality—is far from certain. And although Natalie was troubled by guilt at the first discovery and embarrassment at the second, she was able to work through those emotions and finally "come out" as her sons had before her. As she described so well, that process is as slow and painful for parents as it is for their gay children.

In Natalie's story, we see another aspect of a mother's reaction to a son's gayness—that is, turning that gayness into a scapegoat for other aspects of a son's behavior that a mother doesn't approve of. Natalie was angry at Jeremy when she found out about his sexuality. Although she thought this anger came out of the fact that he was gay, she was wise enough to go for therapy and insightful enough to discover the truth: that it was the number of lovers he had, and not their sex, that made his behavior hard to take. Other mothers might continue to believe that their sons are promiscuous *because* they are gay, not simply promiscuous *and* gay, and if only a nice girl would come along it might all go away!

Gayness is commonly used as a scapegoat in this way, the focus of all maternal discontent. Johnny must smoke dope because he's gay. . . . He doesn't call me on my birthday because he's gay. . . . He gets drunk because he's gay. Gayness becomes a metaphor for other things, for all things "evil." A wise mother will see beyond this and focus on the real issues.

A SON'S STORY

As we've seen here, to truly accept a gay son is not simple. It is a difficult process, perhaps the most difficult a mother will face. How much harder, then, must it be to accept *oneself* as gay, and to face the possibility of rejection, even disownment, from the people one loves best? It takes courage to live a gay life in a straight world; it takes courage to let a mother know that you're "different," that you'll never be the man she imagined. Several gay men told me their own stories of struggle with their sexual identity, with society's stereotypes, with their parents' reactions of disbelief and horror. Many of the sons' stories don't have happy endings. Some sons are disowned, emotionally if not legally; they may give up and go away, or engage in a life-long battle to win over parents who won't be won over. Others never disclose their sexual orientation to their parents, and the relationship is sabotaged by words that won't be spoken. But there are others who do win acceptance, and with it a relationship better than they had known before. The son we will meet here, Gordon, took a long time before he could face himself, and a longer time before he could face his mother. He knew that she loved him but wasn't sure that her love would be enough.

Gordon, now a respected literary agent, was born to older parents. His father was already forty and his mother thirty-five when they had their second child, their first son. Although his mother worked through much of his childhood, Gordon did not feel any lack of attention from her. In his estimation, she was a very giving mother, and treated *both* her children as her favorites. At the same time, Gordon didn't feel overprotected by her. "Hers was the kind of love that didn't overwhelm you, and didn't hold you back," he told me. "It just made me feel very secure, and free to explore. My sister and I would go out, with no grilling about who we would see and when we'd be back. Her trust gave us the courage to venture out."

From the time they were adolescents they would share their experiences at night as they joined their parents around the kitchen table. It became a family ritual: They would all sit down and watch the eleven o'clock news on television, and drink coffee, and talk. They would discuss the day's events, their own day's experiences. They would talk about anything at all, from the political to the personal. But then Gordon made a discovery in his life that he just could not talk about.

As Gordon tells it, "I knew from a very early age that I was gay. I just always knew that I was very very different. And I spent my whole life reconciling how to deal with that, and finally accepting it." Gordon did try dating girls but never found that very comfortable. He even had a serious relationship with a girl in college, lasting more than a year, but it broke up over the question of sex—she wanted it, he didn't. The heterosexual life wasn't for him, and yet he wasn't quite ready to try the alternative. Something was holding him back. "Whenever I found a man attractive sexually, I found it so difficult to deal with, I would just let it go to a certain point and then back away from the friendship. It wasn't that we got into bed and then I would say I was going home. I wouldn't even let myself get into bed."

And he couldn't tell his parents about what he was going through, either the emotional parts of it or the sexual. He couldn't even sit and watch television with them if the subject of the show was homosexuality. He was afraid of what might be going through their minds, that they somehow suspected, and so he would leave the room. He rationalized his silence by the fact that although he was thinking gay, although he was fantasizing gay, he wasn't yet acting gay. So why admit it?

When his attitude toward his sexuality changed, so did his attitude toward telling his parents. For him, the big breakthrough came when he joined a gay synagogue: "It was an incredible environment for somebody so unsure of himself to get into, because all of a sudden here was a totally open, nonpressured, nonsexual situation. A few weeks after I started going there I did strike up an affair with somebody. Two weeks into the relationship I decided I simply had to tell my parents. I remember it was a Wednesday night. It was right before Labor Day weekend, which I was going to be spending with this fellow. It happened over eleven o'clock coffee. My parents and I sat down and the television was on and we were watching the news and the weather. And when that was all over I just got up and walked over to the set, shut it off, and said, 'There is something I really want to talk with you about.' "

He was finally ready to tell them about his gayness, and they were ready to hear it. He was surprised at just how ready. His father took it quietly, as if he had known all along. His mother's response was the bigger surprise. She told him, after only a moment's silence, that this doesn't change anything, that you are still our son, that now we just know more about you.

From Gordon's viewpoint, things *did* change between him and his mother, but all for the better. "What's always been positive between us is even more positive now. After twenty-nine years of hiding, there is now basically nothing I can't talk to her about. The only area I don't share is what I do in bed, which I think is totally irrelevant. What's helped us is that we've always been a bunch of yentas. We've always talked. It was never any problem. The level of communication, the exact subject, may not always have been on the deepest matter. But there was always constant talk. Our lives centered around the kitchen table. That was where the heavy discussions took place. And that's where I was finally able to totally open up."

Since his disclosure, Gordon has experienced almost total acceptance by his parents of his homosexuality. And the acceptance is not just passive, not the laissez-faire attitude, "As long as it makes him happy, so what if it's a man and not a woman?" It's an active recognition of who he is, and whom he loves. As long as his relationships are based in mutual respect and true caring, he feels that his parents rejoice in them, even if his partners are men.

Gordon has found just one limitation to his mother's acceptance: She doesn't want other people in the family to know. It bothers him that she won't discuss it with relatives and close friends, though he believes the day will come when she *will* break that barrier, and perhaps even move forward from acceptance to pride.

"In every other way she's been wonderful about this. If I were straight and not gay, our relationship couldn't be any better. It's interesting, when I look at my friends, I see that the men who are the best adjusted have had similar relationships. Maybe not as immediate as I have. They may have gone through a period of severe rejection by their parents. But because they were so well-adjusted themselves, they could go to their parents and say 'This is me. Here I am,' and eventually bring their parents around. I waited until I could feel that way about myself before I told my parents. It was worth the wait."

Gordon says he was flabbergasted at his parents' accepting attitude, yet considering his past relationship with them, it wasn't really surprising at all. Theirs was a relationship based on sharing, on respect for one another, on love of the other person for who he or she is, not for an image of the ideal son or the ideal parent. Relationships based on honesty are likely to be strengthened—not shattered—by this most honest, and most difficult, of revelations. For Gordon, one of the keys was to fully accept himself before he could hope for his parents to accept him. It was a hard struggle, as it is for so many gay men and women, to admit what they really knew all along, to commit themselves to a way of life that is a contradiction to everything they've been brought up to believe. Gordon waited until *he* was ready, and found that his parents were ready for him.

Gordon is now willing to wait for his parents to take the

final step, the disclosure of his gayness to others. He has recognized that parents have their problems with it too, that what he took twenty-nine years to come to terms with cannot be fully embraced by his parents overnight. Now that he has come out of the closet, he is confident that his parents will not be far behind.

MOTHERS AND SONS TOGETHER

Relationships between mothers and gay sons don't always go so well. The potential is there, with a gay son as well as a straight one, for the worst of relationships. The potential is also there for the best of relationships. A son's gayness simply adds another facet to the mother–son relationship, an extra dimension that can be used by sensitive mothers to enhance it, or by intolerant ones to end it.

Whether the relationship is good or bad, it is always important to the gay son, as his mother can serve as his anchor in a hostile world. Her reaction to his gayness is a true test of her motherhood. Her hostility can work to repress his true nature, inhibiting his ability to love. Her acceptance can help to free him, giving him the courage to confront himself and the world, the self-confidence to love in his own special way. Perhaps it is most important for the adolescent son, the boy still at odds with his sexual nature. To most gay teenagers, who, like any adolescents, seek the acceptance of their peers, being different means being bad. But if gay adolescents feel accepted by their parents, it goes a long way to lessen the traditional isolation gay people feel. It helps the boy to develop into a much more healthy, resilient person. Even as an adult, mother-love helps, as Michael Shernoff, the psychotherapist who works with gays, explains: "A gay man of any age wonders whether his mother's love is unconditional enough to accept him as a 'faggot.' So there's this enormous insecurity. If she accepts it, no matter how old he is, it will help him get over a lot

of that insecurity. The basic unqualified acceptance of a
mother is just so crucial to the healthy development of the
normal human being."

He emphasizes that to tell a parent is to risk losing that
love, a difficult risk that parents should respect. It is also
a chance to build a better relationship than before, a real
opportunity that parents should not pass up. "I stress the
positives to the parents. I tell them to stop asking what they
did wrong and to focus on what they did right. I tell them,
'You obviously are so important to your child, he wants to
share this information with you. He wishes this to be another bridge of communication between the two of you,
another level of intimacy. He is saying that he loves you,
that he trusts you, that he doesn't want to close you out of
his life.' I reassure the parents that they are *not* losing
their son."

As mothers get older, even those who were at first the
angriest about their son's sexuality often come to a rap-
prochement with a gay son. They can no longer tolerate
the distance between them, and they can no longer deny
the cause: that they are being rejected as a parent because
they have rejected their child as a gay adult. And they can
no longer deny the remedy: to accept him on his own
terms, to accept that he can truly love a man as most men
love a woman, to accept him as he is, gayness and all. They
finally understand that to be an important part of their
son's life, they must be able to truly accept that important
part of him.

As I come to the end of this chapter, I reflect back on the
question posed to me at the beginning. The answer I gave
then has become the truth, but a more complex truth than
I could have imagined. Certainly, I would still love my
sons if they were to grow up gay, but I cannot deny my
hope that they won't. And I find myself, against my better
judgment, sometimes watching for the so-called signs, glad
that they prefer baseball to ballet, that they chase around
the playground with other rough-and-rowdy boys, that my

older son, when passing by newsstands, seems properly awed by the wonders of the female form splashed across magazine covers. It seems, for them, that there will be one less complication in their lives, one less injustice to fight against. As for me, I would be spared the emotionally wrenching discovery and the difficult process of adjustment that was described to me by so many women, each with her own story and her own particular pain.

But if it should come to pass that the apparent evidence of heterosexuality was misleading, or a self-protective sham, I too would feel that pain. Hopefully, this would be one step on the road to total acceptance, but I can't know for sure where it would lead me. It's impossible to predict how I would feel at such a revelation. But I do know how I would act. I would act grateful that they could trust me enough to tell me. I would act glad that they had discovered and acknowledged the truth about their sexuality. I would act accepting, because I would know how much they would need my acceptance, and that to do otherwise would be to risk losing them. In time, I would hope, my feelings would follow my actions.

8

The End–Or
the Beginning?

Old age has come, and so has forgetfulness. Adele is a woman in her late seventies who has been suffering from progressive loss of memory. An aide comes in several hours a day to help her manage her day-to-day activities. As a form of therapy, Adele has been given definite chores to do, including the cooking of the evening meal. She and her aide plan the menu together and prepare the food. Six days a week, it's an arduous task, and the aide has to guide Adele through every step of the process. But on Fridays, it's a different story. Adele knows *exactly* what she wants to make, and needs no help in making it. What she plans and prepares are her bachelor son's favorite recipes, the foods she cooked for him when he was a boy, the foods he's continued to praise even as a man. On Friday nights, Adele's son comes over for dinner, and for Adele, there is no forgetting.

As a son can jar an older mother's memory, so too

can he reawaken her feelings of pride in being mother to a male. Having a son, especially an attentive one, can lift the status of an older mother among her friends. It's a sign that she is important enough to rate this grown man's love and concern. His maleness means more with the passing years, and his attentions to his mother seem more of a tribute. The specialness of having a son flowers, not fades, as the seasons go by.

Jerie Charnow, a psychotherapist and an expert on the aged and their families, sees this phenomenon often in the women she works with. They get emotional fulfillment from their sons largely because their sons are men, and in the traditional thinking of many older people, being male brings with it automatic respect and a position of power. Being *with* a male is the next best thing. So an older woman will call up her son and ask him to drive her someplace, not so much because she needs the ride as because she enjoys sitting next to this man, basking in the reflection of his prestige. There may not be many other men in her life, so she depends on her son for this psychological lift.

Charnow, who heads the Consultation Service for Older Adults and Their Families in Roslyn, New York, sees something else going on between men and their older mothers—she sees the women acting differently and even dressing differently for a son than for a daughter. When the daughter is coming over for a visit, for example, no need to change from housecoat and slippers. And no need for elaborate preparations. But when the *son* comes, out come the fresh flowers and the good dishes, on goes the perfume and the good dress. It's almost as if he is a boyfriend coming to call. Even if his wife is with him, even if his children are along, his mother may well still focus her attention on him.

There seems to be something happening in this relationship that happened before, a long time back—a romantic attachment between mother and son, though now more on the mother's part. The various stresses of her older years may have reawakened in her this earlier Oedipal aspect of their relationship, as she sees in her son the men friends of her past and recalls the sensuality of his infancy and boyhood. She can't touch him now, but she touched him then, and part of her remembers.

Although a woman's Oedipal feelings may be evoked as part of a regression into her past, they can serve a positive function in the present. Some mothers use this sexual bond to keep their sons interested in them and willing to do things for them. Dr. Diana Koin is a specialist in geriatric medicine in Portland, Oregon. She has become aware of the rather subtle sexuality of many of her elderly patients, particularly where their sons are concerned. "It seems that older women bring to bear old seductive traits to get their son's help. It operates more subtly than we're used to. It shows up in toned-down kinds of things. For example, instead of getting all dressed up for her husband, she does it to keep her son's attention. She does it to keep him interested, hoping he'll be more willing to help her out if she's pleasant to look at and attractive. It seems bizarre to say it, but it's a healthy kind of phenomenon. Instead of trying to suck him in unwillingly, she's reverting to earlier patterns to try to get through a crisis. It's not being done in a destructive way. The son would never dream it had any sexual overtones whatsoever, nor would the mother recognize it. But it has a familiar ring to it, a familiar flavor. This mother and this son have been down this path before."

Whatever its purpose for mother and son, there is little doubt that Oedipus is alive in old age, reminding the pair of their past relationship and underlining the present one. Dr. Anna Leifer, a Long Island, New York, psychoanalyst, tries to explain the attraction. "Sons become men, and if we're lucky they become men we admire, men whom we enjoy being with. There is a different ambience when a mother is with her son, especially a grown son." Leifer has noticed that she herself has a different feeling when she's with her son than with either of her two daughters. When she goes somewhere with her son, she finds it's more like being with her husband. She feels the pride of getting dressed up, walking alongside of him, holding his arm.

As I spoke with women in their sixties and older, I came upon abundant evidence of the ascendance of Oedipus. As one divorced woman related to me of her only child, her son, "He always compliments me, always. And it makes me feel very good. I'd rather have a compliment from him than from anybody else I know. After all, he's the only man in my life." Another woman, though happily married, is very attuned to her sons' compliments, and tries her best to win them. "They always comment when I get my hair touched up. If they like the color they let me know. If they think there's too much of one tone or the other, they say 'That's not you.' It's important to me that they feel I'm attractive. I don't want to look like an old lady. I want to be youthful looking for them, and I think they're aware of it."

Even in the midst of a medical emergency, one elderly woman, about eighty, heard her son louder than she heard her doctor. She had fallen on her nose, fallen hard, and she was rushed to the hospital. Her son met her in the emergency room. It was a few years back, but she still remembers well what her son said to her doctor: "God, I hope she won't be disfigured. She was such a beautiful woman." "You see," the woman pointed out to me, "he was proud of me. He thought I was beautiful." And she smiled in a most beautiful way.

Some of the women I interviewed complained that their sons gave them *too* much physical affection—but the way they talked about it made me think that they didn't mind it at all. As one woman put it, "My son would sometimes kiss me like his girlfriends, and I would push him away and say, 'Hey Burt, I'm not your girlfriend.' " Another mother had a similar protest: "He gives me too much affection, too much. When he gets in the mood, he kisses me all over. I say, 'Give this to your wife.' He says she gets plenty. He's a very affectionate person, and I do like it. That's something my husband never gave me when he was alive. My son and I were the cuddly ones. We always were, and we still are."

This mother hit on an important point in explaining the emergence of Oedipus in a woman's old age. In many cases, her husband is no longer alive, or too incapacitated to play an important part in her life. The mother–son relationship almost invariably changes if the father is removed from the scene. Often the son takes over some of his father's roles, providing not only affection but protection, financial assistance, someone to trust. Some older women, especially traditional-minded ones, have been brought up to depend on a man for decision-making. And their son may well be the most reasonable and trustworthy man available to them. And so they revive the relationship with their son but cast him more in the role of husband than child. He may resent the demands, or he may enjoy this new-found status and the way his mother's eyes light up when they see him. Clearly in the emotional sense, and more subtly in the sexual sense, the Oedipal wishes of his childhood have come true.

THE MYTH OF ABANDONMENT

Just as the issue of sexuality revives in old age, so does that of separation. Many women approaching their older years fear physical and emotional abandonment, especially by their sons. They've heard the warnings: without a daughter, it's going to be a lonely life; sons are too wrapped up in their own midlife crises to pay much attention to their elderly mothers; before you know it your son will dump you in a nursing home and won't be heard from again. But the idea of children of *either* sex abandoning their elderly parents is finally being exposed as a myth—a cruel myth that has made the coming of old age hard to face. A growing body of research indicates that the ties between the generations are strong, as strong now as they've ever been. Study upon study confirms that most parents and adult children help each other out, keep in touch, and feel genuine affection for each other, and that children don't toss parents aside. Sons as well as daughters provide their elderly parents with a steady flow of emotional support. Says Dr. Amy Horowitz, a specialist in family care of the aged for the New York City Department of the Aged, "Abandonment is such a small minority overall, whether by sons or by daughters. It's an exception to the rule. Most care of older people is conducted by family members, not by strangers."

So most daughters and most sons are available for help. But there is another side to the story. Most older people are happier if they don't expect their children's help, and don't need it. Research conducted on 595 elderly parents, published in *The Gerontologist,* shows that people who expect a lot from their adult children have lower morale than those who don't. And those who don't live close to the "kids" have higher morale than those who do. What most older people find, to their surprise, is that they are still giving more than they are getting. According to Dr. Judith Treas, research associate at the Andrus Gerontology Center and associate professor of sociology at the University of Southern California, "Older people are not as dependent as they think they're going to be. If you look at a parent of seventy-five and a child of fifty-five, there's generally more help and resources flowing from parent to child than from child to parent." The mothers may complain about it, that they still have to give financial assistance to their children, or help out with their grandchildren, but they are actually much more comfortable on the giving end, and glad that they can take care of themselves.

It may seem, as a mother looks anxiously ahead, that her

children will be the foundation of her old age, and that without a daughter she'll be on shaky ground, indeed. But for much of the time the son will need his mother more than she'll need him. And when, finally, her needs exceed his, it's unlikely she'll be abandoned or left lonely. Sons as well as daughters do come through.

But the sexes are not the same, and sons generally do not play the identical role in an older person's life that daughters do. If you notice more daughters than sons taking their elderly mothers on shopping trips, you're not mistaken. And if you see a more loving look pass between mother and son than between mother and daughter, neither are you imagining things.

Dr. Horowitz investigated the different ways in which sons and daughters help out older sickly parents, who really do need help. Her subjects were 131 adult children who served as the primary caretaker of an elderly parent. How did the male children and the female children do it differently? Some of the findings indicated a clear gender gap. When it came to hands-on help, such as cooking and cleaning, dressing and driving, the daughters surpassed the sons. Only when it came to such "male-oriented" activities as financial assistance and management, and dealing with bureaucracies, were sons almost as helpful as daughters.

Other studies have come up with similar results: Sons are not as likely as daughters to actually get in there and do the work. One of the reasons for this gender difference is not hard to fathom. As Dr. Horowitz puts it, the "sexual socialization" of boys hasn't prepared them to be the nurturant, emotional, all-giving adults some of their sisters strive to be. Nor has it prepared them for the domestic duties of basting and baking, and sewing and scrubbing, and otherwise helping out an incapacitated mother. Even if they've figured out, somewhere along the way, how to do those domestic chores, doing them just doesn't seem *right* to the sons—doesn't seem like a man's job. Better to let a woman take care of these things.

THE CHOSEN CHILD

Another reason for a man's "hands-off" attitude is more psychologically complex, rooted in the interactions of his early family life. In the years when the children are young, there is often one child in the family who is "chosen"— given the mission of taking care of the parents, especially the mother, especially as she grows older. This chosen child is most often a daughter. Being chosen is not the same as being favored. In fact, the opposite is often the case. This is the child who feels most unloved, and longs for her parents to recognize her. She takes on the responsibility of "parenting" her parent to prove what a good child she is. She is saying, in effect, "Don't you see how I love you? Why don't you love me?" And she locks out the other children, her rivals, and insists on doing it all, even as she complains that nobody else is helping.

But what the girl is trying to achieve is only one consideration in this common family dynamic. The choice, in reality, is not hers alone to make. The choice is actually made by the family as a whole. Dr. Anna Leifer describes the powerful family forces at work: "The chosen child does not have a choice. Everyone in the family has conspired to make her the chosen one. The forces in the family are unrelenting. She is what her family wants her to be. One reason she's chosen is, yes, she wants the love and she needs the closeness. But there's also a deal struck between the parent, often the mother, and this child, most often a daughter. The fact that the child wants the love is only one part of it."

But why are daughters chosen over sons, chosen to parent the mother, especially in the mother's old age? One reason, Dr. Leifer suggests, comes out of the fact that the daughter has a longer Oedipal period than the son. A girl's primary identification is with the mother, the parent of the same sex, and it needn't come to a sudden break-off. But a son has to cut off his maternal identification at some point to make his primary identification with his father, who most often does not have the predominant nurturing role.

Another reason a daughter is so often the mother's chosen child is that a son is so often the mother's favored child. The mother–son romance of childhood may leave the daughter a resentful outsider, determined to work her way in and keep her brother out. If those rivalrous feelings last into adulthood, the son may be forced to keep his distance, forced by a subtle but powerful message that he should keep away, that his help is not welcome. "If a daughter is always rushing in with help and with advice on day-to-day living, then a learned helplessness develops in the son," says Dr. Treas. "The son begins to feel that he's not the appropriate person to provide help, that he's not even competent to give help." If he gathers up the confidence to try, he may find his sister is in his way.

Ida, a woman in her seventies with a daughter and a son in their forties, is perfectly content with her relationship with her daughter, but she complains that her son doesn't do enough for her. As she talks about the family's past, you can see the part she played in choosing her own future. She remembers her children always fighting. Her daughter, Susan, suspected her brother was taking her friends away from her, and she was quite sure he was taking her mother from her, as well. According to Ida, "I'm not sure that I favored one over the other, but Susan feels that mothers are just crazy about sons, and that I preferred Herbie to her."

Susan has always been her mother's helper, from the start. She would do the shopping for the family and keep the house clean while her mother worked. She is still at her mother's service. Mother and daughter now live in the same apartment building, at the daughter's insistence. And daughter and son are still fighting. While Susan takes care of her mother, Ida takes care of her son: "When Herbie switched careers, I paid for his medical school. Now I'm paying for him to start up a practice. I got a kick when I saw the first sign, 'Dr. Herbert Plummer.' And I thought, 'How much money it cost me to see that!' He doesn't mind taking the money. The first couple of times may have been hard for him. But then it's expected, like welfare. He's accustomed to it now, and he asks for quite a bit. He's the type who thinks he's making a lot of money. He loves to spend. He sends his daughter to a private school. Now if you don't have the money, you don't send your child to a private school. I end up footing the bill. And Susan ends up bawling me out for it."

Ida gives so much to her son, she wonders why he doesn't give her more in return. "I'd like him to call more often, or come up. I complain every once in a while. I let him know I don't like it. Susan must have spoiled me. If she can call me three times a day, he can call me once in seven days. Herb just doesn't give me what I want from him. He doesn't give me what Susan gives me."

Ida may complain that her son is inattentive in her old age, but his current role was largely determined by the family dynamics of decades ago. He was "favored" and his sister was "chosen," and the choice is no longer really his. To visit his mother is to invade his sister's turf, to help her too much is to become the grown man his mother is still not ready for, as she continues to baby him. Each member of the family has followed, unconsciously, his or her chosen path.

Many of the older women I spoke to, women with both a son and a daughter, fit into a similar pattern. They complain that the son is not attentive enough, that their daughter is their "right hand," yet this right hand insists on being a one-handed show. And the son has learned well not to take part, at the risk of being rejected.

Whether a son is disappointing because of sexual socialization or family favoritism, it is not his doing alone. Psychotherapist Jerie Charnow explains how he has been placed in that position: "The problem is that the daughter often doesn't share with the son. She takes it all on as her responsibility because it's written somewhere that she should. And then she builds up tremendous resentment against the brother because of her own overwhelming burdens. He really hasn't done anything wrong. She just never asked her brother, and he wasn't trained to offer. The women were taking care of it. When the women need help, men step in. But the women have to say they need help."

LOVING SONS, DUTIFUL DAUGHTERS

If sons are allowed and encouraged to help, they can be valuable resources to their mothers when they need them the most. Even now, there are areas that most sons do very well in, as Dr. Horowitz's study points up. Sons may not help their mothers as much in a physical way, but the sons who were surveyed saw their mothers and phoned them as frequently as daughters did. And they were just as likely to provide emotional support—90 percent of both sons and daughters would give advice or just talk to the parent when the older person was upset or depressed. Perhaps most important, the sons felt as much affection for the parent as daughters did.

So the feelings are there, and it seems that feelings are what count the most. In an even larger study conducted on 400 Los Angeles women from ages sixty to seventy-five, the mothers rated as most important to them the love, affection, and understanding showed to them by their children; relatively unimportant to them were sacrifices their children made for them, or the provisions of such services as shopping and running errands. From this research, it's apparent that what sons do the best is what mothers appreciate the most.

Dr. Horowitz's study tapped yet another positive aspect of the relationship between older women and their sons. This expert on the aged looked at not only what the children did for their parents but how they felt about doing it. Sons were less likely than daughters to feel that they were neglecting other family responsibilities, that their leisure time was being affected, that their emotional state was suffering, and that their plans for the future were being compromised. In general, helping out their parents was not nearly as stressful for them as it was for daughters. And it wasn't because they didn't do as much. Even sons who were equally involved in caretaking did not feel as much stress.

This isn't to say that men are supermen. There are good reasons why caring for a mother should stress them less and stress a daughter more. For one thing, women generally carry more responsibilities—for their home, their children, their careers—so one more responsibility seems a heavier burden. Also, women generally don't get as much cooperation from a spouse as a man ordinarily does. But whatever the reason, a daughter's feelings of stress put her at greater risk of premature "burnout," of wanting to give it all up because she just can't take it anymore, of finally putting the parent under professional care. So when it comes to caring for an aged parent, sons may not be as eager volunteers as daughters are, but when they do take on the job, they're at least as likely to last the duration. And to do it with a smile.

And they're probably more likely to win a smile in return. Anything they do is generally appreciated, since anything they do is more than what's expected. Says Jerie Charnow, "Because mothers have less expectations of sons, everything that sons do, for the most part, is a gift. Sure, the mother may be disappointed if her son doesn't visit more often, or if he comes with his wife when she would rather see him alone, but the bottom line is that most mothers have few expectations as far as everyday living is concerned. The instrumental things really go to the daughter, even if the daughter can't do them. So the relationship between mother and son tends to be an easier one."

There is still another positive factor to consider in evaluating the mother–son relationship of later life. What most sons *don't* provide—hands-on care—is often better done by someone outside of the family. Having a child tend to one's most intimate needs is not a comfortable feeling. Being bathed by a child, dressed by a child, fed by a child, in a reversal of the way things were in days long gone, is generally an awkward situation for both parent and child, better handled by someone hired to do the job. What many sons offer is more important—the love of someone who really cares, the advice of someone who really wants to help, the support of someone who can be counted on when the need is really there. More important still, a son may well offer his mother a spur to independence as he is less likely to be drawn into a dependent relationship with her—a relationship that many daughters succumb to. As he insists on the freedom to be himself, a person apart from her, his mother is freed to find her own special identity, even as she grows old.

Many women change naturally as they grow older, even without their son as a spur. They find strengths within themselves they never knew they had, as Dr. Gary Seltzer, an assistant professor of family medicine and community health at Brown University Medical School, explains: "Many women who have been very passive all along vis-à-vis their children and their whole life-style assume more responsibility as they grow old. They interact with their children in a more sophisticated way, and that can change the relationship." In the past, it was thought that older people become more childlike, and that their children take on the parental role. But that theory has been refuted. In fact, as Dr. Seltzer suggests, a woman can gain in resources and grow in emotional strength as she ages. Her grown son does not have all the power just because he's a man. She has power, too, because she's a woman who has learned about herself and is no longer afraid to make her presence felt.

Whether a woman has sons or daughters or both says little about the quality of her old age. What says more is who *she* is, what her own development was like, and how she has handled the vicissitudes of her life. For the older woman who is still growing, who is open to change and to new experiences, who can reach out and accept from other people than her family, the gender of her child is of little consequence to her happiness.

BEYOND THE CALL

So far this chapter has dealt with the most typical situation—both sons and daughters "doing" for their parents, with daughters doing more. But there are sons, countless sons, who help out far more than their sisters do, far more than a mother expects, when given the chance. For Frank, a man in his fifties, the chance came when his sister "burned out." Their mother is a physically frail person, independent of spirit, but quite unhappy. For the past twenty years the daughter has taken on most of the burden of her care, running over to help, taking her mother any place she wanted to go. Frank filled in when his sister couldn't. But the situation has gotten worse. Their mother now needs around-the-clock help, and has three different women spelling each other to care for her needs. And the daughter has herself been ill. She feels she just can't keep the system going any longer, and she wants to put her mother into a nursing home. But the son is the reluctant one—so reluctant that he went to a counselor to find out if it's really necessary, and he determined that it isn't. He decided that he will pick it up, and he will keep it going. And he will keep his mother at home. In this instance, the daughter felt that the burden was hers alone, and finally too much for her. When she finally stumbled with it, her brother stepped in to take on the responsibility.

Another son in another family, Claude, has a younger

sister. They were what most adults would call "good" children, never causing any trouble. Now that their mother is widowed and frail, they are still "good" children, especially Claude. While both Claude and his sister pay for their mother's home care, he is the one who visits her every day, who shops for her every afternoon on his way home from work, who takes her to doctors. When they ran into money problems keeping the full-time aides, his sister finally faced the fact that they would have to give it up and apply for Medicaid. But Claude couldn't face it. He refused to acknowledge that a time would come when he couldn't do everything for his mother.

Jerie Charnow often sees both sons and daughters in her practice, and she is often surprised by the sons. "Some of them are so much more nurturing than the daughters are. Again and again I see them doing things for their mothers, giving so much time and tenderness. It's as if they're saying, 'You did your best for me. Now I'll do my best for you.' These were generally the mothers who did a lot for their sons, and yet were able to let them go. Then when the mothers need help they don't have to ask for it. The sons simply give it. I was taken aback by this at first, or should I say surprised by it, by the fact that it's more common than I thought. The mothers are paid homage, and their rewards are tremendous."

Another specialist in the problems of the aged, Professor Leah Lauter of the Adelphi University School of Social Work, also comes across the not uncommon phenomenon of the involved son. She described one particular family in which the older son was the favored child and the younger son the responsible child (similar in role to the daughter who is "chosen"). The younger son told his future wife that no matter what the circumstances, his mother would always have to live with them, and that if she couldn't accept that, they shouldn't get married. He always took care of his mother, always arranged and paid for her vacations. Yet whenever she had spare money, she would give the other son presents. In the end, when she became too ill to stay in the house, and her younger son decided to put her in a nursing home, it was interestingly enough the older, more neglectful son who chimed in, "If you put her in, you're going to kill her." And it was the younger, involved one who retorted, "And where were you for the past fifty years?"

Different sons find different ways of helping their mothers ease through the passage of old age. The mother of one of Dr. Lauter's colleagues had organic brain syndrome—in popular terms, senility. She didn't even recognize her son when he came to visit her at the nursing home, yet he would go regularly, at least once a week. The way he would interact with her was by singing folk songs, a medley of songs from the family's past. They seemed to strike the right chord with her. She would become alert, alive. This was something she could still relate to. He had found this one connection. So this son provided this mother with more than company, with more than money. He provided her a link with her past life.

Professor Lauter has two children of her own, and her son, though only in his early twenties, has already demonstrated some nurturant qualities toward her. When she told him she'd like to retire, but her pension is not adequate yet, he asked, "Why do you need so much money?" She answered him, "Later, if I get sick and have to go into a nursing home, it's going to cost $30,000 a year. So that'll leave nothing for Daddy and me if we have to live separately." That's where he jumped in to the rescue. "Don't worry Mom, when I get my first job as an engineer I'll make $30,000." But, she asked, "What'll you live on?" "Oh, I'll moonlight as an auto mechanic." Professor Lauter laughed as she related this story, but it obviously conveyed something very important to her. "I would never have anticipated my son saying something like that to me. In a sense what he's saying is that he will take some responsibility for my care. That made me feel wonderful. I certainly would not want that to be the case, obviously, but it's really nice to know the sentiment is there. I think the children of this generation, the men and women alike, are learning more about giving to each other, and their parents will benefit from it."

There are stories of sons going beyond, way beyond, the call of filial duty. One woman looked back into her family's past, at the way her father had been with his parents. "I think he was a better son than husband. He and my mother had a business in the suburbs of New Jersey, and his parents lived in the Bronx. It was before the highways were built, so it was quite a long trip. Whenever his parents were sick he would leave my mother alone with the business to go to New York to see if his parents were all right. It might have been a busy day, a day he really should have been in the store, but he left anyway. He felt so strongly about his parents that he contributed to their welfare even when he had to take from us." It sounds as if this woman was not exactly elated that her father was such a good son. It sounds as if she felt he wasn't a good enough father. Sometimes when an adult son is "too good" to his parents, or perceived that way, a price is paid at the other end.

Sometimes perceptions are misleading. Another woman, Royce, the mother of a middle-aged daughter and son, lives in an adult community just a half-hour from her daughter. Her son lives on the other side of the country. It would seem the typical situation of daughter staying close to the nest and son flying off to a distant destiny. But it is her son with whom Royce feels more empathy, more intimacy, and more of a likelihood of living with if the need ever arises. "It's a matter of personalities and life-styles," Royce explains. "I feel much more comfortable in my son's company than I do in my daughter's company. There's a barrier with her. She's up with the Joneses and the Smiths where I don't fit, up in a world where I don't belong. It's like she talks to me about the Rolex and the Tiffany

watches, and I can just as well take a Timex, if you know
what I mean. To put it plainly, she's a social climber. But
my son's down to earth. We live and we think more the
same way."

Royce admits that her son is no longer the little boy she
brought up. His interests are no longer her interests, and
he has grown apart from her in some ways—as adults
should grow apart from their parents. But in some ways she
still feels very close to him, so that the continent cannot
divide them. For proof of his love, she looks back five years
to a time of crisis when he came through. "It was a terrible
time for me. I was going into the hospital to have a lump
on my breast, and maybe more, removed. My son's wife
gave birth on a Sunday to their second child. I went into
the hospital on that Monday. He flew in Monday morning,
and was at my side. And he stayed at the hospital during
my mastectomy, and for about a week more. I needed him
then, and he was there for me. He wasn't with his wife and
new child. He was with me. Now that's a son for you."

Although sons are less likely than daughters to live with
or near a mother, that doesn't mean that the mother–son
relationship need be any more distant. Researchers at the
University of California at Los Angeles tried to determine
the roots of "filial crisis"—tension and strain between the
generations, coupled with a reduction in intimacy. They
found that children who live near or with their elderly
widowed mothers are more likely to be in a crisis situation
with her—that is, crisis in their relationship—than are
children who live at a distance. Still other research indicates that a satisfying relationship between older adults
and their children is related more to the quality of communication than to geographical closeness. A daughter who
invites a mother into her home is not necessarily inviting
her into her heart; a son who lives a bus ride or even plane
ride away may be the child who provides the intimacy that
the mother is looking for.

Jenny, a widow and the mother of two sons and a daughter, has looked beyond the gender of her children to find their own special qualities. Her oldest child, Avery, is the most family oriented of the three. He's the only one who stayed close to home, the one who's at the center of the network of relatives. He divorced his first wife partly because she didn't appreciate this involvement of his; he said that he couldn't be married to anybody who wouldn't be part of his family. His sister, Ellen, lives across the country with her husband. The move hurt their mother, but then, it didn't really surprise her. Ellen had always kept her distance, was never as physically affectionate as the boys. But Jenny is discovering that a mother–daughter bond definitely exists between them. "I can talk to her about my personal needs, about my dating situation, about my sexual needs. She'll zero right in to my social life and things of that nature. Those are things I can't tell my sons." But there are a lot of things she tells her younger son, Arnold, things she won't tell anyone else. "In every other way, I open up most to Arnold. He's the child I can speak to most about my feelings. He's very understanding, and helps me deal with my problems. Even if I get angry at one of the other kids, and I want to say something to them, he's really taught me a lot about how to talk to them." Whether sons or daughters, our children can affect and comfort us in different ways.

FINAL PAYMENTS

Our relationships with our sons do have histories, and those histories will help to determine our future. To a large extent a mother gets back what she gives, and in much the same way. If she gave generously and with joy, she has a lot to look forward to. If she tells her adult child, "I did it all happily, I loved it, I enjoyed bringing you up, I enjoyed taking you to your music lessons," that kind of attitude will be reciprocated. By the same token, if she says, "It was terrible, I had to do it, look at how I suffered for you," it will come back in a similar way.

A mother teaches her child how to parent, and when the mother gets older and may need some caring for, her success or failure will come back to help her or to haunt her. If she did a good job of it, she may well benefit from the gentleness, and kindness, and sense of responsibility she imparted to her children. And she may benefit from the mutual affection that's developed between them. Dr. Amy Horowitz saw it clearly in her study of frail elderly people and their adult children. The children who helped out the most were those who felt their parents had helped *them* out in the past, and those who felt the most affection for their parents. They were the children who went "beyond the call of duty" in assisting their frail parents. In addition, the children who felt the closest to their parents were those who felt the least stressed in helping them out.

The importance of the past was highlighted in yet another study, conducted by Bertha Simos of the University of Southern California in Los Angeles, this one a look at adult children and their view of problems with their aging parents. The children usually saw their parents' interpersonal problems as longstanding ones, resulting from the parent's basic personality structure. The parents were not perceived totally in the present. Instead, their children judged them on the parenting they were seen as having provided—or having failed to provide—during childhood.

Dr. Gary Seltzer also emphasizes the link of the past to the present: "The patterns that have developed previously in the life cycle maintain themselves to a great extent later in life. There is not a great discontinuity between the older and younger years." Dr. Seltzer points out another kind of link—one that was examined in a different context earlier in this book. That is, the link between a woman's experiences with other men in her life and her view of what her experiences with her son will be like: "If a mother has experienced successful emotional support from men during her life, then she's more likely to expect that she'll continue to get it from her sons." She'll approach her son with the conviction that he will be emotionally available to her in her old age; the woman who sees men as nurturant, including the men she brought up, is unlikely to be disappointed.

Another relevant aspect of a woman's past involves how she treated her own parents when they were elderly. Whether it was with respect or with scorn, again there may well be a replay in the mother's own old age, as she gets back from the next generation, in hearts or in spades, what she handed out a generation before. If her son saw her acting generously with her parents, helping them to negotiate the traps and challenges of old age, he is more likely to be giving and generous when her time of need comes around. If he saw her spurning her parents, unwilling to help ease the crises of their older years, he also will likely be too busy to be bothered by the neediness of an elderly mother.

Parents set the example that helps determine how giving their children will be. Lydia, in her midseventies, the mother of a daughter and a son, is an active woman who works as a bookkeeper. She is also a woman content with the attention her children give her. She tries to be modest about it but is obviously quite proud of her own contribution to their generous natures: "They tell it to me themselves. They say that it's my fault, that I taught them, that they learned it from their mother and father. If a friend was in trouble, we'd try to do what we could to help. And that's the way they are. I brought up children who are givers. They're not rich, but they're good, which to me is more important. And it's really been a blessing to me. They both keep watch over me. When I was sick, my son waited on me hand and foot. If he had to go away, he'd see that one of his friends would come over to take care of me. Now, if my son calls and I'm not home at a time he thinks I should be, he starts calling around to all my friends. My children are both very devoted. And they say it's my doing."

As was discussed earlier in this chapter, many older women receive not only material and emotional support from their sons but physical warmth as well—one woman described it as a "shower of kisses." While this may reflect, in part, the underlying sexuality of the mother–son relationship, it is more than a display of Oedipal affection. Jerie Charnow sees it as a type of repayment, a show of gratitude toward a giving mother: "Sons know, if they've had sisters, that as males they've been in a very special position. And now that they're older, they can reciprocate. That's what the shower of kisses is all about. That's what Mama wants, that's what Mama needs, that's what Mama is going to get. They're repaying their childhood debt."

There may also be repayment of a less welcome sort. In cases where mothers weren't so wonderful, in cases where they were downright abusive, their old age may well be a nightmare. Abuse of the elderly is a phenomenon that has only recently begun to receive publicity. Although fathers can be the victims, it is mothers who are most often the battered ones. Although daughters can do the victimizing, it is the son who is more commonly the assailant of an elderly parent. The parent abuser often feels burdened by the responsibility of caring for the older person, a person who is often suffering from mental confusion. While most adult children would feel frustrated by such a situation, they are able to deal with it because of the fondness they feel for the parent and the debt they feel they owe. But the abuser feels a different kind of debt—a debt going back to his (or her) own childhood, when *he* was the abused one. It's become common knowledge that people who were abused as children tend to abuse their own children. Now we are learning that some of the abused vent their vengeance more directly, abusing the very people who victimized them.

There are other forms of mistreatment that fall short of abuse but are not forgotten and are repaid in kind. A mother who has been neglectful may find herself, in later years, sitting beside a phone that never rings, setting a holiday table for one. She has given her son neither the ability nor the desire to be a person she can count on for much of anything, not even for his company, certainly not for her care. At the other extreme is the mother who has held on too tightly to her son. She has encouraged his dependency on her and made him almost part of her. Psychologists would say that mother and son are "fused." But as she grows old she may lose some of her power over him, and he may take the chance to escape, becoming one of the few exceptions to the rule that children *don't* abandon their elderly parents. Or he may react in the opposite way, overprotecting her as she overprotected him. Instead of letting her make her own decisions as best she can, he tries to run her life.

Strangely enough, what can look like the best of mother–son relationships can really be an expression of a son's vengeance toward an overcontrolling mother. Charnow describes how deceiving appearances can be. "These are the cases where Mother was a controlling mother, always telling her son what to do. Suddenly there's a crisis with her, and there he is at her side. He tells her what to eat, what to do, and he hires and fires the girls. He seems to be really devoted. The family and friends and neighbors will all think, 'Oh, what a lovely son,' because he's doing all the right things. But it's the *way* he's doing them. He's taken her over, manipulating her environment completely, doing things for her she's able to do on her own. And she can't escape from it without a confrontation. But she's afraid to confront him because then she might lose his involvement. It's all or nothing. It's a form of revenge that puts the mother in the son's control." Of course, he is probably not psychologically aware of why he is doing what he is doing. But then his mother was probably no more aware when she took over her son's life years earlier, a takeover that was itself planted somewhere back in her own past.

In a relationship as primary and intimate as a mother and a son's, there has almost inevitably been some form of conflict. Sometimes the conflict has been resolved, satisfactorily, in childhood. Sometimes it's gone on, unrelenting, through the years. Other times it's gone underground after the son has moved away from home, away from mother, perhaps to be expressed in altered form to his wife or his children. But when the mother becomes old, and needy, and involves her son in her life again, the quiescent conflicts may be reactivated. With the stresses of old age and the crises of decline and of loss, the conflicts may become more heated than ever. If both mother and son are willing to reevaluate their relationship, to try out new ways of interacting, to reach out for help, there's a good chance of finally resolving the conflicts before it's too late. But sometimes it is already too late, and the conflicts remain.

Bradley is a son who would say he has no major conflicts with his mother. He strenuously defends her past treatment of him and declares his love for her. But the family history he offers has a different story to tell, a story of abandonment and of control between the generations. Initially, Bradley was on the receiving end, as he recalls what a power his mother was in the past: "My mother was definitely the matriarch of the family. She set the curfews and the punishments. If my mom said to come to the table, I'd come to the table. If my mom said to leave the table, I'd leave the table. I just couldn't talk to her. She didn't want to hear about it. It was, 'This is the rule. This is it. You don't like it, you can leave.' I never answered my mother back. I knew what I would get. She really controlled me. I don't remember the incident, but I do remember having a big fight with her. I packed my bags and walked around the block three times. Why did I come back? I had no money. If I had a hundred dollars in my pocket maybe I would have run away."

There was another fight Bradley had with his mother, a fight he remembers better, a fight he lost. It seems Bradley was sent away from early childhood on to various boarding schools, first prep schools and then military schools. He says that he was sent away for his own good; he was so mischievous that his parents were afraid that he wouldn't study at home, or that he would get into trouble. But the time came when Bradley refused to go. "It seemed to me I was hardly ever home, between prep schools and camp. My experiences away weren't always so wonderful. It's not that I was brutalized or emasculated or anything, but all my bad childhood memories came from prep school or camp. Well this one year I said I wouldn't go back. I talked to my dad, and he said, 'Talk with your mother.' It was a classic. My mother said, 'It's either him or me,' meaning that either I leave the house or she would leave the house. So my father said, 'Guess where you're going?' "

Bradley tried to fight his mother's abandoning attitude in another way, attempting to be the son she seemed to want. He considers her very bright, especially with words; he remembers her finishing up the *New York Times* crossword puzzle in fifteen minutes; he hoped to talk his way into her affection, but it didn't work. "I wanted to be like my mom, who has the ability to use twelve-syllable words. I would have liked to have been able to, but I couldn't. I would clam up and walk away flustered. And my mother would get very frustrated with me, say, 'Hey, you don't speak properly,' and she would correct me." Not until he was an adult did Bradley please his mother, when he entered the family business and showed her he could be a success.

The power has shifted between Bradley and his mother. He is now an attractive man in his late thirties, financially independent, socially adept, at least outwardly confident in himself and his abilities. She is a widow, and sick, suffering from a serious heart ailment. Now, it's Bradley who's in control. That fact hit him strongly during one period when he helped to care for his sick mother. "I dressed her, carried her, even bathed her. It was very strange for me, a rude awakening. It's like she went from controlling me to my being in control."

Predictably, Bradley now uses that control in the same way his mother used hers—to send away the person who's dependent, the person who's too much trouble to have around. Bradley says it's because she's better off in Florida than she would be near him in Pennsylvania, but his own words reveal the transparency of his position. "I put my mother down in Florida to live in a high-rise. She didn't want to move there. She doesn't know anyone there. She tells me she's lonely. If she was well, she could have stayed up here with me. But she's so sick, she needs the Florida weather. Besides, I told her the rents up here are too high. And she can't live with my sister because there are too many stairs to climb. But I write to my mother and call her and I try to visit her when I can, though it's not as often as she would like. She was good to me, and I'm trying to be good to her."

It would be hard for Bradley to face the truth about his childhood, or to deal with the rage he has so long repressed at his mother's controlling, rejecting behavior. He was sent away, whether he liked it or not. Now it's his mother who's the problem, his mother who's been given her walking papers, and she doesn't like it at all. Certainly, there's the writing, and the calling, and the sometime visiting, as there was when he was the dependent one. But there's also the physical distance, a distance she had imposed on him, a distance he is now imposing on her, against her will. It is really not a coincidence at all. As happens so often, the mother has dictated the circumstances of her own old age. As she rejected her son, she is now the recipient of his rejection.

GETTING OLDER, GETTING BETTER

But sometimes there are breakthroughs as parents and children get older. Sometimes the conflicts are worked through and a new level of understanding is achieved. According to a *Newsday* survey, many parents and children were found to be quite close when the children were in their twenties. Then they drew apart as the children built their careers, their families, their own separate lives. Finally, when the parents reached their seventies, there was again a real closeness, a coming together of the generations.

It can happen because some older people mellow with time. They want to make up for old hurts before it's too late. It can also happen because adult children often soften toward their aging parents. They now want to make peace while their parents are still alive, to mend things while they can, to save themselves a guilty conscience. And besides, as they're getting older themselves, they can better identify with what their parents are going through. The reconciliation can happen because both parents *and* children have left the power games behind and can base their relationship not on who dominates whom, but on mutual respect and admiration. They can build on the past, rather than let it tear them apart.

That's what the Stanley family has tried to do, and it works. It's a process that has become a tradition on the Thanksgiving holidays. As the clan gathers—the parents and the two grown sons and the in-laws and the grandchildren—they record their thoughts for holidays to come. "Every year we make tape recordings, and everyone says something to commemorate the occasion," Mrs. Stanley relates. "And we replay the old tapes, and we show the old slides we took years ago. We relive all the pleasant times." They are creating a family history of sights and of sounds, a living history that binds together the family's oldest and newest members.

"The Waltons" seem alive and well in the Stanley family

tradition. More often, it is not something as pleasant, or planned, that draws parents and children together again. More often it is something sudden and unexpected and unwanted—more often a crisis. And crisis can be an almost constant condition of old age. Says Dr. Judith Treas of USC, "Old age contains the seeds of change. It brings with it the crises of declining health, of declining income, of the death of a spouse. In those situations, there is the potential for renegotiating a role, for reordering an ongoing relationship." Professionals who work with elderly people actually view crises as opportunities for positive change. The good that can come out of crises can sometimes override the unhappiness they bring. "We always look for crises," points out Professor Leah Lauter of Adelphi University. "Of course we don't want to see them, but when they occur it's an ideal time to work out unresolved issues. People are more open to change during such times."

Jerie Charnow agrees that a crisis is a wonderful opportunity because it brings up all the feelings of the past for all members of the family. She has seen it many times in her practice, when a mother, for example, becomes ill and there is no money to put her in a nursing home, or when there is no one close enough to supervise things and something has to be done. "The children will come here, and one will say, generally the daughter, 'Look, I can't handle it anymore. It's cutting into my time with my family. I've done it for five years, or ten years, and this is just too much, it's the last straw.' Then suddenly you'll hear from the son, who'll say, 'How can you put her in a nursing home? You can't do that to her.' Then there'll be a bloody battle, a whole business, with one saying, 'What do you care about Mom? You've never been around.' And the other saying, 'You were handling it fine. You didn't say you needed me.' Then suddenly they'll be talking about things that happened when they were fifteen, when they were ten. Everyone feels exhausted, everyone feels as though he or she is going around in circles, and just plain frustrated. But then comes the opportunity. They suddenly realize that Mom is not what she was, that sister isn't what she was, she's not a ten-year-old but a fifty-six-year-old lady with grandchildren and a full-time job and a husband who's had a heart attack or whatever." They can see each other more clearly and relate on a much more realistic basis, both the mother with her children and the children with each other.

For Jenny and Arnold, a mother–son pair we met earlier in this chapter, it was two crises coming together that brought them closer: the suicide of the father and the walking out of a long-time lover. Previously, their relationship had not been a smooth one. As Jenny recalls, Arnold had been the most difficult of her three children to raise. After two easy children, she found it hard to cope with his active, assertive ways, and was frustrated in her attempts. Things improved for a while, until his late teens, which came along in the late 1960s—an unfortunate happenstance from his mother's standpoint. He left school, hitchhiked across the country, experimented with drugs, and lived with a young woman. Jenny viewed him as a microcosm of that turbulent period. But then things changed again. Arnold's girlfriend left him. Jenny's husband committed suicide. Jenny tells it from there: "Since that time, Arnold and I established a very unusually close relationship, even though he's married now. It's because we both had to deal with my husband's death, a terrible shock for me and a traumatic event for him. And he was also going through the loss of his girlfriend. We were both experiencing loneliness. We helped each other out then. We came together, emotionally, and have stayed that way." Crisis can bring heartbreak. But it can also bring a change of heart. And the crises of older age can bring a mother and son together again.

THE DEATH OF A SON

In any mother–son relationship, it is inevitable that one will have to cope, ultimately, with the death of the other. But as long as there *is* a survivor, the bond survives. Sons never do totally relinquish their mothers, nor do mothers their sons.

Perhaps the hardest death for anyone to cope with is the death of an adult child. Because of increasing life spans, and the difference in life expectancy between males and females, many mothers do find themselves facing their son's death. In fact, research shows, a woman has a one-in-four chance of surviving a son. It is a devastating loss for a mother, the loss of the dreams she's had for this son, the loss of her own link to future generations. A recent study conducted by Dr. Catherine Sanders of the University of South Florida provides evidence of just how devastating such a death is. Of the 102 newly bereaved individuals questioned, fourteen had lost a child. The ages of these parents ranged up to the midsixties, and that of the children up to the late forties. The study found that the loss of a child—whether a young child or an adult child—produced greater grief than the loss of a spouse or a parent. According to the study, "The impossibility of surviving their child remained foremost in their thoughts and the question of 'Why?' was an obsessive rumination. There was an intense preoccupation with thoughts of the child (whether six or forty-nine) which seemed to absorb all available energy. Several spoke of moving through an unreal world—of life not making sense. Theirs was a raw, visible pain." This study supports the belief that the death of a grown child is the most difficult and longest-lasting grief to bear. And yet, the researcher reports, the parents *did* eventually get on with their lives.

The grief is intense for many reasons. For one, it seems that the natural order of things has been reversed and thus obliterated. A parent *should* die before a child. For it to

happen otherwise seems a cruel joke. It also brings with it
the guilt of the survivor. The guilt is especially strong for
parents because they feel that they should have protected
their child, even an adult child, that they should have pre-
vented this awful thing from happening. What kind of
mother would let a child die? When a mother lets herself
off the hook, when she comes to understand and to fully
accept that there was nothing she could have done, then
the healing begins.

Anne Rosberger is a psychiatric social worker and director of the Bereavement and Loss Center of New York
City, as well as the mother of two sons. She has witnessed
both the tremendous grief at the loss of a son and the re-
covery process: "Women who lose adult children are
shaken to their very roots. They often feel as if they're not
even entitled to be alive. The thought is, 'How can I be
alive if my child is dead?' But some women can move
ahead with their lives and function again. They recognize
that the pain will always be there, but they can find some
pleasure in being alive themselves."

One part of their new lives will be involved in keeping
their son alive in some way, in keeping the bond intact.
That may mean visiting the places they used to go together, looking at the writings or pictures he created, perhaps creating their own writings or artwork to commemorate their sons and ventilate their emotions. For some
mothers it means following their son's profession closely,
perhaps reading the professional journals he subscribed
to, keeping track of his associates' progress, imagining how
he would have progressed if he were still alive. Then, of
course, there is the bond with his family, particularly with
any children he might have. They are now the key to her
immortality, as well as symbol of her son. A grieving
mother will hold on to all the things that seem to bring her
son closer to her; a son cannot truly die as long as his
mother lives.

THE DEATH OF A MOTHER

Although the death of a mother is certainly more in the natural order of things than the death of a son, it can still have a traumatic impact on the survivor. Most research in this area focuses on the effect of a parent's early death on a young child's development, but even when the parent is elderly and the child a middle-aged adult, the sense of loss can be profound. It is a loss that cannot be replaced, a loss that may stir up the most early, primal feelings of abandonment and fears of one's own death. It is as if a layer of protection, a shield, has been stripped away. And the son or daughter stands next in line, seemingly closer to his or her own mortality. The research conducted by Dr. Sanders has shown that in some ways it is even harder to take than the loss of a spouse. It arouses more anger, more loss of control, and more anxiety about death.

The death of a mother, in particular, may arouse especially strong feelings. Studies indicate that it is more likely than the death of a father to lead to severe depression. Anne Rosberger tries to explain here the singular impact of a mother's death: "Both adult males and females tend to see their mothers as a source of protection, and with her passing they feel more vulnerable. In a certain sense it's one of the most intense relationships. It's one in which the parent often subordinates her own desires, her own needs, for those of her children. Perhaps in no other relationship would you find as much of that as in this relationship." And so with a mother's passing, who will put the son's needs above his or her own? Who will make him feel so safe, so secure? Another reason for the intense reaction, the therapist suggests, is that there may be more guilt felt toward a mother than a father, more guilt because she was more likely to be alone and in need in her old age, and so more likely to be disappointed in her children when they didn't come through with everything she expected. While the death of a parent is almost always hard to deal with, and always involves some guilt, feelings of intense guilt and severe unresolved conflict can complicate the mourning process.

If that's all true, why do sons sometimes seem so callous? Men are generally not the ones who wring their handkerchiefs at funerals, or turn for help to cope with their loss. They are the ones who seem to return quickly to business as usual. In one particular instance, a son left the hospital to return to work just as his mother's death seemed imminent while the daughter stayed on, angry at her brother's seeming indifference, leaving her alone at their mother's death. Was it that he didn't care enough to stay? It seemed unlikely, since he had remained living close to his mother throughout her life and had been, in every sense, a "good" son, though with a life of his own. So why this final "abandonment"? Or was it actually something else? Dr. Anna Leifer, the psychoanalyst, offers another possibility: The son felt *so* close to his mother, he simply could not handle the final separation.

That would fit well the way many men handle things, she points out, as she presents another example of the different methods of coping of sons and daughters. This was a family in which the mother was dying of cancer. Her relationship with her adult son and daughter had not been especially good, but they were both deeply affected by her illness and impending death. It was quite unusual for the son to express such emotions—he was the type of man who often cut himself off from his feelings—but these feelings were apparently too intense to keep to himself. Dr. Leifer asks, "In this family, who was affected more, the son or the daughter? Who was in more pain? It's hard to say because people handle their difficulties so differently. This man finally did express his feelings toward the end. On the day of his mother's surgery, he came to the hospital, desperately wanting to see her. He began to walk around in the operating area in a frantic attempt to find her. But she had died during the operation, and that's unfortunately how he finally came upon her. He described it to me in a therapy session, and was very affected by it, and cried. Now the daughter continued in therapy in order to deal with her feelings, but he did not. Does that mean he was in less pain? I just don't know."

Anne Rosberger also points out the different coping styles of the sexes: "In our culture, it's just that men don't seek help as much. They use other means to deal with pain than women do. Often men find themselves coping with all kinds of experiences by working. Women tend not to do this as much, not to bury their feelings in activity as much as men do." Perhaps that's another reason why the son we met earlier left his mother before her death, left to go back to his work. Perhaps in his work he found his solace.

A son's life may be affected in many ways by the death of a mother. One way is in his relationship with his wife. For some men, the wife can move in to take over the role of the mother, filling the void either temporarily or for good. For others, the link between mother and wife is less direct. The grieving son will first review his relationship with his mother, the one who has been his role model of how to interact with women. It's as if he plays back his feelings about the warmth he got from her, the love, all the values that mothers have for sons. He reviews them and then compares them with his feelings about his relationship with his wife. With his mother's death, his wife has become perhaps the only female of real importance in his life, and he concentrates on her, and on their relationship. It's not a focus that usually lasts for long with such intensity, but it may well be a preoccupation during his time of grief.

A man's relationship with other family members may also be affected, for better or for worse. What comes most easily to mind is the "worse," the image of relatives scrambling for their piece of the estate. But in some families the relationships between the children and the surviving parent can actually improve. As the mortality of their parents has become all too clear, the children may learn to cherish the remaining parent for who she or he is, and not to dwell on the flaws. Time suddenly seems too precious to waste on resentments and recriminations. Even relationships between siblings can get better with the death of a parent. It happened for Gary and Daniel, two men in their forties, after their mother died. As Gary tells it, his mother was always the central figure in the family. Everyone else related more to her than to each other. It was as if she had held the family together. But when she died, it didn't fall apart. The brothers, in fact, became closer than ever. "We're really family now," Gary says, "really close and open with each other. The family ties between the two of us are strong. Before, the family revolved in circles around Mother. We all orbited around her. She was the center. Without her, we circle around each other. We're more locked into each other because she's not there. She would be happy to see the way we are."

She'd probably also be happy to know that, even in death, she remains in the family circle. She is certainly very much alive in Gary's memory. "I don't dwell on thoughts of her, but the memory is definitely there. I keep a lot of mementos of her, pictures of her, blankets and afghans she crocheted that I use around the house. I keep them because they're excellent work, and I keep them because she made them. She was also a good cook, and we still make some of her recipes in the house. When we go out to eat with the kids and we order cheesecake, we always try to compare it with my mother's. We still keep her in the circle. And we want to keep her alive in the children's memory."

What has been forged between mother and son cannot be broken by her death. The bond remains as the son internalizes her image, and tries to keep his mother alive, at least in spirit. Eating the kinds of food she used to prepare is comforting; it keeps part of her around. Wrapping himself in her blanket is still to feel her loving warmth. Men often internalize the image of their dead mother. They do it in different ways, such as telling humorous but appreciative stories about her, wanting their wives to cook the same as Mama did, wanting their wives to treat the children as Mama treated him. One grieving son who had a very warm and generous mother took to quoting her a great deal and using certain phrases that were typical of her. He would reminisce about things they had done together, about the songs she liked. He realized that he was trying in these ways to keep her alive in a sense. It was comforting to him to hear the music that she liked, to eat the foods that were associated with her. Food is a particularly salient reminder for many men, perhaps because it's the first way that children know their mother, and it's part of her generosity and protection as well as her control. This is not unhealthy, as Anne Rosberger emphasizes. In fact, it happens most when there has been a good relationship. A mother is not someone who can, or should, be dismissed easily: "Sometimes it's assumed that if you're healthy you'll forget all about her, that as soon as you've gone through your little bit of mourning, you'll get on with the business at hand and forget about the past. As far as I'm concerned, there is something very strange in that kind of reasoning, because this person plays such an important part in your life. To go on with your life as if nothing has happened, nothing has been taken away, is impossible. To expect that is to forget what human needs are, that we're part of a continuing process."

For some sons, a mother's death brings a better understanding of what their relationship was all about. If it was a good relationship, there is the pleasure in going over it, in remembering the joys they shared and the emotional riches they imparted to each other. If it was a turbulent relationship, the son is freed from that turbulence, freed to look back, in peace, at what had been. For some sons, positive things come out of this loss, though at the expense

of their mother's death. Some sons accomplish things they
would never have tried before, take risks they would
never have dared, discover the creativity they never knew
they had. Dr. Milton Kapit, a New York psychoanalyst,
explains how that can happen especially after a "difficult"
mother has died: "There's a lot of energy consumed in
having to maintain a relationship with her. Considerable
tension and anguish go into that. In a sense, her death can
be a relief to the son, and can produce a great release of
energy." Some sons first feel free to marry after the death
of a mother. Andrew Carnegie, America's "steel king," is
a famous example of this. He was so closely tied to his
mother that he wouldn't marry while she was alive. He
finally tied the knot just five months after her death. He
was fifty-one years old at the time. In such cases, there has
often been too tight a bond between mother and son, and
only after the mother's death does the son feel free to find
a mature, adult love. Or he may *think* he's free, only to
seek out the same type of relationship he had with his
mother.

The mother–son bond is one of power and incredible
endurance. It does not end with a mother's death, but as a
mother you can help prepare your sons for that difficult
time. One way is to release them from any feelings of guilt
they may have toward you. In most families there are
questions that go unasked and unanswered. You can help
your sons by encouraging them to bring up anything they
want to settle with you, perhaps things they've harbored
all their lives but have been hesitant to discuss. Another
way to ease their future pain is to let them know that you
not only love them but respect them, that you are proud
to be their mother and proud to have them as sons. It is a
message that they will not outgrow as they move from boyhood into manhood, and out of your home, but always
remain a part of your life.

Bibliography

CHAPTER 1

Preference and Obsession: The Birth of the Mother–Son Bond

Asch, S., and Rubin, L. Postpartum reactions: Some unrecognized variations. *American Journal of Psychiatry*, 1974, *131*, 870–874.

Barry, M., and Johnson, A. The incest barrier. *Psychoanalytic Quarterly*, 1958, *22*, 485–500.

Braverman, J. Personal communication, 1982.

Buhrich, N., and McConaghy, N. Parental relationships during childhood in homosexuality, transvestism and transsexualism. *Australia and New Zealand Journal of Psychiatry*, 1978, *12*, 103–108.

Coombs, L. Preferences for sex of children among U.S. couples. *Family Planning Perspectives*, 1977, *9*, 259–265.

DeMause, L. *Foundations of psychohistory*. New York: Creative Roots, Inc., 1982.

Dinitz, S., Dynes, R., and Clarke, A. Preferences for male or female children: Traditional or affectional? *Marriage and Family Living*, 1954, *16*, 128–130.

Entwisle, D., and Doering, S. *The first birth*. Baltimore: The Johns Hopkins University Press, 1981.

Guttmacher, M. *The mind of the murderer*. New York: Farrar, Straus & Cudahy, 1960.

Hartley, S., and Pietraczyk, L. Preselecting the sex of offspring: Technologies, attitudes, and implications. *Social Biology*, 1979, *26*, 232–246.

Illick, J. Child-rearing in seventeenth-century England and America, in *The history of childhood*, ed. by L. DeMause. New York: The Psychohistory Press, 1974.

Langer, W. Infanticide: A historical survey, in *The new psychohistory,* ed. by L. DeMause. New York: The Psychohistory Press, 1975.

Largey, G. Sex control, sex preferences, and the future of the family. *Social Biology,* 1972, *19,* 379–392.

Marvick, E. Nature versus nurture: Patterns and trends in seventeenth-century French child-rearing, in *The history of childhood,* ed. by L. DeMause. New York: The Psychohistory Press, 1974.

Norman, R. Sex differences in preferences for sex of children: A replication after 20 years. *The Journal of Psychology,* 1974, *88,* 229–239.

Peterson, C., and Peterson, J. Preference for sex of offspring as a measure of change in sex attitudes. *Psychology,* 1973, *10,* 3–5.

Pharis, M., and Manosevitz, M. Parental models of infancy: A note on gender preferences for firstborns. *Psychological Reports,* 1980, *47,* 763–768.

Pogrebin, L. *Growing up free.* New York: Bantam Books, 1981.

Popper, A. Better luck next time. *Parents' Magazine,* 1980, *55,* 64–67.

Rorvik, D., with Shettles, L. *Your baby's sex: Now you can choose.* New York: Dodd, Mead & Co., 1970.

Rosner, F. The Biblical and Talmudic secret for choosing one's baby's sex. *Israeli Journal of Medical Sciences,* 1979, *15,* 784–787.

Strote, M. What are you having . . . ? *Baby Talk,* 1981, *46,* 32+.

Westoff, C., and Rindfuss, R. Sex preselection in the United States: Some implications. *Science,* 1974, *184,* 633–636.

Whelan, E. *Boy or girl?* New York: Pocket Books, 1977.

Williamson, N. Boys or girls? Parents' preferences and sex control. *Population Bulletin,* 1978, *33,* published by Population Reference Bureau, Inc., Washington, D.C.

Winston, S. Birth control and sex ratio at birth. *American Journal of Sociology,* 1932, *38,* 225–231.

CHAPTER 2
Our Fathers, Our Brothers, Our Sons

Arganian, M. Sex differences in early development. In *Individual differences in children,* ed. by Jack C. Westman. New York: John Wiley & Sons, 1973.

Brooks, J., and Lewis, M. Attachment behavior in thirteen-month-old, opposite-sex twins. *Child Development,* 1974, *45,* 243–247.

Clarke-Stewart, K., and Hevey, C. Longitudinal relations in repeated observations of mother-child interaction from 1 to 2½ years. *Developmental Psychology,* 1981, *17,* 127–145.

Colonna, A., and Solnit, A. Infant sexuality. *Siecus Report,* 1981, *9,* 1+.

Davis, G. *Childhood and history in America.* New York: The Psychohistory Press, 1976.

DeMause, L. *Foundations of psychohistory.* New York: Creative Roots, Inc., 1982.

Fallopius, G. De decoraturie trachtaties, cap. 9, *Opera Omnia,* 2 vols. (Frankfurt, 1600), 336–337; Soranus, *Gynecology,* 107.

Feiring, C., and Lewis, M. Temperament: Sex differences and stability in vigor, activity, and persistence in the first three years of life. *The Journal of Genetic Psychology,* 1980, *136,* 65–75.

Forrest, T. The family dynamics of maternal violence. *Journal of the American Academy of Psychoanalysis,* 1974, *2,* 215–230.

Hoffman, L. Changes in family roles, socialization, and sex differences. *American Psychologist,* 1977, *32,* 644–657.

Hoyenga, K. B., and Hoyenga, K. T. *The question of sex differences.* Boston: Little, Brown & Co., 1979.

Kagan, J. Psychology of sex differences, in *The growth of the child.* New York: W. W. Norton Co., 1978, pp. 115–137.

Kleeman, J. A boy discovers his penis. *The Psychoanalytic Study of the Child,* 1965, *20,* 239–266.

Korner, A. Sex differences in newborns with special reference to differences in the organization of oral behavior. *Journal of Child Psychology and Psychiatry,* 1973, *14,* 19–29.

Lewis, M. State as an infant–environment interaction: An analysis of mother–infant interaction as a function of sex. *Merrill-Palmer Quarterly*, 1972, *18*, 95–121.

Lewis, M. Early sex differences in the human: Studies of socioemotional development. *Archives of Sexual Behavior*, 1975, *4*, 329–335.

Loewald, H. The waning of the Oedipus complex. *Journal of the American Psychoanalytic Association*, 1979, *27*, 751–755.

Martinson, F. Eroticism in infancy and childhood. *The Journal of Sex Research*, 1976, *12*, 251–262.

McCandless, B., and Trotter, R. *Children: Behavior and development*. New York: Holt, Rinehart and Winston, 1977.

Moss, H. Sex, age, and state as determinants of mother–infant interaction. *Merrill-Palmer Quarterly*, 1967, *13*, 19–36.

Moss, H., Robson, K., and Pederson, F. Determinants of maternal stimulation to the infant and consequences of treatment for later reactions to strangers. *Developmental Psychology*, 1969, *1*, 239–246.

Phillips, S., King, S., and DuBois, L. Spontaneous activities of female versus male newborns. *Child Development*, 1978, *49*, 590–597.

Roiphe, H., and Galenson, E. *Infantile origins of sexual identity*. New York: International Universities Press, 1981.

Rubin, J., Provenzano, F., and Luria, Z. The eye of the beholder: Parents' views on sex of newborns. *American Journal of Orthopsychiatry*, 1974, *44*, 512–519.

Segal, J. Age of infants and parental sex-role perceptions. *The Journal of Psychology*, 1981, *107*, 267–272.

Sidorowicz, L., and Lunney, G. Baby X revisited. *Sex Roles*, 1980, *6*, 67–73.

Smith, C., and Lloyd, B. Maternal behavior and perceived sex of infant: Revisited. *Child Development*, 1978, *49*, 1263–1265.

Smith, P., and Daglish, L. Sex differences in parent and infant behavior in the home. *Child Development*, 1977, *48*, 1250–1254.

Stoller, R. Primary femininity. *Journal of the American Psy-*

choanalytic Association—Supplement—Female Psychology, 1976, *24*, 59–78.

Thoman, E., Leiderman, P., and Olson, J. Neonate-mother interaction during breast-feeding. *Developmental Psychology*, 1972, *6*, 110–118.

Uddenberg, N. Mother–father and daughter–male relationships: A comparison. *Archives of Sexual Behavior*, 1976, *5*, 69–79.

Uddenberg, N., Englesson, I., and Nettelbladt, P. Experience of father and later relations to men: A systematic study of women's relations to their father, their partner and their son. *Acta Psychiatrica Scandinavica*, 1979, *59*, 87–96.

Will, J., Self, P., and Datan, N. Maternal behavior and perceived sex of infant. *American Journal of Orthopsychiatry*, 1976, *46*, 135–139.

CHAPTER 3
The Oedipal Age

Appleton, W. *Fathers and daughters.* Garden City, N.Y.: Doubleday & Co., 1981.

Armstrong, L. *Kiss daddy good-night.* New York: Hawthorn Books, 1978.

Barry, M., and Johnson, A. The incest barrier. *Psychoanalytic Quarterly*, 1958, *27*, 485–500.

Bender, L., and Blau, A. The reaction of children to sexual relations with adults. *American Journal of Orthopsychiatry*, 1937, *7*, 500–518.

Brain, J. *The last taboo.* Garden City, N.Y.: Anchor Press/ Doubleday, 1979.

Brophy, J. *Child development and socialization.* Chicago: Science Research Associates, Inc., 1977.

Brown, W. Murder rooted in incest, in *Patterns of incest,* R. E. L. Masters. New York: Julian Press, 1963, p. 301–327.

Brunswick, R. The pre-Oedipal phase of the libido development. *Psychoanalytic Quarterly*, 1940, *9*, 293–319.

Burgess, A., Groth, A., Holmstrom, L., and Sgroi, S. *Sexual assault of children and adolescents.* Lexington, Mass.: Lexington Books, D. C. Heath & Co., 1978.

DeMause, L. *The new psychohistory*. New York: The Psycho-history Press, 1975.

Dion, K. Children's physical attractiveness and sex as determinants of adult punitiveness. *Developmental Psychology*, 1974, *10*, 772–778.

English, O., and Foster, C. *Fathers are parents, too*. New York: G. P. Putnam's Sons, 1951.

Frances, V., and Frances, A. The incest taboo and family structure. *Family Process*, 1976, *15*, 235–244.

Harrison, R. *Rex*. New York: William Morrow & Co., 1975.

Janus, S. *The death of innocence*. New York: William Morrow & Co., 1981.

Johnson, M. Sex role learning in the nuclear family. *Child Development*. 1963, *34*, 319–333.

Kagan, J., and Lemkin, I. The child's differential perception of parental attributes. *Journal of Abnormal and Social Psychology*, 1960, *61*, 440–447.

Kleeman, J. Genital self-discovery during a boy's second year: a follow-up. *The Psychoanalytic Study of the Child*, 1966, *21*, 358–392.

Lester, D. Incest. *The Journal of Sex Research*, 1972, *8*, 268–285.

Loewald, H. The waning of the Oedipus complex. *The Journal of the American Psychoanalytic Association*, 1979, *27*, 751–775.

Lukianowicz, N. Incest. *British Journal of Psychiatry*, 1972, *120*, 301–313.

Margolis, M. A preliminary report of a case of consummated mother–son incest. *The Annual of Psychoanalysis*, 1977, *5*, 267–293.

McCandless, B., and Trotter, R. *Children*. New York: Holt, Rinehart & Winston, 1977.

Medical aspects of human sexuality. How can one foster "masculinity" in boys and "femininity" in girls? 1980, *14*, 32+.

Medlicott, R. Parent–child incest. *Australia and New Zealand Journal of Psychiatry*, 1967, *1*, 180–187.

Meiselman, K. *Incest*. San Francisco: Jossey-Bass Publishers, 1981.

Puglisi, J., and Jackson, D. Sex role identity and self-esteem in adulthood. *International Journal of Aging and Human Development*, 1980–81, *12*(2), 129–138.

Rangell, L. The role of the parent in the Oedipal complex. *Bulletin of the Menninger Clinic*, 1955, *19*, 9–15.

Rochlin, G. *The masculine dilemma*. Boston: Little, Brown & Co., 1980.

Rothbart, M., and Maccoby, E. Parents' differential reactions to sons and daughters. *Journal of Personality and Social Psychology*, 1966, *4*, 237–243.

Sagarin, E. Incest: Problems of definition and frequency. *The Journal of Sex Research*, 1977, *13*, 126–135.

Sanford, L. *The silent children*. Garden City, N.Y.: Anchor Press/Doubleday, 1980.

Schwartzman, J. The individual, incest and exogamy. *Psychiatry*, 1974, *37*, 171–180.

Shelton, W. A study of incest. *International Journal of Offender Therapy and Comparative Criminology*, 1975, *19*, 139–153.

Shengold, L. The parent as sphinx. *American Psychoanalytic Association Journal*, 1963, *11*, 725–751.

Shengold, L. Some reflections on a case of mother/adolescent son incest. *International Journal of Psychoanalysis*, 1980, *61*, 461.

Silverman, S. *Public spectacles*. New York: E. P. Dutton, 1981.

Singer, D., and Singer, J. Raising boys who know how to love. *Parents' Magazine*, 1977, *52*, 32+.

Sloane, P., and Karpinski, E. Effects of incest on the participants. *American Journal of Orthopsychiatry*, 1942, *12*, 666–673.

Small, A., Teagno, L., and Selz, K. The relationship of sex role to physical and psychological health. *Journal of Youth and Adolescence*, 1980, *9*, 305–314.

Sroufe, L., and Ward, M. Seductive behavior of mothers of toddlers: Occurrence, correlates, and family origins. *Child Development*, 1980, *51*, 1222–1229.

Wahl, C. The psychodynamics of consummated maternal incest. *Archives of General Psychiatry*, 1960, *3*, 188–193.

Walfish, S., and Myerson, M. Sex role identity and attitudes toward sexuality. *Archives of Sexual Behavior*, 1980, *9*, 199–203.

Weinberg, S. *Incest behavior.* New York: Citadel, 1955.

Yorukoglu, A., and Kemph, J. Children not severely damaged by incest with a parent. *Journal of the American Academy of Child Psychiatry,* 1966, *5,* 111–124.

CHAPTER 4

The Turbulent Teens

Acock, A., and Bengtson, V. On the relative influence of mothers and fathers: A covariance analysis of political and religious socialization. *Journal of Marriage and the Family,* 1978, *40,* 519–530.

Adams, J., ed. *Understanding adolescence.* Boston: Allyn and Bacon, Inc., 1973.

Blos, P. *The adolescent passage.* New York: International University Press, 1979.

Bryt, A. Developmental tasks in adolescence. *Adolescent Psychiatry,* 1979, *7,* 136–146.

Burke, R., and Weir, T. Sex differences in adolescent life stress, social support, and well-being. *The Journal of Psychology,* 1978, *98,* 277–288.

Burke, R., and Weir, T. Helping responses of parents and peers and adolescent well-being. *The Journal of Psychology,* 1979, *102,* 49–62.

Davies, M., and Kandel, B. Parental and peer influences on adolescents' educational plans: Some further evidence. *American Journal of Sociology,* 1981, *87,* 363–387.

Dear Abby. *New York Post,* Nov. 18, 1981, 28.

Dear Abby. *New York Post,* Jan. 29, 1982, 54.

Freud, A. Adolescence. *The Psychoanalytic Study of the Child,* 1958, *13,* 255–278.

Gottlieb, B. *Understanding your adolescent.* New York: Rinehart & Company, 1957.

Matthews, K., and Serrano, A. Ecology of adolescence. *Adolescence,* 1981, *16,* 605–612.

Meissner, W. Parental interaction of the adolescent boy. *The Journal of Genetic Psychology,* 1965, *107,* 225–233.

Metcalf, A. How parents contribute to adolescents' sexual acting out. *Medical Aspects of Human Sexuality,* 1980, *14,* 23–24.

Mohr, G., and Despres, M. *The stormy decade: Adolescence.* New York: Random House, 1958.

Offer, A. *The psychological world of the teen-ager.* New York: Basic Books, 1969.

Oldham, D. Adolescent turmoil: A myth revisited. *Adolescent Psychiatry,* 1978, *6,* 267–279.

Smith, B. Adolescent and parent: Interaction between developmental stages. *The Center Quarterly Focus,* published by the Center for Youth Development and Research, University of Minnesota, 1976, 1–8.

Steinberg, L. Transformations in family relations at puberty. *Developmental Psychology,* 1981, *17,* 833–840.

Steinberg, L., and Hill, J. Patterns of family interaction as a function of age, the onset of puberty, and formal thinking. *Developmental Psychology,* 1978, *14,* 683–684.

Stewart, L. Mother–son identification and vocational interest. *Genetic Psychology Monographs,* 1959, *60,* 31–63.

Troll, L., Neugarten, B., and Kraines, R. Similarities in values and other personality characteristics in college students and their parents. *Merrill-Palmer Quarterly of Behavior and Development,* 1969, *15,* 323–336.

Vandewiele, M. Wolof adolescents' perception of their parents. *The Journal of Psychology,* 1981, *109,* 173–177.

Willis, M. The maligning of adolescence: Why? *Adolescence,* 1981, *16,* 953–958.

Wright, P. and Keple, T. Friends and parents of a sample of high school juniors: An exploratory study of relationship intensity and interpersonal rewards. *Journals of Marriage and the Family,* 1981, *43,* 559–570.

CHAPTER 5

That Other Woman— Your Daughter-in-Law, His Wife

Bates, A. Parental roles in courtship. *Social Forces,* 1942, *20,* 483–486.

Bell, R. *Marriage and family interaction.* Homewood, Ill.: Dorsey Press, 1971.

Bierer, J. The trigamist syndrome. *International Journal of Social Psychiatry,* 1980, *26,* 242–245.

Burgess, E., and Wallin, P. *Engagement and marriage.* Philadelphia: Lippincott, 1953.

Day, I. How I stayed friends with my mother-in-law (Even after divorcing her son). *Ms.,* 1978, 7, 12–13+.

Deutsch, C. Do your parents haunt your marriage? *Parents' Magazine,* 1979, *54,* 24.

Deutsch, C. In-law problems. *Parents' Magazine,* 1980, *55,* 26.

Duvall, E. *In-laws: Pro and con.* New York: Association Press, 1954.

Gaylin, J. How to handle the other woman in his life: His mother. *Glamour,* 1979, *77,* 227–229.

Gottlieb, B. *Understanding your adolescent.* New York: Rinehart & Company, 1957, p. 89.

Jacoby, S. Mothers-in-law: A special kind of love. *McCall's,* 1979, *106,* 18+.

New York Post. Mom washes out a wedding, Oct. 5, 1981, p. 16.

Rangell, L. The role of the parent in the Oedipus complex. *Bulletin of the Menninger Clinic,* 1955, *19,* 9–15.

Roiphe, A. The other woman . . . his mother. *Mademoiselle,* 1982, *88,* 122–3+.

Safran, C. Troubles that pull couples apart: A *Redbook* report. *Redbook,* 1979, *152,* 83+.

Safran, C. The *Redbook* poll on in-laws. *Redbook,* 1980, *155,* 62.

Stinnett, N., and Walters, J. *Relationships in marriage and family.* New York: Macmillan Publishing Co. and London: Collier Macmillan Publishing, 1977.

Waller, W. *On the family, education and war.* Chicago: The University of Chicago Press, 1970.

Weller, S. His mother: How she influences his life—and maybe yours. *Glamour,* 1979, *77,* 270+.

Whitcomb, M. No love for son's wife. *50 Plus,* 1981, *21,* 74.

CHAPTER 6

Why Some Mothers Lose Sons

Botwin, C. Don't lean on your children. *50 Plus,* 1981, *21,* 63.

Framo, J. *Explorations in marital and family therapy.* New York: Springer Publishing Co., 1982.

Fromme, A. The joys and jabs of 50-plus parents. *50 Plus,* 1978, *18,* 52–53.

Kahn, R. Coping with the empty nest after 50. *50 Plus*, 1979, *19*, 54.

Wolfe, L. When was the last time you called your mother? A *New York Magazine* survey of readers and their parents. *New York Magazine*, 1979, *12*, 47–50+.

CHAPTER 7

That Other Man: When His Lover Is Not a Lady

Bell, A., Weinberg, M., and Hammersmith, S. *Sexual preference*. An official publication of the Alfred C. Kinsey Institute for Sex Research. Bloomington, Ind.: Indiana University Press, 1981.

Bennett, K., and Thompson, N. Social and psychological functioning of the ageing male homosexual. *British Journal of Psychiatry*, 1980, *137*, 361–370.

Brown, H. *Familiar faces, hidden lives*. New York: A Harvest/HBJ Book, 1976.

Dailey, D. Adjustment of heterosexual and homosexual couples in pairing relationships: An exploratory study. *The Journal of Sex Research*, 1979, *15*, 143–157.

Ebert, A. *The homosexuals*. New York: Macmillan, 1977.

Fairchild, B., and Hayward, N. *Now that you know*. New York: A Harvest/HBJ Book, 1979.

Fairchild, B. and Hayward, N. My child is a homosexual. *Family Health*, 1980, *12*, 38+.

Gelman, R., and McGinley, H. Interpersonal liking and self-disclosure. *Journal of Consulting and Clinical Psychology*, 1978, *46*, 1549–1551.

Green, R. Childhood cross-gender behavior and subsequent sexual preference. *American Journal of Psychiatry*, 1979, *136*, 106–108.

Hart, M., Roback, H., Tittler, B., Weitz, L., Walston, B., and McKee, E. Psychological adjustment of nonpatient homosexuals: Critical review of the research literature. *The Journal of Clinical Psychiatry*, 1978, *39*, 604–608.

Jones, C. *What about homosexuality?* Nashville: Thomas Nelson, Inc., 1972.

Jourard, S. *The transparent self*. New York: Van Nostrand, 1964.

Jourard, S. *Self-disclosure: An experimental analysis of the transparent self.* New York: John Wiley & Sons, 1971.

Kimmel, D. Adult development and aging: A gay perspective. *Journal of Social Issues,* 1978, *34,* 113–130.

Monteflores, C., and Schultz, S. Coming out: Similarities and differences for lesbians and gay men. *Journal of Social Issues,* 1978, *34,* 59–72.

Morin, S., and Garfinkle, E. Male homophobia. *Journal of Social Issues,* 1978, *34,* 29–47.

Myers, M. Counseling the parents of young homosexual male patients. *Journal of Homosexuality,* 1981/82, *7,* 131–143.

Parents of Gays, Lambda Rising, Washington, D.C., 1975.

Peplaw, L., and Cochran, S. Value orientations in the intimate relationships of gay men. *Journal of Homosexuality,* 1981, *6,* 1–19.

Siegelman, M. Parental background of male homosexuals and heterosexuals. *Archives of Sexual Behavior,* 1974, *3,* 3–18.

Storms, M. Theories of sexual orientation. *Journal of Personality and Social Psychology,* 1980, *38,* 783–792.

Vida, G., ed. *Our right to love.* Englewood Cliffs, N.J.: Prentice-Hall, 1978.

Whitam, F. The prehomosexual male child in three societies: The United States, Guatemala, Brazil. *Archives of Sexual Behavior,* 1980, *9,* 87–99.

Zuger, B. Homosexuality and parental guilt. *British Journal of Psychiatry,* 1980, *137,* 55–57.

CHAPTER 8

The End—Or the Beginning?

The Amazing Randi and Bert Randolph Sugar. *Houdini: His life and art.* New York: Grosset & Dunlap, 1978.

Bankoff, E. *Support from family and friends: What helps the widow?* Presented at the 33rd Annual Scientific Meeting of the Gerontological Society of America, San Diego, 1980.

Berkman, S., and Houser, B. *Filial crisis among the adult children of the elderly.* Paper presented at the Annual Meeting of the National Council on Family Relations, Oct. 15, 1982.

Birtchnell, J. Depression in relation to early and recent parent death. *British Journal of Psychiatry,* 1970, *116,* 299–306.

Birtchnell, J. The relationship between attempted suicide, depression, and parent death. *British Journal of Psychiatry,* 1970, *116,* 307–313.

Brubaker, T., Cole, C., Hennon, C., and Cole, A. Forum on aging and the family: Discussions with F. Ivan Nye, Bernice L. Neugarten and David and Vera Mace. *The Family Coordinator,* 1978, *27,* 436–444.

Brubaker, T., and Sneden, L. Aging in a changing family context. *The Family Coordinator,* 1978, *27,* 301–314.

Cohen, S., and Gans, B. *The other generation gap: The middle-aged and their aging parents.* Chicago: Follett Publishing Co., 1978.

Davidson, W., and Cotter, P. Adjustment to aging and relationships with offspring. *Psychological Reports,* 1982, *50,* 731–738.

Hardt, D. An investigation of the stages of bereavement. *Omega,* 1978–79, *9,* 279–285.

Hausman, C. Short-term counseling groups for people with elderly parents. *The Gerontologist,* 1979, *19,* 102–107.

Horowitz, A. *Sons and daughters as caregivers to older parents: Differences in role performance and consequences.* A version of this paper was presented at the 34th Annual Scientific Meeting of the Gerontological Society of America, Toronto, Canada, 1981.

Horowitz, A., and Shindelman, L. Reciprocity and affection: Past influences on current caregiving. *Journal of Gerontological Social Work,* in press.

Houser, B., Berkman, S., and Long, A. *Filial expectations and outcomes for older women.* Paper presented at the 11th Annual Brigham Young University Family Research Conference, February 1981.

Johnson, E., and Bursk, B. Relationships between the elderly and their adult children. *The Gerontologist,* 1977, *17,* 90–95.

MacDonald, P. Death of a parent. *Glamour,* 1979, *77,* 220+.

Malinak, D., Hoyt, M., and Patterson, V. Adults' reactions to the death of a parent: A preliminary study. *American Journal of Psychiatry,* 1979, *136,* 1152–1156.

Mancini, J. Family relationships and morale among people 65

years of age and older. *American Journal of Orthopsychiatry,* 1979, *49,* 292–300.

Meyer, B. *Houdini: A mind in chains.* New York: E. P. Dutton, 1976.

Mindel, C. Multigenerational and family households: Recent trends and implications for the future. *The Gerontologist,* 1979, *19,* 456–463.

Newsweek, Unveiling a family secret, Feb. 18, 1980, *95,* 104+.

Pincus, L. *Death and the family.* New York: Pantheon Books, 1974.

Quinn, W., and Hughston, G. *The family as an informal support system for the aged.* Paper presented at the 32nd Annual Scientific Meeting of the Gerontological Society, Washington, D.C., 1979.

Ragan, P., ed. of *Aging parents.* Ethel Percy Andrus Gerontology Center, University of Southern California, Los Angeles, 1979.

Revenson, T., and Rubinstein, C. *Debunking the myth of loneliness in old age.* Presented at the 33rd Annual Scientific Meeting of the Gerontological Society of America, San Diego, 1980.

Robinson, B., and Thurnher, M. Taking care of aged parents: A family cycle transition. *The Gerontologist,* 1979, *19,* 586–595.

Sanders, C. A comparison of adult bereavement in the death of a spouse, child and parent. *Omega,* 1979–80, *10,* 303–322.

Seelbach, W. Gender differences in expectations for filial responsibility. *The Gerontologist,* 1977, *17,* 421–425.

Seelbach, W. Correlates of aged parents' filial responsibility expectations and realizations. *The Family Coordinator,* 1978, *27,* 341–350.

Seelbach, W., and Saver, W. Filial responsibility expectations and morale among aged parents. *The Gerontologist,* 1977, *17,* 490–499.

Shanas, E. Social myth as hypothesis: The case of the family relations of old people. *The Gerontologist,* 1979, *19,* 3–9.

Simos, B. Adult children and their aging parents. *Social Work,* 1973, *18,* 78–85.

U.S. News and World Report, Abusing the aged: The unreported crime, Apr. 13, 1981, *90,* 10.

Wall, J. *Andrew Carnegie*. New York: Oxford University Press, 1970.

Ward, R. Limitations of the family as a supportive institution in the lives of the aged. *The Family Coordinator*, 1978, *27*, 365–373.

Watson, J., and Kivett, V. Influences on the life satisfaction of older fathers. *The Family Coordinator*, 1976, *25*, 482–488.

Wood, V., and Robertson, J. Friendship and kinship interaction: Differential effect on the morale of the elderly. *Journal of Marriage and the Family*, 1978, *40*, 367–375.

Index

Brother-sister relationships, 34–36
Bulletin of the Menninger Clinic,
54

Care, *see* Hands-on care
Caring, *see* Intimacy
Carnegie, Andrew, 241
Caron, Dr. Rose, 39
Charnow, Jerie, 206, 214–15, 216,
219, 226, 227, 232–33
Children
"good," 219
grade-school, 74–75
reconciliation with parents,
231–33
Chosen child, and older mother,
212–15
Coates, Dr. Susan, 60
Comfort, for older mother, 218–
223
Communication
on homosexuality, 184–85
with older mother, 222
at wedding, 126
"Companions," vs. "lovers," 186
Compliments, for older mother,
208
Conditional mother love, 167
Conflict resolution, between
older mother and son, 228
Connection, vs. separation, 24
Contentment, vs. jealousy, 126
Control, loss of mother's, 82–85
Controlling mother, vengeance
toward, 227–30
Courting, by teenage sons, 93
Crisis, and reconciliation, 232–33
see also "Filial crisis"
Crying, boys vs. girl babies, 38–
39

Date, Saturday night, 95
Dating game, and teenage boys,
93–96
Daughter, 237
and abandonment fear of older
mother, 210–11
as chosen child, 212–15

guilt at relationship with
mother, 143–44
and nurturing of older mother,
218–23
preference for, 24–26
relationship with father, 30–34,
47–48
see also Dutiful daughter;
Girls; Women
Daughter-in-law, 112–38
allied with mother, 131–33
as other woman, 112–17
relationship with mother, 135–
138
in triangle, 127–31
at wedding, 123–26
Death, 186
of older mother, 236–41
of son, 234–35
Deception, of homosexual son,
179–80
Decision-making, for older
mother, 209
Denial, 186
Dependence
vs. independence, 76, 87, 142,
147
intimacy without, 147
of older people, 210
Depression, at guilt of older
mother, 236
Deutsch, Dr. Cynthia, 138
Devaluation, of rejecting mother,
157
Dickes, Dr. Robert, 57, 60–61, 69
Differences, enjoyment of, 188–
189
"Different" feeling, of homosexual son, 179
Disapproving mother, 116–18
Distance, 141
and older mother, 222–23
Divorce, of son, 133–35, 190
Domestic chores, and daughter of
older mother, 211
Dubinsky, Ted, 51, 165, 188
Dutiful daughter, and older
mother, 215–18

without dependency, 147
and independence, 141–43
with old mother, 221–23
Involvement, and estrangement,
164

Java, Kalangs in, 66
Jealousy
vs. contentment, 126
and marriages, 100
maternal, 59
of rejected son, 158
Jocasta (mother of Oedipus), 50
Journal of Consulting and Clinical Psychology, 183
Journal of Marriage and the Family, 109
Journal of Psychology, The, 42
Journal of Sex Research, The, 71

Kagan, Dr. Jerome, 57, 59–60
Kalangs, in Java, 66
Kapit, Dr. Hanna, 173
Kapit, Dr. Milton, 148–49, 173–174, 241
Kelman, Dr. Norman, 113, 141
Koin, Dr. Diana, 207

Laius, King of Thebes, 50
Lauter, Leah, 219, 220, 232
Leifer, Dr. Anna, 130, 207–8, 212, 237–38
Lesbians, 188
Lester, David, 71
Lewis, Dr. Michael, 39, 40, 42, 43
Lies, of homosexual son, 179
Life, as continuing process, 240
Los Angeles study, 215
Loss
of mother by son, 174–75
of son by mother, 139–51, 172–174
see also Abandonment;
Favored son; Rejected son;
Seduced son; Separation
Love
giving or withholding of, 167
supposed, 163

Lover (male), of son, 190–92
"Lovers," vs. "companions," 186
Loving son, and older mother,
215–18
Loyalties, family, 135

Making amends, 172–74
Male lover, of son, 190–92
"Male-oriented" activities, 211
Manipulation, of seducing
mother, 151–52
Margolis, Dr. Marvin, 68
Marriage
end of son's, 133–35
of mother, 98–101
unhappy, 36–37
Marriage choices, of son
difficulties in, 118–20
reasons for, 120–23
Marriage and Family Interaction,
114
Masculinity, 31, 42, 43, 55, 56
in women, 25
Masturbation, 45, 46, 47
Maternal jealousy, 59
Memory, of dead mother, 239
Men
changing roles of, 146
responsibilities of, 216
Mendelsohn, Dr. Robert, 53, 57, 63
Mental illness, not related to
homosexuality, 178–79
Metcalf, Dr. Aubrey, 77, 92
Middlescent mother, 105–7
Mistreatment, not abuse, 227
Mohacsy, Dr. Ildiko, 45
"Momism," 148
Montgomery, Sarah, 187, 192
Morale, of older people, 210
Mother
bad, 171
blaming, 147–51
controlling, 227–30
disapproving, 116–18
early affection, boys vs. girls,
41–42
early relationships of, 104–5

nudity of, 59–61, 91
reconciliation with children,
231–33
rejection of, 84
see also Older parents
Parents of Gays group, 193, 196
"Passing," of male lover, 191
Patience, of mother, 79
Paul, Dr. Henry, 54, 61
Pelew Islands, brides on, 15
Penis, 45, 46
production of, 40
Perfection, and parents, 173
Physical confrontation, 92–93
Play therapy, 53
Possessiveness, maternal, 113, 115
Power
of older mother, 217
and seductiveness, 64–66
and teenage boys, 80–82
Power shift, from older mother to
son, 229–30
Privacy, 163
and teenage boys, 83–84
Promiscuity, 196, 197
Psychological Reports, 18
Psychology, 18
Psychosis, and incest, 69–70
Public Spectacles (Fosse), 50
Punishing behavior, and femi-
nization, 43
Punishment, and seductive
mother, 64

Rebellion, teenage, 101–2, 104–5
Reconciliation, of children and
parents, 231–33
Redbook magazine, 114, 134
Rejected son, 156–59
Rejecting mother, devaluation of,
157
Rejection
by married sons, 113–14, 121
of older mother, 230
of parents, 84
by teenage boys, 84
by teenage girls, 103
of teenage son, 76

of unwanted son, 26–28, 29
Relief, over homosexual disclo-
sure, 188
Religion, 118
Repayment, of older mother by
son, 223–30
Repetition compulsion, 23
Repression, and incest taboo, 90
Resentment, of seduced son, 153,
154
Responsibilities
of men vs. women, 216
for older mother, 218–23
Revenge, toward controlling
mother, 227–30
Roiphe, Dr. Herman, 46–47
Role model, mother as, 103, 108–9
Roles, of men and women, 146
Rosberger, Anne, 235, 236, 238,
240
Rosenbaum, Dr. Britt, 65, 67, 70–
71, 108

Sambursky, Dr. Joel, 36
Sanders, Dr. Catherine, 234, 236
Saretsky, Dr. Lorelle, 32, 45, 65,
115, 117, 136
Saturday night date, 95
Scapegoats, for unhappy mar-
riages, 36–37
Schonberger, Dr. Joseph, 21, 24
Secrecy, vs. honesty, 189
Secure son, 168–72
Seduced son, 64–66, 151–55
Seductive mother, 61–64, 90–91
sons of, 64–66
Seductiveness, of older mother,
207–9
Segal, Jonathan, 42
Seggev, Dr. Lydia, 23, 25, 26, 28,
79, 100–101
Seltzer, Dr. Gary, 217, 224–25
Seltzer, Miriam, 106, 122–23, 165–
166
Senility, 220
Separateness, 141–42, 163, 165–66
see also Independence
Separation, 106